Puerto Rico

INSIGHT GUIDES
PUERTO RICO

APA PUBLICATIONS L
Part of the Langenscheidt Publishing Group

INSIGHT GUIDE
PUERTO RICO

Editorial
Managing Editor
Carine Tracanelli
Art Director
Ian Spick
Picture Manager
Steven Lawrence
Series Manager
Rachel Fox

Distribution

United States
Langenscheidt Publishers, Inc.
36–36 33rd Street 4th Floor
Long Island City, NY 11106
orders@langenscheidt.com

UK & Ireland
GeoCenter International Ltd
Meridian House, Churchill Way West
Basingstoke, Hampshire RG21 6YR
sales@geocenter.co.uk

Australia
Universal Publishers
1 Waterloo Road
Macquarie Park, NSW 2113
sales@universalpublishers.com.au

New Zealand
Hema Maps New Zealand Ltd (HNZ)
Unit 2, 10 Cryers Road
East Tamaki, Auckland 2013
sales.hema@clear.net.nz

Worldwide
Apa Publications GmbH & Co.
Verlag KG (Singapore branch)
38 Joo Koon Road, Singapore 628990
Tel: (65) 6865 1600.
apasin@singnet.com.sg

Printing

Insight Print Services (Pte) Ltd
38 Joo Koon Road, Singapore 628990
Tel: (65) 6865 1600.

©2009 Apa Publications GmbH & Co.
Verlag KG (Singapore branch)
All Rights Reserved

First Edition 1987
Fourth Edition 2009

CONTACTING THE EDITORS
We would appreciate it if readers
would alert us to errors or out-
dated information by writing to:
Insight Guides, P.O. Box 7910,
London SE1 1WE, England.
Fax: (44) 20 7403 0290.
insight@apaguide.co.uk

www.insightguides.com

ABOUT THIS BOOK

The first Insight Guide pioneered
the use of creative full-color
photography in travel guides in
1970. Since then, we have
expanded our range to cater for our
readers' need not only for reliable
information about their chosen destination but also for a real understanding of the culture and workings
of that destination. Now, when the
internet can supply inexhaustible
(but not always reliable) facts, our
books marry text and pictures to
provide those much more elusive
qualities: knowledge and discern-
ment. To achieve this, they rely
heavily on the authority of locally
based writers and photographers.

Insight Guide: Puerto Rico is struc-
tured to convey an understanding of
this island-nation, its people and
culture as well as to guide readers
through its attractions:

♦ The **Features** section, indicated
by a pink bar at the top of each
page, covers the cultural history of
the island in a series of illuminating
essays on the Puerto Rican people,
their cuisine, festivals, language,
and art scene.
♦ The main **Places** section, indicated by a blue bar, is a complete
guide to all the sights and areas
worth visiting. Places of special
interest are coordinated by number
with the maps.
♦ The **Travel Tips** listings section,
with a yellow bar, provides full information on transportation, accommodations, restaurants, activities from
culture to shopping to sports, an A–Z
section of essential practical information, and a handy phrasebook
with Spanish words and expressions.
An easy-to-find contents list for Travel
Tips is printed on the back flap, which
also serves as a bookmark.

Map Legend

— · —	International Boundary
— · —	National Park/Reserve
— — —	Ferry Route
✈ ✈	Airport: International/Regional
🚌	Bus Station
❶	Tourist Information
† † †	Church/Ruins
ℭ	Mosque
∩	Cave
▯	Tower
★	Place of Interest
⚑	Beach
▲	Mountain Peak
🗼	Lighthouse
※	Viewpoint
✉	Post Office
⌇	Crater

The main places of interest in the Places section are coordinated by number with a full-color map (e.g. ❶), and a symbol at the top of every right-hand page tells you where to find the map.

The contributors

This book was commissioned by **Carine Tracanelli** at Insight Guides' London office. To oversee the work in Puerto Rico, she enlisted the help of **Ebedet Negrón**, lifestyle editor for Puerto Rico's English-language daily, the *Puerto Rico Sun*. Boston University graduate, bilingual Negrón updated all the text, including the Features and the Travel Tips.

This new edition was edited by Tracanelli and **Mick Meikleham**, a freelance editor and regular contributor to Insight Guides. It builds on the earlier editions produced by **Barbara Balletto, Christopher Caldwell, Gerry Tobin, Tad Ames, Natalia de Cuba Romero, Gabrielle Paese, Susan Charneco**, and **Larry Luxner**, who refined the original text written by a team including Luxner, Caldwell, **Sarah Ellison Caldwell, Webster** and **Robert Stone, Angelo López, Adam Cherson, Hanne-Maria Maijala, Kathleen O'Connell, Eleonora Abreau-Jiménez**, and **Susan Hambleton**.

The majority of the photographs were taken especially for this edition by Insight regular **Glyn Genin**, who captured the beauty of the island and its people. The design was refreshed by **Nicola Erdpresser**.

This book was proofread by **Neil Titman** and the index was compiled by **Helen Peters**.

Contents

LEFT: Old San Juan is awash with color.

Maps

Travel Tips

THE BEST OF PUERTO RICO: TOP SIGHTS

From Indian heritage sites to colonial gems, and sandy beaches to extraordinary ecological sites, here is a rundown of Puerto Rico's most spectacular attractions

△ **El Morro** was one of a ring of forts that held the key to Spanish power in the Caribbean. The watchtowers of the fortress look out to sea and inland across San Juan Bay to the coastal plains beyond. *See page 117.*

▽ **Museo de Arte de Puerto Rico**, San Juan. This converted hospital in Santurce houses works by well-known Puerto Rican artists dating back to the 17th century, as well as regional and international works. The museum is also home to Pikayo, one of the city's best restaurants for gourmet Creole cuisine. *See page 127.*

△ **Río Camuy Cave Park** has one of the most dramatic subterranean cave systems yet discovered. Trains take passengers between caves and sinkholes that have taken the Camuy River millions of years to erode. *See page 173.*

◁ **Playa Luquillo**, east of San Juan, is popular with families and a safe place for children to swim. The kiosks sell afternoon snacks. *See page 144.*

△ **El Yunque** receives more than 100 billion gallons of rain per year, making it the perfect habitat for 26 unique animal species. *See page 141.*

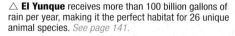

▽ **Phosphorescent Bay** is known for its glowing waters. It has a high concentration of bioluminescence, generated by microscopic organisms in the water. Take a boat trip out into the bay to agitate the trillions of dinoflagellates, and watch them light up. *See page 236.*

△ **Arecibo Observatory** sits in the heart of the karst country, a region of archetypal limestone erosion, and has the largest single-dish radio telescope in the world. It has been silently scanning the universe, making maps of distant solar systems, and listening for messages from other planets since 1960. *See page 168.*

▷ **Tibes Indian Ceremonial Park** is one of the Caribbean's most important Amerindian archeological sites. Visit the museum to find out more about the Amerindian peoples. *See page 210.*

THE BEST OF PUERTO RICO: EDITOR'S CHOICE

Dazzling beaches fringed by coral reef, steamy rainforests harboring unique flora and fauna, and elegant architecture are all waiting to be experienced in Puerto Rico. Here, at a glance, are the editor's top tips for making the most of your visit

BEST BEACHES

and mangroves in front of the beach. It's also a quiet beach so relaxation guaranteed. *See page 189.*

● **Playa Boquerón** is one of the loveliest beaches on the island. The fine sands of the wide, curving bay back onto a palm grove, and coral lies beneath its calm waters. *See page 190.*

● **Isla Verde** is a minute from all the main resort hotels in San Juan. This white-sand beach is one of the most popular on the island. *See page 128.*

● **Rincón** is a surfer's paradise, best visited from October through April. *See page 184.*

● **Playa Luquillo** *See pages 7 & 144.*

● **Playa Buyé** in Cabo Rojo is the perfect getaway spot with its crystal clear water, palm trees,

FUN FOR CHILDREN

● **The Museo del Niño** (Children's Museum) in Old San Juan is a hands-on, educational activity center for kids of all ages. Children can create crafts, play dress-up in a model town and learn the basics of Puerto Rican culture. *See page 111.*

● **Parque de Bombas** Ponce. The whole family will marvel at the old-fashioned red-and black-striped firehouse that is in the center of the town square. *See page 205.*

● **Arecibo Lighthouse and Historical Park** A fun and educational excursion, with an observation bridge over a

small tank containing sharks and rays, replicas of a Taíno village, a pirate's ship, and a mini zoo. *See page 166.*

● **Mayagüez Zoo** Puerto Rico's only place to see lions, tigers, and bears, as well as explore a forest-style cave in the zoo's new conservation center for reptiles and amphibians. *See page 187.*

● **Parque de las Ciencias** Located in Bayamón, this science museum has displays on archeology, transportation, health and marine ecosystems. A plaza houses models of rockets from NASA. *See page 133.*

TOP: Playa Boquerón. **ABOVE:** fun times.
RIGHT: the pirate ship in the Arecibo Historical Park.

SNORKELING AND SCUBA-DIVING

with tropical fish. The coral reef is close to shore. *See pages 182–3.*

● **Fajardo** is known for its calm, clear waters, and cays and reefs. Icacos offers a narrow stretch of bone-white beach and a coral underworld 20ft (6 meters) below the sea where you can see elkhorn, staghorn, brain, star, and other corals. *See page 145.*

● **Caja de Muertos** This island off the coast of Ponce has beautiful coral in calm blue Caribbean waters with a fairly slow current. *See page 210.*

● **Vieques** is unique for its contrasts: rich in marine life in some parts, and completely void in others due to US naval activities. Follow the fish for the best diving spots, but even snorkelers can glimpse sea turtles, rays, and the brightest blue coral near Vieques's Sun Bay. *See page 233.*

● **Isla Mona**, often called the Galapagos of the Caribbean, has marine life you won't see close to the big island's shores. *See page 239.*

● **Rincón, Aguadilla, and Jobos** on the island's west coast have unparalleled beauty. Beginners and experienced divers will love the Rincón area: it is surrounded by a rocky bottom some 120ft (36 meters) down. Aguadilla's Crash Boat Beach offers great snorkeling near the old dock and in the caves and reef nearby. West of Jobos, you'll find underwater caverns teeming

ABOVE: iguana in Las Cabezas de San Juan Preserve.
LEFT: exploring Puerto Rico's amazing underwater world.

FOREST AND NATURE RESERVES

● **Las Cabezas de San Juan Nature Preserve** An environmental paradise where you can observe most of Puerto Rico's natural habitats. *See page 146.*

● **El Yunque** *See pages 7 & 141.*

● **Guánica Forest Reserve** Known for its bird life as well as its endangered plant species. Some 750 plant and tree species grow here – 16 of them indigenous. *See page 213.*

● **Boquerón Nature Reserve** is a mangrove forest and noted bird-life habitat. *See page 190.*

● **Toro Negro Forest Reserve** Up in the mountains, this reserve provides great views of both coasts. *See page 226.*

MONEY-SAVING TIPS

● The Puerto Rico National Parks Service operates small economy cabins in Humacao, Arroyo, Anasco, Boquerón, and Maricao (Monte del Estado). These no-frills cabins have kitchens and bathrooms, but you supply sheets and towels. They are popular with Puerto Rican families in the summer, but are easier to reserve during the high tourist season from November through May. Check availability at www.

parquesnacionalespr.com. For those looking for economy without sacrificing comfort, the 17 *paradores*, or small inns, of Puerto Rico are ideal; visit www.gotoparadores.com.

● Puerto Ricans are experts at having a good time without spending a lot of cash. There is no charge to use any of Puerto Rico's beaches, save small parking fees. On the weekends, Old San Juan abounds with free activities, from

kite-flying near El Morro to live music at Paseo de la Princesa. Visit www.gotopuertorico.com for details.

A HEADY MIX

Multi-faceted history, colorful culture, breathtaking scenery, and distinctive rhythms make Puerto Rico a truly "rich port"

Before Columbus christened the island of San Juan Bautista (St John the Baptist) in 1493 and Juan Ponce de León switched its name with that of the capital, Puerto Rico (Rich Port), the original settlers – the Taínos – knew it as **Borikén**, the great land of the valiant and noble Lord. Puerto Ricans today often call the island Borinquen, from Borikén, spawning the terms *boricua* and *borincano*.

Puerto Rico is home to close to 4 million people, with more than a million in the greater San Juan metropolitan area alone. It is a vibrant, modern, bilingual, and multi-cultural society molded by Spanish, African, Indian and US influences. Once Spain's most important military outpost in the Caribbean, it has blossomed into a truly marvelous vacation destination.

Located in the northeastern Caribbean, east of the Dominican Republic and west of the Virgin Islands, Puerto Rico is the smallest by land area and second-smallest by population of the four Greater Antilles (Cuba, Hispaniola, Jamaica, and Puerto Rico). It is 100 miles (160km) long and 35 miles (56km) from north to south.

The climate is close to perfect, averaging 83°F (22.7°C) in winter and 85°F (29.4°C) in summer, and as a result of its varied landscape, the island has three kinds of weather: a tropical climate on the north-coast beaches; endless rain in the lush forests of the mountainous center; and a dry heat along the southern coast.

Since the first inhabitants arrived thousands of years ago, this beautiful island has been home to Indians, Spaniards, Africans, and more. Over four centuries the Spanish laid the foundations of the island's culture. They constructed towns, roads, fortresses, and churches. African slaves were brought in to work the land, and they in turn contributed to the island's language, customs, music, and culinary traditions.

PRECEDING PAGES: playing saxophone on the beach in Isabela; sunset on the church square in Humacao. **LEFT:** Carnival celebrations in Ponce. **ABOVE:** Puerto Rican beauty. **RIGHT:** feeding the pigeons in Old San Juan.

Puerto Rico overflows with traces of its past: in Taíno carvings, colonial architecture, first-class cuisine, and even in farming techniques. And the island has kept up to pace with the rest of the world – as its various designer stores, museums and art galleries, symphony halls, communications technology, and championship golf courses all attest.

Cultural cocktail

In Puerto Rico, everyone comes from somewhere else. Although the Taíno population had all but vanished within a few years of Spanish colonization, a few poor Spanish farmers intermarried with some remaining Amerindians. Few of these, known as *jíbaros*, remain today, but their cultural imprint survives. Later, African slaves arrived on the sugar plantations, as well as other Caribbean islanders seeking jobs. Spanish loyalists sought refuge here, fleeing Simón Bolívar's independence movement in South America.

The French also flocked to Puerto Rico, leaving behind upheavals in Louisiana and Haiti. Even farmers from Scotland and Ireland ended up on the island, hoping to benefit from its rich sugar-cane economy. Chinese workers came to build roads in the 1800s; they were followed by Italians, Germans, and Lebanese. In 1898, US expatriates sought the island as a home and more recently Cubans, Dominicans, and Argentinians have settled here.

Although English is spoken, Spanish is predominant – but it, too, is a mix, with words borrowed from the pre-Columbian Amerindian tongue and modern-day English.

After the struggles of independence, and power tussles with the Dutch and English, Puerto Rico eventually arrived at a strangely fruitful relationship with the United States.

Puerto Rico is essentially a crossroads of Hispanic and Anglo cultures. Despite its very diverse influx of cultures, Puerto Rico has been a part of the United States since 1898, and Puerto Ricans have been US citizens since 1917.

Many US corporations have bases on the island, and 2½ million Puerto Ricans spend their working lives on the mainland. Nevertheless, the island likes to keep its distance: in repeated referendums (plebiscites) Puerto Ricans have voted against becoming America's 51st state.

Island spirits

Although Puerto Rico is mainly Roman Catholic, its Christianity is blended with some Taíno and African traditions. *Espiritismo* – once banned by Spanish colonial rulers – flourishes in many pockets of the island. Some believe that *jípia*, or spirits of the dead, sleep by day and roam the island at night, searching for wild fruit to eat. Even today, modern homes will have a bowl of bright plastic fruit in the kitchen to appease the spirits.

Puerto Rico is an enigmatic, spiritual, magical destination, where the familiar mixes naturally with the exotic. This distinctive, heady mix is examined, explored, and celebrated in the following pages. ❏

ABOVE: Friday night is party night. **TOP:** taking a break from grocery shopping in San Juan. **RIGHT:** *vejigante* fiesta mask dancer.

THE PEOPLE OF PUERTO RICO

Nearly everyone comes from somewhere else.
But the wide range of ethnic types has forged
a proud and dynamic Hispanic culture

There is a song, one among many, which stands as the most evocative of what it means to live in the paradise which is Puerto Rico. Written by José Manuel Rivera, *Mi Tierra Borincana* extols with deceptive simplicity the reasons to endure the *tapones* (traffic jams) in San Juan, the ineptitude of bureaucracies, and even the preciousness of certain resources – water in particular – that Continentals (non-Puerto Ricans from the mainland who come to live here) all too frequently take for granted.

"How beautiful it is, to live in this dreamland! And how beautiful it is to be the master of the coquí's song!" as the song says. *"What an advantage it is to reap the coffee of this great gift!"*

In a sense the lyrics are an illusion, yet in another they're very real. For while life on the island for natives and immigrants alike is not what it was 20 or even 10 years ago – there is more crime and unemployment in the bigger cities; its working class works harder for what seems to be less and less – its lure, for those who truly love Puerto Rico, is not diminished.

Data from the 2000 census indicates that 85.4 percent of Puerto Ricans speak Spanish, 14.4 percent speak English and 0.2 percent speak languages other than Spanish or English.

Living anywhere within the commonwealth requires a balance of cleverness, common sense, and hard realism for Puerto Ricans and Continentals alike. Opulence is hardly uncommon

LEFT: patriotic graffiti.
RIGHT: a typical smiling Puerto Rican welcome.

among those who can afford it – in the wealthier suburbs of San Juan, for example, a modest-looking three-bedroom house with a small yard can cost upward of $200,000 – but even so, the display of wealth isn't encouraged.

Puerto Rican people are a friendly and passionate lot, vivacious and expressive in their conversations – and their dancing. Music and food are two elements which the people use to help them celebrate life to the fullest.

Pleasure and leisure

What's important here is a sense of belonging, acquired largely through willing readjustment to Puerto Rico's pace. And the attitude behind it is certainly a healthy one. In Puerto Rico, work is seen not as an end in itself, but merely as a means to fund subsequent enjoyment. Weekends are taken very seriously, and major holidays, especially Christmas, even more so. In the United States, Christmas lasts perhaps a week; on the island the celebrations begin in late November and don't completely stop until mid-January.

In addition to Christmas Day, Puerto Ricans celebrate Three Kings Day, or Epiphany, on January 6. Local children cut grass (to feed the Wise Men's camels), put it in boxes and place these under their beds on January 5, just before they go to sleep. The next morning, the grass is gone and gifts have been left mysteriously in its place – much to the innocent delight of the youngsters throughout the island.

During this extended holiday period, it's presumed by residents that there will be company, people coming from far away to visit or just neighbors stopping by from roughly December 15 (also the official start of the Puerto Rican tourist season, which ends on April 15 of the following year) until the last *pasteles* are eaten and the last glasses of *coquito* (a delicious mixture of milk, rum, vanilla, cream of coconut and cinnamon) consumed.

LA BORINQUEÑA: THE NATIONAL ANTHEM OF PUERTO RICO

La tierra de Borinquen
donde he nacido yo
es un jardín florido
de mágico primor.

Un cielo siempre nítido
le sirve de dosel
y dan arrullos plácidos
las olas a sus pies.

Cuando a sus playas llegó Colón
Exclamó lleno de admiración:
"Oh! oh! oh! esta es la linda

tierra que busco yo."

Es Borinquen la hija,
la hija del mar y el sol,
del mar y el sol,
del mar y el sol,
del mar y el sol,
del mar y el sol.

The land of Borinquen
where I was born
is a flowering garden
of exquisite magic.

A sky, always clear, serves
as its canopy and placid
lullabies are sung by the
waves at its [Borinquen's] feet.

When at her beaches Columbus
arrived full of awe he exclaimed,
"Oh! oh! oh! this is the lovely
land that I seek."

Borinquen is the daughter, the
daughter of the sea and the sun.
Of the sea and the sun. (x4)

Local produce

Although the University of Puerto Rico's School of Agriculture continues to experiment with ways of growing the kinds of produce that now have to be imported, fruits and vegetables that are easily found in the United States are widely available in supermarkets. Yet there are still trucks along most major road selling homegrown oranges – *chinas* – at about $8 for a large bag. Despite the incursion of a horde of mainland products of dubious nutritional repute, *comida criolla* is still the food of the day in most households.

The traditional cuisine is heavy food, rich with an invigorating assortment of beans, from *arroz*

con habichuelas (rice with beans) and *arroz con gandules* (pigeon peas) to *lechón asado* (whole roast suckling pig) prepared almost exclusively for holidays and family gatherings, and its counterpart, *pernil* (fresh picnic ham in most Stateside butcher shops and supermarkets). Both the suckling pig and ham are seasoned with *adobo*, a thick, fragrant paste of garlic, vinegar, peppercorns, and herbs such as cilantro and oregano.

Strangely, for a place with so much marine life – grouper, yellowtail, spiny lobster, squid,

LEFT: in the week leading up to Ash Wednesday and the start of Lent, Ponce – Puerto Rico's second-largest city – celebrates Carnival, with cultural performances, parades, and general festivity. **ABOVE:** selling oysters.

sea snail, conch, and shark – Puerto Ricans prefer chicken and pork. However, red snapper *(chillo)*, shrimp *(camarones)*, and lobster *(langosta)* are enjoyed by the locals, as is salt cod – known as *bacalao* – which is a staple. Seafood lovers will find plenty of good restaurants to choose from, as well as local *fondas*, where specialties such as *mofongo relleno* (fried mashed plantain) with *mariscos* (seafood) are firm favorites. The most popular local snacks include *alcapurrias*, meat or crab fritters *(see also Puerto Rican Cuisine, page 61)*.

Poverty and crime

Despite the progress, the island's poverty is still a sad and consistent fact of life. It explains in part the decorative but restrictive iron grillwork known as *rejas*, found on almost every home. As in most modern countries, it's wise to be cautious. Petty crime is a reality; however, violent crime is generally restricted to poorer areas and is almost unheard of in tourist areas.

Surveys consistently show that voters are far more concerned about increasing crime than anything else. The government has taken measures to increase the number of police officers and to put harsher prison sentences into force for drug dealers; it has also carried out an increasing number of drugs and arms raids. Criminals are punished with the full weight of the US federal law.

Barrios and barriers

In the meantime, Puerto Ricans have responded to crime and gaps in police protection by closing entire neighborhoods to outsiders. Today, all new residential development is gated. Older neighborhoods, such as Parkville, Caparra Heights, and Torrimar, long ago barricaded their streets with electronic gates. The closed neighborhoods, unheard of 20 years ago, are considered essential in order to protect property. Until the crime rate comes down, the trend is sure to continue.

Puerto Rico's ills may also be attributed to sheer overpopulation. Because of high birth rates and medical advances that caused the death rate to plummet shortly after the Spanish-American War, Puerto Rico's population jumped to about a million by 1900, and now stands at more than 4 million. This gives a population density of nearly 1,100 per sq mile (425 per sq km), among the world's highest.

Puerto Rico is divided into 78 municipalities. In terms of population, the largest *municipio* is San Juan, with more than 430,000 people; the smallest is offshore Culebra, with only 2,000.

Driving in Puerto Rico is on the right-hand side, unlike in the nearby Virgin Islands. Adding to the confusion is the fact that the island adheres half-heartedly to the metric system, which means that all distances are posted in kilometers, and gasoline is sold by the liter. Nevertheless, temperatures are still given in Fahrenheit, and speed-limit signs are still in miles per hour. This is unlikely to change as long as Puerto Rico remains under the US flag.

SANTERÍA

Santería and its Puerto Rican variant, *espiritismo*, descend from traditional religious practices associated with the Yoruba region of Africa. The Yoruba religion was transferred to Cuba during the European trade in West African slaves during colonial times. Although many of the most salient aspects of the source religion of the Yoruba are preserved in *Santería*, it has also developed into its own unique tradition, largely due to the syncretism with other religious practices. The most famous is between the Yoruba tradition and Catholicism. In this practice, *santeros* conflated the traditional gods, known as the Orishas, with the Catholic saints.

Español sí, inglés no

A far more contentious issue is the language debate. For 90 years the island had two official languages, Spanish and English. Then, in 1991, former Governor Rafael Hernández Colón – citing Puerto Rico's "cultural heritage" – abolished English as an official language. This won him much praise from the *independentistas*, but sparked an outcry from local educators and businessmen.

The controversy heated up further when Hernández Colón's pro-statehood successor, Pedro Rosselló, took office in January 1993. One of the first things he did was restore the official status of English, making Puerto Rico once again bilingual. However, regardless of the law, fewer than a quarter of Puerto Ricans are completely bilingual; outside the big cities you will find it useful to know at least a few basic Spanish words and phrases to help you get around.

Puerto Rico is a place of which it can truly be said everyone comes from somewhere else. There are the traces of Taíno and Carib blood left in the fine, high cheekbones of many of those whose families have lived on the island for generations. In fact, in the town of Loíza, east of San Juan, the evidence of the island's slave-trading days is impossible to ignore. There are women with skin the color of *café con leche*, who have tightly curled hair that is naturally auburn, and children with liquid-blue eyes and blond hair whose faces are exotically beautiful, thanks to any number of forebears – including traders, pirates, artisans, slaves, and colonists.

Patriotism

Despite all varieties of political difference, pride is universal and strong. Though US flags fly alongside all Puerto Rican flags in public places (by law), and schoolchildren sing *The Star Spangled Banner* before *La Borinqueña*, the island's own beautiful anthem, being Puerto Rican always comes first. This isn't without its paradoxical side. The people who've chosen to live here, Puerto Ricans and Continentals alike, love the island intensely yet know that things are far from perfect – which is where patience and common sense come into play. The Ports Authority (Autoridad de Puertos), for example, is the only municipal agency that consistently makes a profit. Yet those who rely on the ferries it operates between Fajardo, Vieques and Culebra have a well-honed sense of humor toward its less-than-pristine fleet. It might take two hours. It might take six. *Así es la vida*. That's life.

Along with the islanders' resilient humor, there is also an ongoing sense of rebellious resentment in the face of authority, especially towards the US Navy. This became acute in 1970, when Culebrans were kept off Flamenco Beach – as they had been for decades – during

> *Although officially adopted in 1952, Puerto Rico's flag was first used in 1895; its "lone star" was the "guide of the patriots".*

naval ordnance. Protesters stormed the island, including independence advocate Rubén Berríos, along with a group of his cohorts, who camped out on the island for almost a year. It seems that the protests succeeded. The Navy finally left the island in May 2003.

Poetry, poverty, and politics

In conclusion, Puerto Rico is a place where beauty coexists on occasions with squalor; a place where politics and poetry often merge; a place where its most celebrated leaders, among them Luis Llorens Torres and Luis Muñoz Marín, were also poets.

practice bombing runs. "Enough," said 2,000 people all at once. The red flag went up to keep people off the beach; the majority of the population headed straight for it, loaded with picnic coolers. They were going to picnic until the US Navy stopped its target runs so close to their beach. Three years later, the Navy finally agreed to leave Flamenco Beach alone.

In 1999, the controversy of the naval presence in Vieques blew up as David Sanes, a civilian worker for the Navy, was accidentally killed by

LEFT: the pace of life is slow in Puerto Rico.
ABOVE: a group of elders enjoying a game of dominoes in a San Juan park.

The island's poorer residents cherish the things that have no price tags: family, friends, and the pleasure, challenging as it can be, of living here. There is poverty, certainly, a chronic ache to those who love their island. But art flourishes here too, with the craftworkers, musicians, painters, and sculptors. It gives Puerto Rico's beauty a face which is proud yet edged in sadness, exotic yet utterly recognizable.

The country's national anthem, *La Borinqueña* (*see page 20*), which, unlike other nations' songs that speak of military might and triumph over adversaries, sums up the flavor. It celebrates a reality which is at the same time an ideal, *"a flowering garden of exquisite magic. A sky, always clear…"* ❏

DECISIVE DATES

ANCIENT TIMES

4500 BC
Archaic tribes land in Puerto Rico, probably from Venezuela's Río Orinoco delta.

AD 200–1200
The Igneri inhabit the island.

1200–1500
The Taíno Indian civilization flourishes.

AGE OF EXPLORERS

1493
Columbus lands and claims the island for Spain.

1508
Juan Ponce de León establishes settlement at Caparra.

1510
King of Spain appoints Ponce de León governor of San Juan Bautista, as Puerto Rico is then known.

1516
Entrepreneurs construct the island's first sugar factory.

1520s
The island is officially called Puerto Rico.

1521
Caparra settlement moved to present-day Old San Juan.

1531
Puerto Rico sends its first sugar exports to Spain.

1532
The army begins building La Fortaleza.

1539
The Spaniards begin building El Morro fortress.

1598
Ginger replaces sugar as main cash crop; influenza epidemic wipes out most of the able-bodied population of San Juan.

1625
The Dutch lay siege to San Juan, but soon retreat.

1797
British forces try to take San Juan; they retreat only a few weeks later.

1812
Spain grants conditional citizenship to island residents.

1813–18
Trade grows to eight times its previous level.

1887
Luis Muñoz Rivera becomes one of the founders of the Autonomist Party.

1897
Spain declares Puerto Rico an autonomous territory.

ENTER THE US

1898
Spanish-American War; US troops bring the island under American jurisdiction.

1899
Hurricane San Ciriaco devastates the island's sugar and coffee industries.

1910
Muñoz Rivera elected Resident Commissioner to US House of Representatives.

1917
Jones Act extends US citizenship to Puerto Ricans.

1922
Nationalist Party is founded.

1936
Two Nationalist gunmen kill San Juan's police chief.

1937
Nationalist protesters killed in "Ponce Massacre."

1938
Luis Muñoz Marín, son of Luis Muñoz Rivera, forms Popular Democratic Party.

1942
Puerto Rico Industrial Development Co. established.

POST-WORLD WAR II

1946
Jesús Piñero is the first native governor in the island's history.

1948
Muñoz Marín takes office as first freely elected governor.

1950
Nationalists try to kill President Truman in Washington, and stir up revolt at home.

PRECEDING PAGES: cane-fuelled stream train on a sugar plantation. FAR LEFT TOP: Juan Ponce de León. FAR LEFT BOTTOM: Puerto Rico harbor, c.1700. LEFT: US troops entering Ponce during the Spanish-American War, 1898. ABOVE LEFT: scene from the "Ponce Massacre", 1937. ABOVE RIGHT: workers on a plantation near Ponce, 1938. RIGHT: Governor Luis Fortuño's inauguration.

1952
Puerto Rico made a US commonwealth (July 25).

MODERN TIMES

1964
Muñoz Marín resigns from political office.

1976
Carlos Romero Barceló elected governor.

1978
Police kill two young *independentistas*, sparking the Cerro Maravilla scandal.

1991
Hernández Colón abolishes English as one of Puerto Rico's two official languages.

1992
Governor Pedro Rosselló restores English as an official language.

1993
Voters elect to retain commonwealth status.

1998
Hurricane Georges wreaks havoc on the island. Voters reject statehood after a third national plebiscite.

2000
Sila María Calderón elected as first female governor.

2003
US Navy pulls out of Vieques after more than six decades of military exercises.

2006
Budget crisis and fiscal reform.

2007
Archeologists working on a dam project outside Ponce find important pre-Columbian Taíno site containing unprecedented petroglyphs, as well as hundreds of graves.

2008
Luis Fortuño is elected as latest governor of the island.

BEGINNINGS

By the time the Spanish came, the native peoples had created a sophisticated culture with ingenious farming techniques and fine handicrafts

The Taíno, the first people that Christopher Columbus encountered in the New World, evolved about AD 1200 from an intermingling of groups that had migrated into the Caribbean many centuries earlier, primarily from the Orinocan-Amazonian Basin of South America. The Taíno became the dominant culture in the region and lived on the large islands of the Greater Antilles: the Bahamas, Cuba, Hispaniola (Haiti and the Dominican Republic), Jamaica and Puerto Rico.

The earliest archeological remains were discovered at a large limestone cave near Loíza, close to the northeast coast. This cave, known as Cueva María de la Cruz, was excavated in 1948 and 1954 by Puerto Rican archeologist Ricardo Alegría. Carbon dating yielded artifacts related to a preceramic culture which went back to the first century AD.

Shells fashioned into gouging tools for use in the manufacture of dug-out canoes suggest that the first Indians rowed over from Venezuela,

Archeologist Dr Ricardo Alegría was born in 1921. He is also a learned scholar and cultural anthropologist and is known as the "Father of Modern Puerto Rican Archeology".

where similar relics have been recovered. There was unquestionably steady communication and trade between the Caribbean islands.

In his journal Columbus describes a Taíno canoe which seated three men abreast and 70 to

LEFT: ancient Taíno stones at Caguana.
RIGHT: mask at Tibes Ceremonial Park.

80 in all. "A barge could not keep up with them in rowing," he wrote, "because they go with incredible speed, and with these canoes they navigate among these islands."

A stratified society

Part of a well-defined Indian culture that extended throughout the Antilles, the Taínos in Puerto Rico lived in a rigidly stratified society. A great king lived on the island of Hispaniola, and district *caciques* – chiefs – governed the districts of Puerto Rico, which the natives called *Borinquen* – "Island of the Brave Lord." Each district had a centrally located capital village where the *cacique* resided. As in medieval Europe, heredity determined status within society, which comprised *nitaínos*, or nobles who advised the *caciques* and enjoyed certain privileges; commoners; and *naborias*, or slaves.

Taíno villages ranged in size from around 100 people to thousands. The Indians spent the great majority of their time out of doors, yet they built large bell-shaped thatched houses in which as many as 40 family members slept. These were built around a large open space reserved for public ceremonies and for *batey*, which the Spanish referred to as *pelota* – a ball game. The house of the *cacique* was the largest in town and always fronted on this public square. At Tibes, in Ponce, an Indian village has been reconstructed from ancient ruins.

The Taínos believed in a polytheistic order of creation. Yocahú, the Supreme Creator, commanded all the gods, the earth and its myriad creatures. The angry god of the winds, Juracán, invoked the eponymous hurricanes. In the central square, the Indians observed religious worship and participated in ceremonial tribal dances.

Ceramic icons and clay idols displayed in anthropological museums are evidence of the religious past. South of Arecibo, at the 13-acre

STUDY SHEDS LIGHT ON PUERTO RICAN IDENTITY

The concept of Puerto Rican identity has been pondered, defined, and redefined time and time again. Who is Puerto Rican? What is a Puerto Rican? Where do *boricuas* come from? It seems the debate over these questions will never end. Now add genetic testing to the mix. Since 1998, professor Juan Carlos Martínez Cruzado and his team from the University of Puerto Rico in Mayagüez have conducted DNA studies on Puerto Ricans in search of their Indian heritage.

Using a strand of hair and its root, they zero in on mitochondrial DNA, passed down intact from generation to generation. Initially, the study began in Maricao's Indieras area, where a good number of people have specific Taíno-like traits. His studies revealed that the Indian heritage is more prevalent than had been expected. With that in mind, Martínez and his team broadened the study to encompass the island – this time, testing cheek swab samples from 800 people chosen randomly throughout Puerto Rico.

In 2008 his group found that 61 percent had, in effect, Taíno DNA. What's more, of 19 identified lineages, about 10 were traced to pre-Columbian Indians.

That suggests that Puerto Rico's Taínos may have survived much longer than previously thought, and it could mean there was a much larger population of Taínos than has been thought to have existed.

Martínez Cruzado hopes to continue the DNA testing throughout the Caribbean region.

(5-hectare) Caguana Indian Ceremonial Park, used for religious purposes eight centuries ago, there are stone monoliths, 10 *batey* balls, and other artifacts.

Tending the earth

Traces of Taíno agriculture remain in Puerto Rico. Their ingenious method of sowing a variety of plants in earthen mounds called *conducos* is still employed by some farmers. The *conduco* system mitigated the problems of water distribution: water-intensive crops were placed at the bottom of the mounds and those requiring good drainage at the top.

A golden age

In the time left over from farming, fishing, and hunting, the Taínos developed various handicrafts. Early Spanish settlers in the region greatly admired the Indian woodwork: dishes, basins, bowls, and boxes. Most prized of all were the ornate *duhos*, carved wooden thrones used by the *caciques*. The Great Taíno Cacique made a gift of a dozen of these to the Spanish Crown in the 1490s. Indian weavers used cotton and other fibrous plants to make colorfully dyed clothing, belts, and hammocks. But the handicraft that aroused greatest excitement among the Spanish was the gold jewelry that the Indians wore as

Cassava bread, the staple of the Taíno diet, was made by grating and draining the root, which was then formed into loaves and baked. They also relied heavily upon yams, and among the plants the early settlers sent back to Spain were maize, beans, squash, and peanuts.

Using *macanas* – stout double broadswords still used by Puerto Rican farmers – and pointed sticks, the Taínos cleared the thick woods and sowed their fields. Various sources of animal protein supplemented the starchy diet: fish and sometimes pigeon or parrot.

rings in their ears and noses. They neither mined nor panned for gold. When the Spaniards, smitten with desire for the precious metal, coaxed the natives into leading them to their sources, they were taken to beaches where gold nuggets from the ocean floor occasionally washed ashore.

Recent findings have shed more light on these indigenous peoples. The Institute of Puerto Rican Culture has amassed large collections of stones, pottery, tools, and skeletal remains. Archeologists are deciphering information from ongoing digs. In Old San Juan, at the Institute, artifacts and indigenous exhibits, together with a miniature model of a Taíno village on display at Casa Blanca, give some insight into the way of life of the early people in the Old City. ❑

FAR LEFT: traditional Taíno dwelling. **LEFT:** Taíno carving.
ABOVE: this clearing in Caguana Indian Ceremonial Park was used by the Taínos as a ball court.

THE SPANISH SETTLERS

At first the Spanish treated the Taíno population well, but soon the natives were enslaved as their invaders lusted for gold. Then came the trade wars

Fifteen years passed between Columbus's discovery of the island of Borikén on November 19, 1493, and serious attempts to settle it. He came across the island by chance during his second voyage while he was trying to reach Hispaniola. Naming it San Juan Bautista, Columbus claimed it for the Spanish Crown and promptly departed. From 1493 until 1508, the approximately 30,000 Taínos living on the island enjoyed a period of benevolent neglect: from time to time, Spaniards sailed to San Juan from Hispaniola seeking to barter with locals for food. These encounters were always friendly.

Enticing gold

One Spaniard who visited the island was Juan Ponce de León. The natives' ornaments and gold trinkets caught Ponce de León's eye. He felt sure that the area was rich in gold, and he secretly scouted the southern coast for mining sites. In the early summer of 1508 Ponce de León and the Spanish governor of the Carib-

Columbus and his crew were the first Europeans to encounter the Taíno people. It was Columbus who called the Taínos "Indians", an identification that has grown to encompass all the indigenous peoples of the Western Hemisphere.

bean, Nicolás de Ovando, signed a clandestine agreement which granted Ponce de León rights to mine the island on condition that he would yield two-thirds to the king. Secrecy was of the

LEFT: Ponce de León, Puerto Rico's first governor.
RIGHT: Diego Colón and a bust of his famous father.

utmost importance: Christopher Columbus's son, Diego Colón, had inherited the rights to exploit the island, but his family's desire for wealth had proved dangerous in the past. Physical abuse, dissolution of tribes, and starvation of the inhabitants of Hispaniola had been followed by rebellion and bloodshed.

In July 1508, Ponce de León and a band of 50 men – among them Luis de Añasco, the namesake of the river and village – set off for the island of San Juan Bautista. As they sailed eastward along the northern coast, they made friendly contact with the natives, and Agueybaná, the head *cacique* of the island, provided Ponce de León with an entry which ensured safe passage for him and his crew. Finally, after six long weeks of searching, the intrepid explorers found a suitable site for settlement. In a valley several miles inland on an arm of the Bayamón River, Ponce de León founded the island's first European town, Caparra. In official documents, it was referred to as Ciudad de Puerto Rico.

Relations between the natives and the Europeans proceeded well. Panning the river beds produced enough gold to persuade Ponce de León that the island merited permanent settlement. He had hoped for a small, strictly controlled group of Spaniards to live and work

The enslaved natives were divided and placed "under the protection" of 48 *hidalgos* (minor aristocracy, from *hijo de algo*, meaning "son of a somebody"). A combination of feudalism and capitalism, this was the *encomienda*

> The term Arawak (from aru, the Lokono word for cassava flour), was used to designate the friendly Amerindians encountered by the Spanish in the Caribbean. These include the Taíno, who occupied the Greater Antilles and the Bahamas.

among the natives without committing abuses or arousing hostility. However, as soon as King Ferdinand caught wind of Puerto Rico's excellent prospects he directed a number of family friends there. Meanwhile, Diego Colón also entered the scene. Incensed that Ponce de León had grabbed the island for himself, he granted titles to two of his father's supporters – Cristóbal Sotomayor and Miguel Díaz – and subsidized their establishment on the island.

San Juan Bautista was now destined to suffer what Ponce de León had tried to avoid. By a colonial ordinance called a *repartimiento*, one of Colón's men enslaved 5,500 natives, ostensibly to convert them to Christianity but in reality to press them into labor.

system, and it was employed throughout Spain's 16th-century New World empire.

Across the northern coast the Spanish opened mines and panning operations, all supported by the free labor of the natives.

The king appointed Ponce de León governor in 1510 but did not empower him to relinquish the *repartimiento*. The mining business proliferated, though there was so much competition for gold that the few who profited were men like Ponce de León, who made their fortunes selling food and supplies to the miners.

Moreover, not even Ponce de León himself could check the Spanish settlers' abuse of the natives, especially in the more remote western end of the island.

Indigenous resistance

During the winter of 1511, violence erupted, and guerrilla warfare soon spread through the island. Ponce de León responded immediately. Within a few days of the initial outburst he and his captains had captured nearly 200 Natives, whom they subsequently sold into slavery, branding them on the face with the king's first initial. By June, peace once again reigned.

For a few years, the search for Puerto Rican gold continued at the expense of the Natives' freedom, and until 1540, when the sources dried up, San Juan Bautista remained one of the New World's foremost suppliers of gold to Spain. To assuage the wounded sensibilities of Juan Ponce de León for stripping his office down to little more than a title, King Ferdinand gave him permission to explore the virgin peninsula northwest of the Antilles which the Spanish called La Florida.

As people continued to immigrate to the island of San Juan Bautista they brought new commercial enterprises with them. The days were gone when *hidalgos* left their homeland to strike it rich in New World gold mines. Gradually, the settlers turned their energies to agriculture. Land was plentiful and easy to come by, water was abundant and the climate mild. Labor posed a problem at first, for the natives had disappeared quickly following the institution of the *repartimiento*. Epidemics of European diseases had quickly swept through the communities of enslaved natives, devastating the population.

Those Indians who escaped fled into the mountainous interior or across the sea to join the tribes of coastal South America. However, West Africans, imported by Portuguese slavers and supplied by the Spanish Crown, provided an affordable replacement.

LEFT: engraving of Ponce de León mortally wounded while exploring Florida.
ABOVE: slave labor created the plantations.

Peasant roots

Two sorts of farm developed. Some islanders, denied political and social status because they were *mestizos* (the progeny of a white and an Indian or black), were unable to obtain large land grants and credit. They resorted to subsistence farming and on their tiny plots raised cassava, corn, vegetables, fruit, rice, and a few cattle. Generally, *mestizos* cleared fields in inland regions that would not compete with the large coastal plantations. Puerto Rico's sizeable peasant class blossomed from the seeds of these 16th-century subsistence farmers.

In addition there were, of course, owners of large plantations. Usually of purely European ancestry, these immigrants and Creoles (born on the island) were chiefly interested in profit. After experimenting with a variety of crops, including ginger and tobacco, they finally settled on sugar as being the most dependable and profitable cash crop. It was relatively new to Europeans, but their sweet tooth appeared to be insatiable.

In 1516, entrepreneurs constructed the island's first *ingenio* – a factory in which raw cane is ground, boiled, and reduced to sugar crystals. A decade and a half later, Puerto Rico sent its first sugar exports to Spain. Ferdinand's successor, Holy Roman Emperor Charles V, was so encouraged by it that he provided a number of techni-

cians and loans for the industry's growth. Peripheral industries burgeoned as well: demand for timber to fuel the *ingenios* and food to fuel the laborers soared, and where sugar is processed, so inevitably rum is produced. Determined to squeeze all the profit out of their sugar cane, the Spanish settlers built distilleries soon after harvesting the first sugar crop.

By 1550, there were 10 active *ingenios* on the island, but the restrictive policies of the mercantilist King Philip II led to a major crash in the industry during the 1580s. Eventually it recovered, but throughout Puerto Rico's history sugar would be not only one of the island's pre-eminent products but also one of its most troubled industries.

Horses and husbandry

After the collapse of the sugar trade, ginger emerged as the most successful product, and despite edicts from the monarch – who preferred the cultivation of sugar – it flourished until the market bottomed out through a surplus. Animal husbandry was another lucrative industry. The armies that conquered Peru, Central America, and Florida rode Puerto Rican horses, and island *hatos* (cattle ranches) supplied the local garrisons with meat.

The possibility of foreign aggression remained a constant threat. By the 1520s, the economic and strategic promise of the island – now officially called Puerto Rico – had become apparent. Moreover, the individual with the clearest sense of Puerto Rico's potential and importance was gone. Juan Ponce de León had been fatally wounded in an encounter with Florida Indians in 1521; his remains are interred in the Cathedral of San Juan. Without a leader close to the Spanish king, defensive measures were hard to obtain.

In the year of Ponce de León's burial, the colonialists transferred the capital city from the site chosen by him to a large natural bay to the north, renaming it San Juan. Mosquitoes had plagued settlers incessantly in the old river-bank town, and the site proved too small to support increased river traffic as agriculture and industry developed.

Advantageous as the new location was for shipping, it left the people vulnerable to foreign invaders. In the 16th and 17th centuries the French, English, and Dutch dedicated themselves to unseating the powerful Habsburg

THE MIGHTY LION

Born around 1460 in San Servos, Spain, Don Juan Ponce de León is known essentially for three things: the discovery of what is now Florida, the conquering and governing of Puerto Rico, and his never-ending search for the mythical Fountain of Youth. Historians believe he sought not only the age-restorative waters but also gold and silver thought to be at the site of the fountain. He explored many regions, including the Bahamas and Bimini, in his quest, but a poisoned arrow shot into his stomach brought his explorations to an abrupt halt. His epitaph, by poet and historian Juan de Castellanos, reads "Here lie the bones of a Lion/mightier in deeds than in name."

monarchs both at home and abroad. As part of this campaign, they launched attack after attack on Spaniards in the New World. Many of these attacks were carried out by privateers.

Fortifications

Encouraged by rumors of impending assault by French war vessels, San Juan officials in 1522 initiated the construction of the port's first garrison. The wooden structure had not been completed before they realized it would be insufficient in the face of an attack. The island's first real defensive edifice was not completed

La Fortaleza did little to supplement the defenses already provided by Casa Blanca. Before it had been completed, army officers informed the crown that it had been built in "a poor place" and begged the appropriation of funds for another fortress. El Castillo de San Felipe del Morro (or, simply, El Morro) was the product of their entreaties. Placed on the rocky tip of the San Juan Peninsula, the fortification, which was finished in the 1540s, did much to assuage the fears of the northern capital's residents.

But Puerto Ricans had more to be concerned with than the French alone. The celebrated "sea

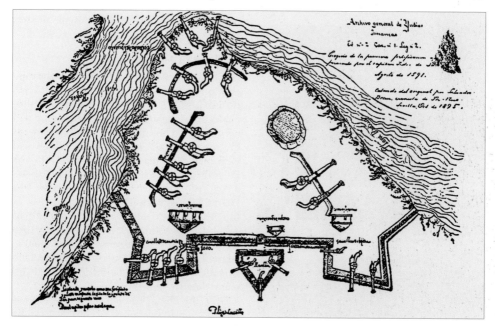

until 1530, when descendants of Ponce de León built a house of stone, Casa Blanca, designed to provide a refuge for colonialists in the face of foreign aggression. The house still stands in Old San Juan. But not even Casa Blanca fulfilled the defensive needs of the settlement, particularly given the expected large-scale population growth. Two years later, the army began building La Fortaleza, sometimes known as Santa Catalina. Today it houses the offices of the governor of Puerto Rico, and it holds the distinction of being the oldest executive mansion in the Western Hemisphere.

LEFT: foreign navies were a constant threat, hence the heavy fortifications at El Morro (**ABOVE**).

dogs" of Queen Elizabeth, Francis Drake and Captain John Hawkins, forcibly seized dozens of Spanish cargo ships traveling between the Antilles and Spain. In 1585, open war broke out between the two nations. England's well-known defeat of the Spanish Armada in 1588 left Spain permanently disabled as a naval power.

More defenses

Towards the end of the 16th century, Puerto Rico received cursory attention. The Council of the Indies, the bureaucracy that oversaw the enforcement and administration of Spanish colonial policy in the Western Hemisphere, conferred upon the governor the title of Captain-General and directed him to improve the island's military preparedness. Governor Diego Menéndez de Valdés exercised tremendous initiative during the 1580s. A number of fortresses were constructed during his tenure, including El Boquerón and Santa Elena in San Juan. Menéndez ordered the refurbishing of the land bridge La Puente de San Antonio – now La Puente de San Gerónimo – and the strengthening of La Fortaleza. He also requisitioned artillery and ammunition, expanding the troop count from 50 to 209 men.

Menéndez stepped in just in the nick of time. A string of English assaults launched with the intention of capturing Puerto Rico was

thwarted, thanks to sturdy defenses. A historic confrontation in the autumn of 1594 resulted in an English defeat. During one of these battles a cannonball shot through the side of Francis Drake's ship and mortally wounded John Hawkins, who was with Drake in his cabin. Drake was forced to retreat.

Yet the English would not give up. While the Spanish king nearly doubled – to 409 – the number of troops at the San Juan garrison of El Morro, the veteran sea warrior George Clifford, third Earl of Cumberland, secretly planned an assault. He was aided by an influenza epidemic in 1598, which wiped out most of the able-bodied population of San Juan. As a result, the city was seriously unprepared for the imminent attack.

Influenza's revenge

From a point 80 miles (129km) east of the capital, Cumberland's troops marched toward San Juan in June, easily taking fortifications as they proceeded. On July 1, the defenders who had been forced to hole up in El Morro surrendered the town. But the same scourge which had weakened the Puerto Ricans now struck the English conquerors. More than 400 English soldiers died of influenza within six weeks. The Puerto Ricans promptly availed themselves of the British state of weakness. Refusing to acknowledge Cumberland's authority, they engaged relentlessly in skirmishes on the outskirts of the town. On August 27, Cumberland withdrew from the island, destroying two plantations in his wake.

Next, the Dutch entered the picture. Determined to bring Spanish dominance of the

---

BARTOLOMÉ DE LAS CASAS

Bartolomé de Las Casas, O.P. (1484–July 17, 1566), was a 16th-century Spanish priest, and the first resident Bishop of Chiapas. As a settler in the New World, he was galvanized into action by witnessing the torture and genocide of the Native Americans by the Spanish colonists. He became famous for his advocacy of the rights of Native Americans, whose cultures especially in the Caribbean he describes with care and attention. He initiated what became known as the Black Legend, which formed images of the Spaniards as predatory colonists and the Indians as innocent victims.

His first-hand interpretations of Taíno cultures as feudal have been criticized 500 years later by Marx-influenced historians since they do not fit neatly into their theoretical vision of the progress of society. However, his descriptions of *caciques* (chiefs or princes), *bohiques* (shamans or clerics), *ni-Taínos* (noblemen), and *naborias* (common folk), clearly show a feudal structure.

Bartolomé de Las Casas's book *A Short Account of the Destruction of the Indies (Brevísima Relación de la Destrucción de las Indias)*, published in 1552, gives a vivid description of the atrocities committed by the conquistadors in the Americas – most particularly, the Caribbean, Central America, and what is now modern Mexico – including a great number of events to which he was actually a witness.

Caribbean to an end, they commissioned Boudewijn Hendrikszoon to take over the island. Hendrikszoon's fleet of eight vessels arrived in San Juan harbor on September 24, 1625. In the course of the next three days the Dutch slowly advanced, forcing a Spanish retreat into El Morro.

The siege of San Juan lasted a month. Finally, the courageous captains Juan de Amezquita and Andrés Botello led surprise attacks on the Dutch trenches on October 22. The next 10 days of battle left the Dutch fleet severely damaged – one ship destroyed and the troops depleted. The island was confirmed as a Spanish domain.

In the 1630s and 1640s, King Philip IV of Spain realized his plan to fortify the entire city of San Juan: seven fortresses were linked by a line of stone walls. The natives were inducted into the provincial district militia.

In control

Having seen off the English and the Dutch, the island was now relatively safe from invaders, and attention was turned to the problem of establishing a strong economic base. But, as a Spanish colony, Puerto Rico was allowed to keep open only one port – San Juan – and was barred from trading with non-Spanish powers. These strictures seriously limited the chances for economic growth.

In the mid-16th century, when the influx of African slaves diminished, Britain threatened Spain on the high seas, and when non-Spanish producers in the West Indies developed more efficient sugar production, the sugar industry collapsed. Virtually nothing was exported in the 1560s and 1570s.

Smugglers all

Ironically, what turned the flagging island economy around was the circumvention of the Spanish mercantilist policies that had been the cause of Puerto Rico's problems to begin with. Refused permanent concessions by the crown, the planters and merchants on Puerto Rico engaged increasingly in illicit foreign trade. Local produce – sugar, livestock, tobacco – was exchanged for slaves, staples, tools, and other manufactured goods. By the mid-17th century almost everyone, from clerical authorities to

LEFT: relics at Casa Blanca, Puerto Rico's first fort.
RIGHT: the patron saint of sailors.

soldiers, from friars to peasants, was involved in smuggling. The coastal towns of Aguada, Arecibo, Cabo Rojo and Fajardo grew into busy centers of illicit international trade.

Word of the proliferation of contraband activity and privateering in Puerto Rico eventually got back to Spain. Recognizing that the island's problems were critical, the king sent a commissioner, Alejandro O'Reilly, to evaluate the state of Puerto Rico. O'Reilly's report of 1765 was remarkably comprehensive and perspicacious. He reckoned the island's population had reached about 45,000: 40,000 free men and 5,000 slaves. Most of the urban inhabitants lived

in northeastern coastal towns and earned their livelihood through smuggling and the black market. Smuggling was so prevalent that O'Reilly could report extensively on prices, supply, demand, and distribution.

In 1765, a Spanish council met to review O'Reilly's report and to formulate a solution to the Puerto Rican problem. Recognizing the need for a stronger enforcement agent to curb contraband trade, Spain more than doubled the *situado* and installed Don Miguel de Muesas as governor. He was instructed to create a sturdy domestic economy. By building bridges and roads, by strengthening defenses, and by improving public education, he hoped to promote agricultural prosperity and domestic self-sufficiency.

Despite the ability with which O'Reilly pleaded Puerto Rico's case, Spain continued to see the development of the island's economy as secondary to its importance as the first naval fortification in the New World empire. Further, a population boom – largely attributable to immigration – had more than tripled the number of residents on the island by the turn of the century.

Meanwhile, Great Britain had its eye on Puerto Rico and was showing a readiness to acquire it. In 1797, after Napoleonic France and Spain had declared war on Britain, a British fleet of 60 vessels manned by 9,000 troops under the command of General Abercrombie landed at Boca de Cangrejos. On April 17, they took Santurce and quickly laid siege to the walled capital. Militia detachments from around the island arrived and launched a counterattack. Abercrombie ordered a retreat on May 1.

Shifting control

Napoleon's invasion of Spain in 1808 sent shock waves through the empire and led to a complete reorganization of colonial rule. As control over the transatlantic territories became weakened, several countries in the Americas won independence from Spain. A provisional assembly called the *Cortés* was convened in Spain to rule in the name of the deposed King Ferdinand VII. Fearing that Puerto Rican separatists who sympathized with the rebellious colonialists in South and Central America – Mexico and Venezuela particularly – would instigate revolutions at home, the *Cortés* invited Puerto Rico to send a delegation to Cádiz in 1809.

An island Creole by the name of Ramón Power Giralt went as the colony's emissary and was elected vice president of the assembly. He pushed for reforms designed to ameliorate the social and economic ills of the island. Puerto Ricans gained status as Spanish citizens; tariffs on machinery and tools were dropped; a university was founded; and measures were taken to improve the island's industry. The *Cortés* disbanded in 1814 when Napoleon retreated and King Ferdinand VII returned to the throne. But the king, wary of the independence fever pervading the colonies, left in place a fair number of Power

THE SETTLEMENT OF CAPARRA

The Caparra ruins, located in the sector of the same name in the municipality of Guaynabo, consist of the remains of the first permanent settlement established on the island by Juan Ponce de León in 1509, which was called Caparra or Ciudad de (city of) Puerto Rico.

Although it had good breezes, the site lacked an important element: easy and direct access to the bay, which was vital for its subsistence. The most direct access was through the mangrove swamps that formed a nearly impenetrable barrier – Caparra was not destined to become the most important city on the island.

Little is known of the physical layout of this first Spanish settlement in Puerto Rico. With few exceptions, the majority of the structures of the city of Caparra were built with perishable materials.

The town was built around a public plaza, which was the site of business and gatherings. The residences were huts or small houses. There were also corrals, stables, and warehouses.

In 1519, the settlement of Caparra was moved to the islet of San Juan, located at the entrance of the bay, a site that was less vulnerable to attacks from the Taíno natives and with better access for transporting merchandise. Over time, people forgot where the exact site of the old town was located. The name of the area remained, however, Pueblo Viejo, or Old Town.

Giralt's reforms in a *cédula de gracias* (royal decree) that was granted in 1815.

In 1807, the US president, Thomas Jefferson, placed an embargo on all trade with the Spanish West Indies, which as a result cut exports by more than half, but after Napoleon Bonaparte's invasion of the Iberian Peninsula Jefferson lifted the embargo.

Not long after it was lifted, new difficulties floated into Puerto Rican harbors. Trying to respond to the threat Napoleon's armies posed on Spain's borders, the Spanish governor called upon its colonies to ship an extraordinary supply of resources which could be used to outfit

and maintain its own troops. With most profitable products going to Spain, Puerto Rico's economy suffered. And added to all these woes was the war of 1812 between Great Britain and the United States.

Increasing independence

The recovery following this tumultuous period included tremendous growth in the island economy. Power Giralt's economic reforms remained in place and, for the first time since their institution, began to have a real effect. Not

---

LEFT: slave market in Puerto Rico. **ABOVE:** the US flag flies prominently outside the University of Puerto Rico. **RIGHT:** replica of a Spanish galleon in Arecibo's Museo de Arte e Historia.

only was trade with the wealthy United States permitted, but the tariffs were also decreased significantly. The *cédula de gracias* declared by Ferdinand VII in 1815 ended the Spanish trade monopoly in Puerto Rico by permitting trade with other countries. However, according to the dictates of the king, only Spanish vessels were allowed to carry on the exports.

Once again, the colonial governors took exception to Spanish policy. Disobeying the king's orders, they gave right of entry to ships regardless of their origins. Also, under a civil intendancy plan instituted by Power Giralt, an independent official was appointed to oversee

financial affairs, rather than their being left in the hands of the governor. Alejandro Ramírez Blanco filled the post first. During his tenure he opened several ports, abolished superfluous taxes, and increased the export of cattle.

Between 1813 and 1818 Puerto Rican trade expanded to approximately eight times its previous level, and in 1824 the king finally relinquished the last vestiges of mercantilism, conceding the right of Puerto Rican ports to harbor non-Spanish merchant ships. The future of the Puerto Rican economy became clear to many. Spain was neither a reliable nor a tremendously profitable trading partner, and the more Puerto Rico moved away from its dependence on the mother country, the faster its economy would develop. ❑

SELF RULE AND THE UNITED STATES

"It wasn't much of a war, but it was all the war there was,"
said Teddy Roosevelt. Even so, the Spanish-American
War marked a turning point for Puerto Rico

In 1820 the population of Puerto Rico was estimated at 150,000. By 1900 it had mushroomed to about a million. The character of society had changed drastically; for the first time, agitators for Puerto Rican autonomy were vocal and posed a serious threat to the Spanish government. Increasingly, the royally appointed governor and the army would be identified as impediments to the achievement of Puerto Rican independence. In 1820 Pedro Dubois had scarcely initiated a recruitment program when he was discovered by the government. The governor incarcerated Dubois at El Morro and had him executed before a firing squad.

Three years after the Dubois incident, another event in the struggle for autonomy took place. After the restoration of Ferdinand to the throne in 1814, a series of governors with absolute power ruled Puerto Rico. On the first day of 1820, an army commander declared the liberal reformist constitution of 1812 to be still in effect. One by one officials of various districts

BETANCES.

When the US acquired Puerto Rico, only an eighth of the population was literate, and only one in 14 children attended school.

joined him. The already weak king, hoping to avoid an all-out revolution, had to concede, and decided to resurrect the *Cortés*, disbanded in 1814. José María Quiñones went to Spain as the representative from Puerto Rico in 1823. He submitted a plan to introduce more autonomy

LEFT: battling in the Spanish-American War. **RIGHT:** "subversive beard" Dr Ramón Emeterio Betances.

to the island colonies, particularly in the administration of domestic affairs.

Reign of oppression

The *Cortés* approved the Quiñones proposal, but its intentions fell to pieces before it could see them through. In 1823 the constitutional government of Spain collapsed. The king returned to absolute power and appointed the first of 14 governors of Puerto Rico who exercised total authority over the colony, collectively staging a 42-year reign of oppression and virtual martial law.

The first of these dictators was Miguel de la Torre. Hanging on to the governorship for 15 years, Torre imposed a 10pm curfew and established the *visita* – an island-wide inspection network that allowed him to keep abreast of activity in the colony and maintain tight security. Although Torre's reign was oppressive, it had some benefits. He took control of the country's development, built roads and bridges

> The Treaty of Paris gave Puerto Rico to the US, beginning a long relationship between the two countries. One of the long-term effects of the Treaty of Paris was that many Puerto Ricans immigrated to the US, especially New York City.

movement. It was a troubled time for the island; between 1848 and 1867, seven consecutive military dictators governed the island, taking advantage of the institutions put into place by the Torre administration. To add to the colony's misery, in the 1850s a cholera epidemic swept across the island, claiming the lives of 30,000. Ramón Emeterio Betances, a doctor renowned for his efforts against the epidemic, was exiled in 1856 for his criticism of the colonial authorities.

Intimidated by the growing separatist fervor in Puerto Rico and Cuba, and by the Dominican Revolution in 1862, the Spanish Crown invited Puerto Rico and Cuba in 1865 to draft

and brought in huge numbers of slaves to foster sugar production, contributing significantly to the lasting development of the local economy.

Subversive beards

In 1838 a group of separatists led by Buenaventura Quiñones plotted a putsch. Word of the conspiracy leaked out and several of the participants were executed; the others were exiled. Declaring beards subversive, the new governor banned the wearing of facial hair. Subsequent governors passed laws aimed at the suppression of blacks (following the historic slave rebellion on Martinique) and instituted the *libreta* laws which required all inhabitants of Puerto Rico to carry passbooks and restricted unauthorized

a colonial constitution in the form of a "Special Law of the Indies." The documents which emerged called for the abolition of slavery, freedom of the press and speech, and independence on a commonwealth basis. While the crown dragged its feet in granting these concessions, in Puerto Rico the angry governor, José María Marchessi, exiled several leading reformists, including the recently returned Betances. Fleeing to New York, they joined with other separatist Puerto Ricans and Cubans.

From New York the autonomists directed the independence movement during the 1860s and 1870s under the aegis of the Puerto Rican Revolutionary Committee. Covert satellite organizations formed in villages and towns across Puerto

Rico, centering around Mayagüez. On September 23, 1868, several hundred men congregated at a farm outside the northwestern mountain town of Lares. Marching under a banner that read *Libertad o Muerte. Viva Puerto Rico Libre. Año 1868* ("Liberty or Death. Long Live Free Puerto Rico. Year 1868"), they took the town and arrested its officials. They elected a provisional president and proclaimed the Republic of Puerto Rico. The republic would be short-lived. Troops sent by the governor met the rebel front at San Sebastián and won an easy victory. Within six weeks the echoes of the "Grito de Lares" – "the Shout of Lares" – had died com-

pletely, although it has retained lasting symbolic importance in the Puerto Rican independence movement.

Brief independence

Puerto Rico did enjoy a brief flash of autonomy in 1897. The Autonomist Party voted to fuse with the monarchist Liberal Party of Spain after forming a pact with its leader, Mateo Sagasta, which guaranteed Puerto Rican autonomy if the Liberals came to power. On the assassination of the Spanish prime minister Sagasta became Spain's leader; he immediately declared Puerto Rico an autonomous state.

ABOVE: 19th-century Spanish currency.

Adopting a two-chamber constitutional republican form of government, as agreed with Sagasta, the Puerto Ricans elected a lower house of assembly and half of the delegates to the upper house. The governor was still appointed by Spain, but his power was restricted. The new government assumed power in July 1898. Later that month General Nelson A. Miles of the United States landed on the southern coast with an army of 16,000 men. It was the beginning of the Spanish-American War and the end of short-lived Puerto Rican autonomy.

The US steps in

"It wasn't much of a war, but it was all the war there was," Teddy Roosevelt reflected on the Spanish-American War. On August 31, 1898, Spain surrendered. The Puerto Rico campaign had lasted only two weeks, the whole war less than four months. General Miles tried to assuage the inhabitants' anxiety about annexation as a United States protectorate, however, telling them: "We have come … to promote your prosperity and to bestow upon you the immunities and blessing of the liberal institutions of our government." His assurances did not pacify everyone. Emeterio Betances, now aging, issued a warning to his fellow people: "If Puerto Rico does not act fast, it will be an American colony forever."

On December 10, 1898, the Treaty of Paris, which settled the final terms of Spain's surrender, was signed. In addition to a large reparations payment, the United States won Puerto Rico and the Philippines from Spain, but Puerto Rico wasn't exactly a grand prize at the time. Its population had reached about a million. A third were blacks and mulattos who generally had little capital or land. Two percent of the population owned more than two-thirds of the agricultural land, yet 60 percent of the land owned was mortgaged at high interest rates.

It ain't over till it's over

The United States set up a military government, and Puerto Rico was placed under the charge of the War Department. Assuming a hard-headed approach to underdevelopment and a lagging economy, the first three governors-general enjoyed almost dictatorial power. They introduced American currency, suspended defaulted mortgages, and promoted trade with the United States. They improved public health, reformed tax laws, and overhauled local government.

But to many Puerto Ricans, autonomy was still vital. A leading autonomist leader, Luis Muñoz Rivera, organized a new party in an attempt to reach a compromise between the separatists and the US government. The Federal Party and its ally, the new Republican Party, advocated cooperation with the United States, especially in commercial matters, full civil rights and an autonomous civilian government. But not even the conciliatory approach that Muñoz Rivera endorsed satisfied the McKinley administration. The colonial governor-general, George W. Davis, reported to the president that "the people gen-

Things began to look up in 1900, when the Secretary of War, Elihu Root, proposed a program for the gradual introduction of autonomy for Puerto Ricans which President McKinley endorsed. However, though Puerto Rico was suddenly closer to autonomy than it had been since before the Spanish-American War, the path to home rule was not yet clear.

The big debate

For the next 48 years, Puerto Rico and the US had a strange colonial-protectorate relationship. While it was widely acknowledged that the latter possessed enormous wealth from which

erally have no conception of political rights combined with political responsibilities."

As if political turmoil were not enough, Mother Nature interfered in the form of Hurricane San Ciriaco in 1899. Three thousand people died, and the damage to property was immense. The hurricane devastated the vital sugar and coffee crops and left a quarter of the island's inhabitants without homes. The US Congress awarded only $200,000 to the island in relief payments.

Puerto Rico faced an unhappy future. The economy was on the brink of collapse, the hostilities with inept American administrators continued, and there were the apparently insurmountable difficulties of widespread illiteracy and poverty.

the former stood to benefit, Puerto Ricans also feared that Betances's prediction would come true – that Puerto Rico would be swallowed up culturally and economically if its bonds with the US were to strengthen.

Puerto Rico looms large in recent American history. It was the first non-Continental US territory and served as the test case for the formation and implementation of colonial policy.

Special interest groups in the United States polarized into two lobbies. The agricultural contingent, fearing competition from Puerto

ABOVE: US and Puerto Rican flags fly harmoniously over El Castillo de San Cristóbal.
RIGHT: American medical officers at Coamo Springs.

Rican producers whose labor costs were lower, allied with racists who dreaded the influx of the "Latin race" which would result from granting US citizenship to Puerto Ricans. And as proof of Benjamin Franklin's observation that politics makes strange bedfellows, these opponents of the administration's Puerto Rican colonial plan found themselves under the blankets with liberal Democrats who opposed all imperialism.

The burgeoning of a colony

With the passing in 1900 of the Foraker Act (*see box below*), Puerto Rico took on a brand new colonial status, but reception of the Act

could have been better. An immediate challenge to its constitutional legality brought it before the US Supreme Court, where the majority declared that constitutionality was not applicable in an "unincorporated entity" like Puerto Rico. Dissenting Chief Justice Fuller wrote that it left Puerto Rico "a disembodied shade in an intermediate state of ambiguous existence."

Reluctant US citizens

On the eve of the United States' entry into World War I in 1917, President Wilson approved the Jones-Shafroth Act granting US

THE FORAKER ACT

On April 2, 1900, US President McKinley signed a civil law that established a civilian government in Puerto Rico. Although officially known as the Organic Act of 1900, it was more commonly referred to as the Foraker Act for its sponsor, Charles Benson Foraker.

The new government had a presidentially appointed governor, an Executive Council comprising both Americans and Puerto Ricans, and a House of Delegates with 35 elected members.

There was also a judicial system with a Supreme Court. All federal laws of the United States were to be in effect on the island. In addition, a Resident Commissioner chosen by the Puerto Rican people would speak for the colony in

the House of Representatives, but have no vote. The first civil governor of the island under the Act was Charles H. Allen, inaugurated on May 1, 1900, in San Juan.

An initial 15 percent tariff was imposed on all imports to, and exports from, the United States, and the revenues would be used to benefit Puerto Rico. Free trade was promised after two years.

The colonial government would determine its own taxation programs and oversee the insular treasury. Ownership of large estates by American corporations was discouraged by prohibiting businesses to carry on agriculture on more than 500 acres (200 hectares). However, this clause was rarely enforced, and capital-rich firms from the US moved in.

citizenship to all Puerto Ricans. This Act affronted many Puerto Rican statesmen. For years they had pressed for a break from the US and now, in blatant contradiction of their demands, Congress was drawing them in even more. Muñoz Rivera, the Resident Commissioner, had beseeched Congress to hold a plebiscite – but to no avail.

Catch-22

The "Catch-22" of Puerto Rico's relationship with the US had emerged full-blown. The more political maturity the colony showed, the more fervently Nationalists agitated for independ-

ence. The more hostile to the US the colony seemed to American lawmakers, the more reluctant they were to give any ground.

During this period of strong antagonism between Puerto Rico and the United States, the island's economy and population actually grew rapidly. Improved health care resulted in a significant drop in the death rate.

Meanwhile, employment and production increased, and government revenues rose. Big American corporations pocketed most of the profits from this growth, and Congress assured them of continued wealth.

In contrast, the average Puerto Rican family earned between just $150 and $200 a year; many *jíbaros* had sold their own little farms to work for farm estates and factories.

The Labor Movement

Pablo Iglesias, a disciple of Samuel Gompers, one of the great fathers of American trade unions, led the move to organize Puerto Rican laborers. By 1909 the labor movement, organized under Iglesias's leadership as the Free Federation, identified itself with the labor union movement in the US. It even assumed the task of Americanizing Puerto Rico.

"The labor movement in Porto [*sic*] Rico," Iglesias wrote, "has no doubt been, and is, the most efficient and safest way of conveying the sentiments and feelings of the American people to the hearts of the people of Porto Rico."

A 1914 cigar strike and then a 1915 sugarcane strike brought useful publicity. Iglesias was subsequently elected to the new Senate of Puerto Rico in 1917.

EXODUS TO HAWAII

The 1899 floods caused by 28 days of continuous hurricane rain damaged the agricultural industry and left 3,400 dead and thousands of people without shelter, food, or work. As a result, there was a shortage of sugar from the Caribbean in the world market and a huge demand for the product from Hawaii and other sugar-producing countries. To meet the demand, plantation owners began a campaign to recruit laborers in Puerto Rico.

On November 22, 1900, the first group of Puerto Ricans, consisting of 56 men, began their long journey to Maui, Hawaii. The trip was long and harsh. They first set sail from San Juan harbor to New Orleans, Louisiana. Once in New Orleans, they were boarded on a railroad train and sent to

Los Angeles, California. From there they set sail to Hawaii. According to the *Los Angeles Times*, dated December 26, 1901, the Puerto Rican workers were mistreated and starved by the shippers and the railroad company. They arrived in Honolulu, on December 23, 1900, and were sent to work in different plantations on Hawaii's four islands.

By October 17, 1901, 5,000 Puerto Rican men, women, and children had made their new homes on the four islands. Records show that, in 1902, 34 plantations had 1,773 Puerto Ricans on their payrolls; 1,734 worked as field hands, and another 39 were clerks or overseers (foremen).

Today there are almost 30,000 Puerto Ricans or Hawaiian-Puerto Ricans living in Hawaii.

Trouble-shooting

The Great Depression nearly undid Puerto Rico. For the poorest island of the Caribbean the desperation of the 1930s caused sugar-cane workers to go on strike nationally in 1934 -- an unsuccessful strike that would eventually lead to the formation of the Puerto Rican Communist Party.

Two hurricanes accompanied the collapse of the economy – San Felipe in 1928 and San Cipriano in 1932 – destroying millions of dollars' worth of property and crops. Starvation and disease took a heavy toll on the population during the Depression. Across the island, tion was that (according to both American foreign policy and international law) the United States' claims on Puerto Rico were in fact illegal, since Puerto Rico was already autonomous at the time of occupation.

The strength and seriousness of Albizu Campos's Nationalist organization were made abundantly clear on February 23, 1936. Two of his followers, Hiram Rosado and Elías Beauchamp, shot and killed the chief of police of San Juan. The assassins were arrested and summarily beaten to death, and Albizu Campos and seven key party members were imprisoned in the Federal Prison in Georgia.

haggard, demoralized people waited in long queues for inadequate government food handouts. But out of the poverty and deprivation, a new voice emerged.

It belonged to Pedro Albizu Campos, a former US Army officer and a graduate of Harvard Law School. He was of a generation of Puerto Ricans who were children at the time of the United States' takeover. Equipped with a great understanding of the American system, he used it to become a leader of militant revolutionaries. Albizu Campos's accusa-

LEFT: the Puerto Rican national crest.
ABOVE: dissident Pedro Albizu Campos arrested in Puerto Rico.

A year later, however, the party was still strong. Denied a permit to hold a demonstration in the town of Ponce, a group of Albizu Campos's followers dressed in black shirts assembled to march on March 21, 1937. As the procession moved forward to the tune of *La Borinqueña* – the Puerto Rican anthem – a shot rang out. The origin of the gunfire has never been determined, but within moments police and marchers were exchanging bullets. Twenty people were killed and another 100 wounded in the panic-stricken crossfire that ensued. The governor called the affair "a riot"; the American Civil Liberties Union labeled it "a massacre." The event is still remembered today as *La Masacre de Ponce.* ❑

MODERN TIMES

Colony or commonwealth? Or independent state?
Luis Muñoz Marín helped decide the issue with
the innovative "Operation Bootstrap"

The United States began to export Puerto Rico's share of the New Deal in 1933, but it was not a winning hand. President Franklin Roosevelt sent a string of appointees to the Governor's Mansion in San Juan, but their efforts proved inadequate and aggravating to many Puerto Ricans. Then, from amidst the crumbling political parties, a brilliant star in Puerto Rico's history appeared.

Luis Muñoz Marín, son of the celebrated statesman Luis Muñoz Rivera, had served in government since 1932 and had used his charm and connections with the American political elite to bring attention to the plight of the colony. In 1938, young Muñoz Marín founded the Partido Democrático Popular (PDP), running on the slogan "Bread, Land and Liberty," and adopting the *pava* – the broad-brimmed straw hat worn by *jíbaros* – as the party symbol. In 1940, the *populares* took over half the total seats in the upper and lower Houses.

A people's governor

Muñoz Marín, elected leader of the Senate, decided to try to work with the new governor to achieve recovery. The appointee, Rexford Guy Tugwell, was refreshingly different from his predecessors. Able to speak Spanish and evincing a genuine compassion for the Puerto Ricans, he seemed promising. Muñoz Marín's good faith paid off. By improving the distribution of relief resources and by proposing a plan for long-term economic development, contingent upon continued union with the United States, Muñoz Marín convinced Tugwell that

PUERTO RICO WANTS YOU

LEFT: coffee bean sculpture in Yauco, hub of the coffee industry in Puerto Rico. **RIGHT:** Uncle Sam's daughter.

Puerto Rico was finally ready to assume the responsibility of electing its own governor.

As a first step, the United States appointed Puerto Rico's resident commissioner, Jesús Piñero, to the post. In 1946, Piñero became the first native governor in the island's history. Simultaneously, the US unveiled plans for the popular election of Puerto Rico's governor, demonstrating new confidence in the colony.

The people elected Muñoz Marín, of course. In 1948 he took office as the first popularly elected governor and put forward his proposal for turning Puerto Rico into an associated free state. Learning from the newly independent Philippines, where instant autonomy had crippled economic and social progress, the US delayed endorsing Muñoz Marín's plan.

However, in 1950, President Truman approved Public Law 600, the Puerto Rican Commonwealth Bill. It provided for a plebiscite in which voters would decide whether to remain a colony or assume status as a commonwealth. As the latter, Puerto Rico would draft its own constitution, though the US Congress would retain "paramount power." In June 1951, Puerto Ricans voted three to one in favor of the commonwealth.

Two disturbing events punctuated the otherwise smooth transition to commonwealth status. On the very day that President Truman signed Public Law 600, a group of armed Nationalists marched on the Governor's Mansion, La Fortaleza. In a brief skirmish a policeman and four Nationalists were gunned down. Simultaneously, outbursts in five other towns left over 100 casualties, including 27 dead. The violence extended beyond Puerto Rican shores. Two Puerto Ricans from New York traveled to Washington and made an attempt on the president's life a month later. In March 1954, four Puerto Rican Nationalists fired into the House of Representatives from the visitors' gallery, wounding five Congressmen.

Muñoz Marín resigned from political office in 1964 but his party remained in power. In 1966, a commission determined that commonwealth, statehood, and independence all deserved consideration. Seven months later the PDP, pushing for a decision, passed a bill mandating a plebiscite. Muñoz Marín re-entered the fray in support of continuing as a commonwealth. He argued that Puerto Rico had been placed fourth in the worldwide rate of economic progress only due to its relationship with the US. Further, he claimed, statehood could easily bring an end to the independent culture of Puerto Rico. His arguments held sway; two-thirds of the ballots in 1967 were cast for commonwealth status.

Eggs in one basket

Muñoz Marín had long ago recognized that the key to averting future economic catas-

POPULAR CULTURE: A PUERTO RICAN HALL OF FAME

For decades, Puerto Rico has made its presence known in the world of film, music, and sports. From José Ferrer to Benicio del Toro, Hollywood has seen its share of Puerto Rican artists shine. Ferrer was the first Puerto Rican to win an Oscar, for his performance in Cyrano de Bergerac in 1950. The actor, who made his debut on Broadway in 1935, also won a Tony Award for playing the title role in Edmond Rostand's Cyrano.

Actress, singer, and dancer Rita Moreno became the second Puerto Rican to win an Oscar for her fiery performance in the 1961 film West Side Story. To this day, she is the only female to have won an Oscar, an Emmy, a Grammy and a Tony award. Other actors such as Raúl Juliá and Benicio del Toro have followed in their footsteps. While Juliá never

received an award in life, he is known for his memorable performances in such films as Puerto Rico's La Gran Fiesta, Kiss of the Spider Woman and Romero.

Del Toro, who has made his mark as both an actor and a producer, became the third Puerto Rican to win an Oscar for his performance in Traffic. He has also won a Golden Globe and a Screen Actors Guild Award, among others. Other famous Puerto Rican actors include Jennifer López, Jimmy Smits, Rosie Pérez, and Roselyn Sánchez.

Celebrities on the music scene include guitarist and singer José Feliciano, mambo musician Tito Puente, pop artists Ricky Martin and Chayanne, and reggaetón artist Daddy Yankee, whose break-out hit Gasolina has traveled the world.

trophe lay in avoiding a dependence on agriculture. Relying heavily on one or two crops left Puerto Rico subject to too many risks: weather, foreign production, and interest rates. The government established the Puerto Rican Industrial Development Corporation in 1942 to oversee the development of government-sponsored manufacturing. When the state plans floundered, the administration canceled the program and initiated a brand new plan, known as Operation Bootstrap. Aimed at developing an economy based on rum, tourism, and industry, the program sent dozens of PR agents to the mainland on promotional tours extol-

Operation Serenity

As a complement to Operation Bootstrap, the government instituted a program entitled "Operation Serenity," which had the uplifting of the arts as its objective. Programs to promote both music and art were administered by the

> *Puerto Ricans in the US number about 3 million today, though ignorance of their culture is endemic, as illustrated in Rosie Pérez's 2006 documentary* Yo Soy Boricua, Pa'que tú lo Sepas!

ling the Puerto Rican climate, geography, economy, and people.

During the early years of Operation Bootstrap, manufacturing jobs quadrupled to over 20,000, but between 1950 and 1954 over 100,000 Puerto Ricans moved to the mainland to take advantage of the postwar labor market. In New York, Puerto Ricans became the archetypal Latinos, later celebrated in *West Side Story*. A slowdown followed the resumption of peace, but in 1955 manufacturing contributed more to the economy than agriculture for the first time ever.

Institute of Puerto Rican Culture. The thinking at the time was that "man cannot live by bread alone." Poster-making got its debut at the Department of Community Education, where serigraph and lithograph techniques were developed with a certain success. Puerto Rico's newfound skill of poster-making promoted government instructional films and art exhibits, and also portrayed local history. A large group of artists and filmmakers were thus able to develop their skills through the Community Education programs.

Today, the production of Puerto Rico's imaginative posters goes back to those days in the 1950s when the islanders began to pick themselves up from their meager conditions.

LEFT: Luis Muñoz Marín, Puerto Rico's brilliant political star and the first popularly elected governor.
ABOVE: Rita Moreno in *West Side Story*.

Meetings and Conventions

With a state-of-the-art Convention Center and dozens of hotel meeting facilities, Puerto Rico is an ideal destination for conventions

In the words of Ramón Sánchez, executive vice president and chief operating officer of the Puerto Rico Convention Bureau, a non-profit organization that markets Puerto Rico as a meetings and conventions destination: "Puerto Rico has

the air access, the infrastructure, with the hotels, roads, and convention center, plus there is no passport required from the United States."

Puerto Rico is the most accessible island in the Caribbean, with more than 1,300 weekly non-stop flights from the United States, its main market.

The Puerto Rico Convention Center, which opened in November 2005, is located in the heart of San Juan and offers panoramic views extending from Old San Juan to Condado, with the beach only a mile away. Its elegant modern architecture evokes some of the island's tropical characteristics such as the signature wave-like facade. At 580,000 sq ft (54,000 sq metres), it is the largest convention center in the Caribbean, with the capacity to accommodate groups of up to 10,000 people.

In 2007, it won the Prime Site Award of Excellence awarded by the publishers of *Facilities and Destinations Magazine. India Today Travel Plus* Magazine recently selected the Puerto Rico Convention Center as the Top Convention Center of the World from a list of eight venues.

Puerto Rico boasts more than 1.2 million sq ft (111,500 sq metres) of meeting space with more than 13,300 rooms and a variety of top-name hotel brands such as Hilton, Sheraton, Marriott, and Ritz-Carlton. There is aggressive hotel development on the island, which includes the construction of three hotels at the Convention Center District and the introduction of such brands as Mandarin Oriental, Fairmont, and Regent, among other luxury names.

Many hotels and resorts throughout the island have either revamped or added meeting space, such as El Conquistador Resort in Fajardo, the Wyndham Río Mar Beach Resort in Río Grande, the Hilton Ponce Golf & Casino Resort, the Condado Plaza Hotel, and the Caribe Hilton Hotel in San Juan.

Bring your event to Puerto Rico

The PRCB acts as a facilitator for groups interested in bringing their meetings or conventions to Puerto Rico. From the moment a meeting planner or representative contacts the PRCB, it provides them with all the information necessary to help them decide whether Puerto Rico is the right choice. It can tell you everything from where to meet to what to do, where to stay and where to eat. The PRCB has sales offices in Puerto Rico, Chicago, Miami, New York, and Washington DC.

Once a potential client contacts the bureau, the PRCB gathers all of the necessary information: the number or rooms wanted, the date of the event, the amount of space needed, whether they are looking for special rates, transportation, etc.

With that information, the PRCB can line up the hotels based on the client's needs and send out requests for proposal. Once the hotels respond with their proposals, the PRCB sends them to the client, after which the client either makes a decision and begins to negotiate with the hotel or comes to Puerto Rico for a site inspection, according to Sánchez. To book your convention or meeting in Puerto Rico, contact any of the PRCB sales offices. In Chicago, tel: 312-840 8090; Miami, tel: 305-471 0202; New York, tel: 212-265 9500; Washington DC, tel: 202-457 9262, and Puerto Rico, tel: 787-725 2110, or email: info@meetpuertorico.com. ❏

LEFT: the new Puerto Rico Convention Center, San Juan.

Tax holiday

Operation Bootstrap later evolved into Section 936, a clause in the US Internal Revenue Code that partially exempted manufacturers from having to pay federal income tax on profits earned by their subsidiaries in Puerto Rico. Although 936 was phased out in 2005, some 2,000 factories still operate throughout the island, churning out everything from Microsoft software to Bumble Bee tuna, all for the huge American market.

In 1985, when Section 936 was first threatened by congressional budget-cutters, former governor Rafael Hernández Colón came up with a novel approach to save it: he offered to

Critics of the island's political system say the same Operation Bootstrap that created jobs for island residents also contributed to the system's current bloated payroll and Puerto Ricans' belief that the government must provide for them.

In 2006, Governor Aníbal Acevedo Vilá, faced with a $738 million fiscal year-end shortfall, ordered a two-week partial government shutdown that put 100,000 people out of work.

While it is hoped that the budgetary woes will eventually be resolved by the implementation of the island's first ever sales tax on consumer goods and services – initially set at 7 percent – the work stoppage actually sparked an economic slump.

link 936 to President Reagan's Caribbean Basin Initiative (CBI), a trade program designed to help the struggling economies of Central America and the Caribbean. As a result of the deal, Section 936 was extended for 20 more years, and Puerto Rico ended up funding at least $100 million worth of development projects per year in selected beneficiary nations.

The island's heavy dependence on US federal aid programs and local government jobs have led some to call Puerto Rico a "welfare state."

ABOVE: The Arecibo Observatory – the world's largest radio telescope – is a testament to modern Puerto Rico.
RIGHT: painting of a gourd player in the Old Customs House Museum in Arroyo.

Today, Puerto Rico has a 93 percent literacy rate – higher than most states and a big improvement over 1898, when only an eighth of the population could read.

Luxury tourism

Although manufacturing still accounts for 42 percent of economic output, the island's low-cost lure has disappeared.

Now Puerto Rico may be forced to reduce the government payroll and compete in the global economy. Indeed, one option being explored is to place greater emphasis on luxury tourism, with the planned construction of five-star resorts and vacation homes. Tourism currently accounts for just 7 percent of the island's GNP.

Despite economic troubles, residents, even the poorest, enjoy a relatively high standard of living; Puerto Rico has a per-capita income of around $14,000. Though far less than the poorest US state, Mississippi, it tops most Caribbean islands and outranks any Latin American nation. In fact, the island's per-capita income is said to be grossly underestimated, owing to the Treasury department's inability to capture, via income tax, a thriving underground economy of cash and bartering.

The belief in an underground economy is fueled by visible prosperity. Virtually every Puerto Rican owns a TV and telephone; there are 1.5 million cars on the island, almost one for every two inhabitants; and fuel consumption is half of the Caribbean total.

On the other hand, Puerto Rico is plagued with serious problems such as overpopulation, high unemployment (14 percent), water contamination, deforestation, a high incidence of HIV/Aids, and a high crime rate. Sociologists blame many of the island's problems on the identity crisis caused by Puerto Rico's unusual political status.

Lack of independence

Under commonwealth status, Puerto Ricans are exempt from US federal income tax, though they do pay personal income taxes to their own government and are subject to the US Army draft. Proportionately more Puerto Ricans died in Vietnam than Americans – all having been sent there by a president for whom they could not vote. To date more than a quarter of a million Puerto Ricans have served in the US Armed Forces.

Because Puerto Rico is not an independent nation, there is no Puerto Rican passport; travel to the US mainland is unrestricted. Some 2.5 million now live in the US, about half of them in New York City.

Although island residents cannot actually vote in American presidential elections, they can vote in the Democratic and Republican primaries. They also elect a resident commissioner to the US House of Representatives who has a voice – but no vote – on legislative matters.

GLOBAL WARMING AND HURRICANES

Global warming isn't to blame for the recent jump in hurricanes in the Atlantic, concluded a 2008 study by a prominent federal scientist. Not only that, but warmer temperatures will apparently reduce the number of hurricanes in the Atlantic according to research meteorologist Tom Knutson.

In the past, Knutson raised concerns about the effects of climate change on storms. His recent paper has the potential to heat up a simmering debate among meteorologists about future effects of global warming in the Atlantic.

Many climate-change experts have tied the rise of hurricanes in recent years to global warming and the hotter waters that fuel them. Another group of hurricane experts claim there is no link. They attributed the recent increase to a natural multi-decade cycle. What makes this study different is Knutson, a meteorologist with the National Oceanic and Atmospheric Administration's fluid dynamics lab in Princeton, NJ. He has warned about the harmful effects of climate change and has even complained in the past about being censored by government.

He said his new study, based on a computer model, argues "against the notion that we've already seen a really dramatic increase in Atlantic hurricane activity resulting from greenhouse warming."

The study, published in the journal *Nature Geoscience*, predicted that by the end of the century the number of hurricanes in the Atlantic will fall by 18 percent.

Puerto Rican politics

Contrary to popular belief, Puerto Rico's No. 1 pastime isn't baseball – it's politics. Everywhere you'll find people enthusiastically discussing and arguing about the political situation. The pros and cons of statehood, commonwealth, and independence – as well as the activities of politicians – dominate most conversations.

There are four main political "players": the Popular Democratic Party, the New Progressive Party, the Puerto Rican Independence Party, and the Puerto Ricans for Puerto Rico Party.

The PRPR was formed in 2003. Recently certified by the State Elections Committee, it debuted

The year 1998 marked the 100th anniversary of the US presence in Puerto Rico, and a December plebiscite saw about 51 percent voting for the fifth alternative on the ballot – "None of the Above" – narrowly defeating the 46 percent who opted for statehood. Less than 3 percent favored independence. The status controversy continues, with incoming government administrations promising to bring the issue up in US Congress for a permanent resolution.

Weather woes

In September 1998, Puerto Rico sustained huge losses as Hurricane Georges wreaked its havoc.

in the November 2008 elections and got 2.3 percent of the votes. The party's focus is on stopping urban sprawl and redeveloping cities into livable spaces. The PRPR does not have a status preference, though it does support a status resolution.

The PIP pushes for complete independence. Though highly visible, it garners few votes. The NPP and the PDP dominate the political landscape. Like the PIP, the NPP and PDP platforms are status-driven. NPP supporters seek statehood while PDP members favor the current commonwealth status.

LEFT: prelude to disaster: waves crash on the rocks near San Juan as Hurricane Georges draws near.
ABOVE: a political statement on a hidden wall.

The death toll was 12, and about 80,000 homes were destroyed. When Georges struck, the island had just recovered from four other hurricanes that caused great devastation. Immediately afterwards, Puerto Rico was declared a disaster area by former US President Bill Clinton. The estimated loss in property was $2 billion. The US Congress allocated $74 million in emergency funds, while a group of Federal Emergency Management Agency officials was on hand within days to help residents. The sting of severe weather conditions lingers into the 21st century. In 2004 parts of Puerto Rico suffered from flooding when the island was hit by tropical storm Jeanne, which picked up strength and became a hurricane when it hit the Dominican Republic and Haiti. ❏

PUERTO RICAN CUISINE

**Processed foods are threatening to squeeze out local dishes.
But you can still find tasty concoctions from Taíno roots,
African flavors, and Spanish traditions**

Carib and Spanish destruction of Puerto Rico's native Taíno tribes, for all its ruthlessness, was far from complete. It has been said that Puerto Rican society today reflects its African and Indian origins more than its Spanish ones, and there is much truth in that. Non-Spanish ways live on in customs, rituals, language, and all aspects of life, and one can see in many facial features the unfamiliar expression of the Taínos, a race otherwise lost to us forever. But nowhere is the Taíno influence more visible, or more welcome, than in Puerto Rican cuisine, one of the great culinary amalgams of our hemisphere.

Imagine a Taíno man – call him Otoao and set his caste at *naboria*, one of the higher agricultural castes in the Taíno hierarchy – rising one sunny morning after having won a glorious victory the previous day over the invading Caribs. This victory was cause for an *areyto*, the Taíno ritual that either preceded or followed any happening of even the remotest importance. Births, deaths,

> In Puerto Rico, adobo *is a seasoned salt that is generously sprinkled on meats and seafood prior to grilling or frying.*

victories, defeats... it's *areyto* time. Like other socio-religious Taíno festivals, *Areytos* required intricate preparations for whatever food and drink was to be served, and, as a *naboria*, Otoao was in charge of hunting and fishing for the tribe.

PRECEDING PAGES: coconut is a key ingredient in Puerto Rican cuisine. **LEFT:** fresh local produce. **RIGHT:** complimentary drinks at the Bacardi Distillery in Cataño.

Not that Otoao's wife Tai had it terribly easy. As a *naboria* woman (a woman's caste was determined by that of her husband), Tai was responsible for the cultivation and harvesting of the fields (*conucos*) as well as the preparation of the meals. These were elaborate, and the Taínos managed to get an astounding range of food on the banquet table.

The menu that evening included roast *jutías* (young guinea pigs) seasoned with sweet red chili peppers, fried fish in corn oil, fresh shellfish, and a variety of freshly harvested vegetables. Among the vegetables were *yautías* (starchy tubers similar to potatoes and yams), corn, yams, cassava and the same small red chili peppers used to season the *jutías*. Bread was *casabe*, a mixture of pureed cassava and water cooked between two hot rocks. For dessert, the Taínos had fresh fruit picked from the extensive variety available on the island. The culmination of the celebration was the drinking of an alcoholic beverage made from fermented corn juice.

This activity was accompanied by the ceremonial inhalation of hallucinogenic fumes thought to make the warriors fitter for battle. The Taínos made hallucinogens of many sorts, the most common of which used the hanging, bell-shaped flowers of the *campana* tree to make a potent and mind-bending tea.

Most of the dietary staples of the Taínos survive in the Puerto Rican cuisine of today, albeit some in altered form. Puerto Rican cooking is now an amalgam of Taíno, Spanish, and African traditions. Much of this intermingling took place early in the island's history, with Spanish colonists incorporating a variety of their own ingredients and techniques into the native cuisine, most of which were found to blend surprisingly well. A tremendous addition to this culinary mélange was made by the Africans brought as slaves shortly thereafter.

African tradition is responsible for what is perhaps the greatest achievement in Caribbean

A MELTING POT OF FOOD DELIGHTS

Chef Roberto Treviño strives to deliver more than great food and service. The co-owner of Budatai says that being a part of the local culinary landscape means that he is committed to doing the right thing for the current food movement.

"People enjoy new dishes, flavors, more than many other things. Each dining experience must be unique," Treviño explains. "I have to make sure I do everything I can so that customers can take something exciting with them. I like preparing a combination of dishes that pushes your own culinary experiences," he adds enthusiastically. "Eating is entertainment."

Treviño believes Puerto Rico is a hotbed of food delights, a literal "melting pot."

"There is a certain sophistication in this island's culinary culture. We have a great selection of foods," he says. Treviño describes how the sophisticated palate of Puerto Ricans allows him to keep his creative juices flowing. "The Spanish influence here is so strong, but also perfectly complemented by African, Caribbean, and Latin American flavors".

Budatai, a fairly new restaurant located in the San Juan neighborhood of Condado, features a blend of Asian-inspired foods with subtle hints of Latin and Caribbean spices and flavors. The name is a combination of the words Buddha, spelled Buda in Spanish, and Tai, the Japanese word for red sea bream.

cooking – the combination of strikingly contrasting flavors which in other culinary traditions would be considered unblendable. One of these savory concoctions is *pastelón*: ripe plantains layered between well-seasoned ground beef and usually served with rice.

Food from around the world

As different ingredients and cooking techniques were introduced to the island by its early settlers, a local culinary tradition began to take shape. Most important of the early imports were the Spanish cattle, sheep, pigs, goats, and other grillable creatures, which the islanders had never

ginger, onions, potatoes, tomatoes, garlic, and much more. These products, along with those already present, were to mold what was to become the Puerto Rican culinary tradition.

It is ironic that included in these imports are several for which Puerto Rico was to become renowned. Puerto Rican coffee was long considered the best in the world by Europeans. And the plantain, arguably the most popular staple in Puerto Rican cuisine, is something of a national symbol – almost as the leek is to the Welsh. A man who is admired for honesty and lack of pretension is said to have on him the *mancha del plátano*, or "stain of the plantain."

tasted but took to with zeal. Along with the animals came an almost infinite number of vegetables, fruits, and spices from the farthest reaches of Spain's vast colonial empire. A subtler, but no less important, influence on the food supply was the introduction of European farming methods and agricultural equipment.

Surprisingly, many of the agricultural staples that look indigenous to the island were in fact brought to Puerto Rico from elsewhere. Among the great variety of crops imported were coffee, sugar cane, coconuts, bananas, plantains, oranges,

LEFT: simple café fare. **ABOVE:** scooping up at Ponce's The King Cream ice-cream shop. **RIGHT:** the menu is on the wall in this Vieques restaurant.

Myths and misconceptions

Puerto Rican cuisine is as eclectic as it is varied. Local food has earned an undeserved reputation for being fiery and spicy. In fact, although it is prepared with a multiplicity of richly varied spices and condiments, Puerto Ricans tend to season their food in a subtle manner. The base of a majority of native dishes is the *sofrito*, an aromatic sauce made from pureed tomatoes, onions, garlic, green peppers, sweet red chili peppers, coriander, anatto seeds, and a handful of other spices. This *sofrito* adds a zesty taste to stews, rice, beans, and a variety of other dishes, but only the blandest of palates would consider it to be piquant.

Native Caribbean flavors are evident in the majority of Puerto Rican recipes. The most popular dinner dishes are stewed meats, rice, and beans, and a huge selection of fritters. Rice dominates many local main courses; expect a big heap with *arroz con pollo* (chicken served with rice sometimes cooked in coconut milk). Popular desserts include *flan* (custard), made of cheese, coconut, or vanilla; and *guayaba con queso* (candied fruit slices with cheese). Fruit is popular and plentiful, and includes mango, papaya, and passion fruit.

Social traditions of old

Puerto Ricans have very successfully kept alive not only the culinary but also many of the

social traditions of their Taíno forebears. Christmas time on the island is not complete without rice, *gandules* (pigeon peas), *lechón asado* (roast suckling pig), *pasteles* (*tamales* made from plantains and *yucas* filled with a meat stuffing), and, as dessert, a *majarete* made with rice flour, coconut milk and pulp, sugar, and spices. During Lent, seafood dishes include the traditional *serenata*: codfish in a vinaigrette sauce served with tomatoes, onions, avocados, and boiled tubers.

Though Puerto Rico is far too small to have many truly regional cuisines, a number of dishes are limited to particular areas of the island. For example, seafood dishes tend to be accompanied by *sorrullos* (corn fritters) in most of the restaurants on the south coast. The same is true of the great variety of fritters available in the food shacks of Luquillo, a most rewarding 30-minute trip from San Juan for anyone interested in local cuisine. Bayamón and its environs offer a truly unusual snack in *chicharrón*, a sort of massive pork crackling sold on the highways in and out of the city. It's an acquired taste, but once you've acquired it, you'll understand why there are so many hefty individuals wandering the streets.

Modest, mouthwatering meals

The island offers a great variety of restaurants for tourists and local consumers. Typical restaurants serving local food are only rarely luxurious or expensive. In fact, among Puerto Ricans, a rule of thumb applies that the shabbier the establishment, the better the food. The best native creations are found at modest little local *fondas*, where the prices are as reasonable as the food is distinguished. In a *fonda*, you can pick up a generous

PUERTO RICAN ARROZ CON POLLO (SERVES 6–8)

A 3–4lb (1.2kg) chicken; 2 tsp salt; 4 tbsp oil flavored with *achiote*; 1oz (28g) cooked bacon, crumbled; 2oz (56g) cooked ham, chopped; 1 onion, chopped; 2 garlic cloves, minced; 2 *ajies dulces*, chopped; 2 tomatoes, chopped; 1 green bell pepper, chopped; ½ cup (100g) pitted green olives; 1 tbsp capers, chopped; 1 tsp dried oregano; 1½ cups (12fl oz) tomato sauce; 4 cups water (32 oz/1l); 2 cups (370g) white rice; salt to taste; ½lb (225g) cooked asparagus, cut; 1

cup (250g) cooked petits pois; ½ cup pimento (85g), chopped.
1. Cut chicken in pieces, wash, and salt. Brown in a large fry pan until golden.
2. Heat oil in stewpot at medium heat. Stir in bacon and ham. Brown for 3 minutes, stirring. Remove and set aside.
3. Stir in onion, garlic, and *ajies dulces*. Stir over medium heat until onion softens, about 3–5 minutes.
4. Add chopped tomato, green bell pepper, olives, capers, oregano, and tomato sauce. Stir for 2 minutes.

5. Add one cup of water and reserved chicken. Cook for 15 minutes over medium heat, turning occasionally.
6. Raise heat to high, and add remaining 3 cups water. When it comes to a boil, add rice, and mix well. Bring to a boil again. Lower heat to medium and allow to cook uncovered, until water is absorbed. Season as necessary.
7. Lower heat, cover, and cook for a further 20 minutes.
8. To serve, top with asparagus, petits pois, and red pimento on top.

plate of rice and beans, *biftec criollo* (steak), *tostones* (fried plantains), salad, a can of beer, and dessert for about $12. At the low end of the economic scale are delicious sandwiches made with a mixture of red meats, cheeses, tomatoes, and other ingredients. Among the most popular are *cubanos* and *media noches*. The *cubano* consists of pork loin, ham and Swiss cheese on *pan de agua* (similar to French bread), while the *media noche* is smaller and uses egg bread. At the pricey end of the scale is *asopao*, probably Puerto Rico's most widely loved native dish. This thick stew can be made with chicken, pork, or seafood, and is invariably worth every penny paid for it.

restaurants can be found, and sushi is gaining in popularity.

While Puerto Ricans love to eat in *fondas*, it does not mean their palates are unsophisticated. Restaurants in Old San Juan, Isla Verde and the Condado attract thousands of food lovers annually with their fusion of traditional island ingredients, international flavors, and gourmet presentation. Chefs such as Pikayo's Wilo Benet and Roberto Treviño, co-owner of Budatai (*see panel page 62*), are internationally renowned for their innovative cooking. The culinary trends have inspired food festivals in Old San Juan, the largest of which is the SOFO (South of Fortaleza

International cuisine

Puerto Rico has become a proving ground for all sorts of global cuisine. Chinese food has become a staple, with fast-order restaurants everywhere. Spanish restaurants, too, abound. The Spanish-style Puerto Rican *panadería* (bakery) has a wide assortment of delicacies. The famous Cuban sandwich is very popular, as are Spanish *tortillas*. Italian food is probably consumed more than any other type. Pizza parlors can be seen everywhere, and home delivery is common. Mexican eateries run hot and heavy in the San Juan area. Even Thai and Japanese

Street) Culinary Fest (tel: 787-723 7080). The Puerto Rico Hotel & Tourism Association celebrated its second annual foodie extravaganza, "Saborea Puerto Rico", in April 2009 at Escambrón Beach. More than 50 of the island's top restaurants, a wide range of wines, renowned chefs, and the sounds of the Puerto Rico Philharmonic Orchestra were at hand to serve up a weekend full of unforgettable enjoyment.

If "gourmet" international food is not your style, the franchise fast-food boom has played a significant role in motivating local eateries to dispense wide varieties of food such as plantain fritters, stuffed potatoes, and seafood salad, while employing novel merchandising techniques to promote them. ❏

LEFT: street-corner temptations in Boca de Congrejos.
ABOVE: barbecue on Playa Rincón.

ISLAND ART

It's the range that surprises. Flamboyant modern painting sits alongside remarkable folk art and a vast Taíno legacy of ancient art

Puerto Rico's art scene offers delights to the mind and senses as meaningful and alluring as those of its landscape. This may mean entering a room of carved religious figures *(santos)* in the middle of a bustling city and finding yourself enveloped in their holy silence; or wandering into a museum or gallery in Old San Juan, only to find yourself as taken by a beautifully landscaped 17th-century courtyard as by what you see on the walls; or talking to a local artist or scholar and finding that his passion for the island and its craftsmen is yours.

To be sure, there are frustrations. In San Juan the problem centers around a glut of good things; finding the best is often a confusing task, with charlatans working next to some of the great artists of the day. Difficulties out on the island are more logistical, with many of Puerto Rico's fascinating local museums hiding in outbuildings on the edges of towns. But even the most cursory foray into the island's artistic past and present will be rewarding.

Museum isle

The Institute of Puerto Rican Culture in Old San Juan owns a vast amount of the island's cultural inheritance, and can guide you to almost anything you fancy. Old San Juan itself is particularly fortunate as an artistic center; besides its museums, it has a dozen contemporary art galleries, a few co-operatives, and craft shops of all descriptions.

If buying art interests you as much as just looking at it, Old San Juan is certainly the

spot to begin your shopping spree. You'll find fine *santos* and other crafts at Puerto Rican Art & Craft, and prints as well as paintings at Sin Título, Coabey, Atlas Art, and Botello. You can also see the work of future arts luminaries at the exhibition hall of the School of Visual Arts (Escuela de Artes Plásticas) in front of El Morro fort.

New Museum of Art

The Museo de Arte de Puerto Rico in Santurce, which opened in 2000, has given the island great prominence as the cultural leader in the region. This converted hospital, designed in the 1920s neoclassical style, is a masterpiece in itself.

LEFT: street art for sale in Old San Juan.
RIGHT: the Porta Coeli Church in San Germán houses an important collection of religious art.

The building houses a 400-seat theater, upscale restaurant, meeting rooms, and a lavish garden. Works by well-known Puerto Rican artists date back to 1600, and the collection also includes regional and international works.

The museum of the University of Puerto Rico in Río Piedras, San Juan, exhibits only a fifth of its collection, but that small proportion is of top quality, from pre-Columbian art to the strongest and most respected painters of the present day.

But the last word on international art must go to the Museo de Arte de Ponce, envisioned by the late Governor Luis A. Ferré and executed by architect Edward Durrell Stone. Here, in a series of dramatically sunlit hexagonal rooms, art reflects the full range of the drama of human life, from the simplest of faces in Jan van Eyck's *Salvator Mundi* to an overpopulated *Fall of the Rebel Angels* to Rossetti's wonderfully confrontational *Daughters of King Lear*. The museum is closed for renovations until 2010. *(See also page 208.)*

Art for heart's sake

Many of Puerto Rico's greatest achievements have been in the folk arts, and these retain a broad appeal. *(See pages 72–3.)* Most notable are the Puerto Rican *santos*, arguably the island's

CIRCA: PUTTING PUERTO RICO ON THE INTERNATIONAL ART MAP

In only a few years Puerto Rico has gone from a prolific but isolated art scene to making a name for itself on the international landscape. The change has been due in part to CIRCA, an international fair that joins art with artists, art collectors, and art galleries from Puerto Rico and around the world. CIRCA '08 had more than 60 exhibitors, including 43 local and foreign galleries, from all parts of the United States, Germany, England, Australia, Holland, Costa Rica, Mexico, the Dominican Republic, Canada, Spain, Colombia, and Italy.

What art lovers and the public in general saw during the four days of the fair was an eclectic and provocative display of contemporary aesthetic and ethnic discourses.

Photography was the obvious centerpiece of CIRCA '08,

with impressive works presented by photographers such as Carlos Betancourt, Marta María Pérez Bravo, Hendrik Kerstens, Mitra Tabrizian, Wilberto Otero, Favián Vergara, Rafi Claudio, Marcos López, Juan Erlich, and Jason Mena.

Painting was also well represented by, among others, Matthias Koster, Ivo Lucas, Jonathan Meese, Claudio Gallina, Hugo Lugo, Alan Reid, Rafael Trelles, Iván Girona, and Michael Linares. In the field of sculpture/installation, Fabián Marcaccio, Jorge Marín, Adelaide Paul, Mariana Montagudo, Jorge Zeno, and Karlo Ibarra presented notable pieces.

The fourth edition, CIRCA '09, was again held at the Puerto Rico Convention Center in Isla Grande in April. Go to circapr.com for more information.

greatest contribution to the plastic arts. These wooden religious idols, evoking an uncanny spiritual quiet, vary greatly in size and shape. The baroque detail of the earliest pieces reflects both their period origins and the tastes of a Spanish clientele. But as Puerto Rico began to develop a stronger sense of colonial identity, as well as an artisan tradition, *santeros* began to carve figures of a striking simplicity.

The proof of the healing powers of *santos* is said to be attested to by the presence of *milagros* ("miracles"), small silver appendages in shapes of parts of the body. These were donated by people who had prayed to particular saints for

batú, a more civilized version of the balancing game favored by Mexico's Mayans, in which one had to keep a small ball suspended in the air for long periods of time, hitting it only with shoulders, head, and ankles. This version is only "more civilized" on the strength of the fact that

> *Galería Botello is an oasis on busy Cristo Street in Old San Juan. Its cool, arched halls, refreshing patio, and collection make it a sanctuary. Check out Angel Botello's iconic sculptures and paintings.*

intercession in healing parts of the body. You can find such *santos* in the Cristo Chapel in Old San Juan. Though *santos* by the great masters are difficult to come by, there's hardly a home on the island where you won't find at least one *santo* of some sort, greatly revered and passed on from generation to generation.

Ancient heritage

The Caguana Indian Ceremonial Ballpark near Utuado gives haunting echoes of pre-Columbian life and culture. Here, early Taíno Indians played

the early Taínos were not sacrificed to the gods if they dropped the ball, as their Mexican counterparts were. The dolmen-like stones surrounding the *bateyes*, or playing spaces, show great feeling for the ideal spatial relationship between art and nature.

Similar evidence of the vast Taíno legacy is found at the university museum in Río Piedras, which holds the cultural heritage of the island. Recent digs have been especially abundant in discoveries, some of them dazzling in quality. Amid the expected – amulets, potsherds, tools – are some baffling curiosities, like stone collars: great solid yokes at once regal and unwearable. In one intriguing case concerning Puerto Rico's early Taínos, men bend and sway

LEFT: town square mosaic in Loíza, a town known for its rich African heritage. **ABOVE:** street mural in San Juan – proof that art isn't confined to museums.

together in entranced harmony. In another are two partially exposed skeletons, a few broken possessions at their sides.

For all the diversity of Puerto Rico's many cultural traditions, it was not until the 18th century that the island produced its first major artist in the Western tradition: José Campeche (1752–1809). In spite of never having left the island and having been exposed to European painting only through prints, Campeche still managed to create paintings of mastery. His religious works show a weakness for sentimentality, with their glut of *putti* and pastel clouds, but the inner peace which Campeche succeeds in

displaying in his main holy figures dispels all possible doubt as to his stature as a truly inspired and talented artist.

There are two such masterpieces in the Ponce museum, but it is in a formal portrait which hangs in the Institute of Puerto Rican Culture that one sees Campeche at the height of his powers. The eponymous *Governor Ustariz* stands in a magnificent room, with sunlight entering from behind. In his left hand are the first plans to pave the streets of San Juan; outside in the distance are men laboring busily to make his dream into a reality. It is truly a triumphant picture.

Local hero

A more accessible painter, and something of a local hero in Puerto Rico, is Francisco Oller (1833–1917). His work is housed in all three main sources: the Institute itself and the museums at Ponce and Río Piedras. To this day, the extent of his influence on Puerto Rican painting is immeasurable.

Unlike Campeche, Oller lived and traveled abroad throughout his life. He studied under Courbet, was a friend of both Pissarro and Cézanne, painted European royalty, and yet remained loyal to – and fiercely proud of – his island homeland. He was a Realist with Impressionist ideas, able to paint gorgeously everything he saw. He was adept at all genres: portraits, still lifes, and landscapes – such as *Hacienda Aurora*, resonating with the vibrant colors of Puerto Rico which are just as much in evidence today.

A piece of work which defies reproduction is Oller's *El Velorio* (The Wake). An enormous painting, it covers an entire wall in the university museum and illuminates the common man's universe in a fashion that recalls the work of Brueghel the Elder. Here people laugh, cry, drink, sing and dance, while on a lace-covered table an almost forgotten, stone-white dead child lies strewn with flowers.

Oller's legacy to Puerto Rican painters has been one not only of technique but also of theme. Since his time, island painters have taken an overwhelming pride in Puerto Rico's diverse populace and landscape. Miguel Pou and Ramón Frade were among the earliest to follow Oller's lead, doing some spectacular genre work in the early part of the 20th century.

At the Institute, Frade's painting *The Jíbaro* is a splendid homage to Puerto Rico's country farmers. Shyly surveying us with a bunch of plantains in his arms, this tiny old fellow appears to be a giant, with the land miniatured at his feet and his head haloed by a cloud.

The 1940s saw a rise in printmaking, which has left that medium one of the most vibrant in Puerto Rico to this day. Funded by the government, printmaking projects lured a slew of fine artists, many of whom are still active. Of particular note are Rafael Tufiño, Antonio Martorell, José Rosa, and Lorenzo Homar. Posters by Ramón Power illustrate some of the clarity and strength from which the best of Puerto Rican artists continue to draw.

istically touched by landscape. Reflectively, she seems to have loosed a phantom of tropical hubris as she opens the drawer of a nearby table.

The large fraternity of Puerto Rico's artists show reverence for the island and its people. Color plays an integral part. The art of Augusto Marín, Angel Botello, Francisco Rodón, and Mari Mater O'Neill can be bought in Puerto Rico and in New York auction houses for hefty prices.

The late Rafael Tufiño's woodcut ink prints tell the story of Puerto Rican life at mid-century. A group of Tufiño's pictures are often on display at the Tourism Company's headquarters in Old San Juan. Luis Cajiga paints dazzling flam-

Over the past 30 years, almost all Puerto Rican artists have studied abroad, and the consequence has been a broadening and an increasingly avant-garde range of attitudes. Some artists have remained abroad, like Rafael Ferrer, whose work is as popular in New York as it is in San Juan, and Paris resident Ricardo Ramírez. Others have returned to work and teach, producing an art with a Puerto Rican flavor. Myrna Báez falls into this category, her canvases interweaving past and present, inner and outer space. Her *Homage to Vermeer* shows a lone figure in an interior surreal-

boyant trees and humble *piragua* vendors. Jorge Zeno's and Sylvia Blanco's imaginative techniques are good examples of surrealistic art, while John Balosi's sculptures and paintings of horses are treasured for their originality.

Viewing opportunities

Gallery nights, when many of Puerto Rico's talented young artists are discovered, are held in Old San Juan on the first Tuesday of each month from 6–9pm.

Another excellent occasion to get more than a taste of local talent is at the San Juan Biennial Graphic Art Exhibition, which covers the spectrum of imaginative techniques and styles of Caribbean artists.   ❏

LEFT: grand stairway at the Museo de Arte de Ponce. **ABOVE:** modern sculpture in Bayamón. **RIGHT:** colorful mural in Ponce's Museo de la Historia.

FOLK ART WITH A FLAVOR ALL ITS OWN

Many of Puerto Rico's handicrafts have evolved out of necessity, and focus on function as well as form, but some of it is just plain fun...

Puerto Rico's most exquisite form of "folk art" actually borders on "fine art": *santos*, the carved religious figures that have been produced here since the 1500s. *(See page 69.)* But over the centuries, the country's folk art has expanded into many other areas, with today's artisans producing a great variety of paintings, non-religious sculpture, jewelry and many other more quirky – and collectible – artifacts.

Usually bursting with bright colors, Puerto Rican folk art has an almost childlike quality. Many times folk artists base their themes on the nature around them: roosters, iguanas, and the tiny *coquís* (tree frogs) are frequently depicted.

Old San Juan is the best place to see – and purchase – local folk art. The Institute of Puerto Rican Culture is a great source of information about the country's arts and crafts, but buyers should head for the two weekend craft markets – one on Plaza de la Dársena in front of Pier 1 (11am–10pm) and the other in Paseo de la Princesa (noon–8pm). Just before Christmas each year, the Bacardi Artisans Fair, a major event held in the distillery grounds, features more than 100 booths displaying everything from stone necklaces to musical flutes. The fair is packed with artists and craftspeople, as well as stalls selling local food and drinks.

ABOVE: *El Gallo* (The Rooster; oil on paper) by acclaimed Puerto Rican painter Óscar Ortiz. This contemporary artist has been praised for his mature and controlled tropical color palette. Roosters are a recurrent theme in Puerto Rican folk art.

BELOW: a real mix and match – folk-art displays inside the Museo de la Historia in Ponce.

LEFT: art historians view the carving of *santos* as Puerto Rico's greatest contribution to the plastic arts. *Santeros* use clay, gold, stone, or cedarwood to carve figurines representing saints, usually from 8 to 20 inches (20–50mm) tall. Perhaps the most popular group of *santos* are the Three Kings *(pictured)*. Some of the best *santos* on the island can be seen at the Capilla del Cristo in Old San Juan.

BEHIND THE *VEJIGANTE* MASKS

An unusual – and popular – form of folk art in Puerto Rico is the grotesque, colorfully painted masks that are one of the highlights of the island's many festivals. Artisans (such as the *ponceño* above) have been producing the horned, spike-toothed, speckled papier mâché creations for centuries – some historians believe the practice dates back to ancient Taínos; others link it to medieval Spain or tribal Africa. Traditionally the masks were black, red, and yellow – symbolic of hellfire and damnation. Brightly costumed *vejigantes* don the masks and roam the streets at Carnival time, in an attempt to scare sinners back into the church. Ponce and Loíza are the island's mask-making centers; their carnivals provide a chance to see masks in action.

ABOVE: this craftsman specializes in carved wooden bird figurines. Puerto Rican markets abound with handmade crafts with a natural theme.

RIGHT: master craftsman Carmelo Martell plays an intricately decorated *cuatro*, Puerto Rico's national instrument.

RHYTHM OF THE TROPICS

Salsa is king, but the sounds range from the percussion of traditional instruments to the classical music encouraged by Pablo Casals, who made his home here

Just before he died, the world-renowned Argentinian composer Alberto Ginastera visited Puerto Rico in order to attend the world première of one of his works commissioned by the Pablo Casals Festival. During an interview at the Caribe Hilton, Mr Ginastera's thoughts turned to the song of the *coquí*, the tiny frog that is found only in Puerto Rico and is famous for its persistent and ubiquitous nocturnal calls. "It is the only natural song that I know of," said Mr Ginastera, "which is formed of a perfect seventh." The *coquí* sings a two-note song – "co… kee!" – and these two notes are a perfect seventh apart. It should come, therefore, as no surprise that the island's natural sounds have their unique man-made counterpart. The music of Puerto Rico is salsa.

From settlement to salsa

Puerto Ricans have always excelled in music, and the somewhat haphazard course of the island's history has given it a multitude of

Salsa literally translates as "sauce": in a musical sense, it is the hot and spicy "sauce" that makes parties happen.

traditions from which to build a distinctively Puerto Rican sound. The earliest settlers were as enthusiastic about their music as any Spaniards; but, deprived of their native stringed instruments, found themselves in the position of having to create their own. As a result, there

LEFT: Ismael Rivera Festival fun in San Juan.
RIGHT: folk music figures prominently in island life.

are at least half-a-dozen stringed instruments native to the island.

In the absence of many tonal instruments, the settlers were forced to make do with simple percussive ones, which are ready to hand in the various gourds, woods, shoots and beans native to this land. The arrival of West African slaves, who brought with them a well-developed and long history of percussion-based music, accelerated this trend.

Even now, Puerto Ricans are very adept at making music with whatever happens to be within grabbing distance. No one *owns* a musical composition in Puerto Rico, as one does in other countries. Play a Puerto Rican a piano tune he likes in a bar room or café, and you won't believe your ears when you hear the rhythmic sounds he gets out of a spoon, a wood block, a bead necklace or even his knuckles on the table.

No lack of formality

To be fair, there is a somewhat formalized genre of this very type of music. It's collectively called *bomba y plena*, but the two are completely different types of music that are coupled with dance. Together, they are the most popular forms of folk music in Puerto Rico.

The *bomba* is purely African in origin and came over with the black slaves who were forced

to work on the country's sugar plantations. It's essentially a marriage of drumming and dancing: one egging the other on in a rhythmic competition of sorts. The northeastern town of Loíza is a particularly good place to experience a typical *bomba*.

Plena, on the other hand, is a blend of elements from the island's many cultures – even ancient Taíno – and generally involves a handful of musicians creating different rhythms on an amazing variety of hand-held percussion instruments. Some resemble hand-held tympanis, some Irish *bodhrans*, some tambourines. Many of them are homemade, and have become a type of "folk art," as well as functional instruments. The custom of *plena* originated in Ponce, but you can hear its distinctive sounds at any patron saint's festival and occasionally at Plaza de Armas or Plaza de la Dársena in Old San Juan.

Traditional music is still performed widely, especially during holidays and festivals. At family get-togethers, there are usually guitarists, *güiro* (gourd) players and pianists playing the long-established music of the people – particularly such standards as *Flores Negros* and *Somos Novios*. Television and radio stations showcase popular singers and groups, such as Luis Fonsi, Kany García, and Ednita Nazario. Stars Chayanne, Ricky Martin, and Daddy Yankee command large audiences at concerts held at the Coliseo de Puerto Rico and Centro de Bellas Artes or at town plazas.

Contemporary music ranges from the traditional-but-modern sounds of *plena libre* to merengue singers like Olga Tañón, Elvis Crespo, and Melina León. The 21st century brought a new beat, reggaetón, a uniquely Puerto Rican fusion of hip hop, with sounds ranging from reggae to rock to salsa, all with a sophisticated beat. Artists like Wisin & Yandel, Tego Calderón, Ivy Queen, Don Omar, and Calle 13 not only hold sway in the island's top radio stations and clubs, but have crossed over into the global market as well.

Classical sounds, too

This is not to neglect the achievements of this small island in the more traditional forms. It is a haven for the opera, and has its own company; Justino Díaz, the island's finest male vocalist, has impressed critics from New York to Milan, and Puerto Rico's "Renaissance Man," composer Jack Delano (who died in 1998), made his mark on the classical scene.

THE PUERTO RICAN CUATRO

The *cuatro* is found in South America and the West Indies. The Puerto Rican *cuatro moderno* has five double courses (10 strings in all) and looks like a Cuban *tres*. It is an instrument of the *jíbaros*, rural farmers, and also the name of the music they played on *cuatros* and *güiros*. It is also used to accompany *aguinaldos*, the Puerto Rican Christmas songs, performed by musicians traveling from house to house. The instrument is roughly violin-shaped, and the strings are made from steel, tuned from low to high B E A D G, with the B and E in octaves. It is played with a flat pick and it sounds like a cross between a 12-string guitar and a mandolin. It is a national culture icon of Puerto Rico.

The Puerto Rico Ballet Company stages classics as well as original local productions at the Centro de Bellas Artes (Performing Arts) in Santurce, while the Puerto Rico Symphony Orchestra – despite being relatively young – is among the best in the Caribbean, and has premièred works by some of Latin America's finest composers, many of them at San Juan's Casals Festival, the Caribbean's most celebrated cultural event, held for two weeks in January each year. The orchestra and the Children's Chorus have drawn much attention internationally.

Pablo Casals

It is Pablo Casals who, more than any other Puerto Rican resident, is responsible for the upsurge of interest and proficiency in classical performance in Puerto Rico in recent years. Born in Catalonia in 1876 of a Puerto Rican mother, Casals was recognized around the time of World War I as one of the greatest cellists of his era. After leaving Spain in 1936 as a protest against the Civil War, he settled in the French Pyrenees, where the first Casals Festival was held in 1950. He visited his mother's homeland in 1956, and spent the final years of his life in Puerto Rico.

In 1957, at the invitation of Governor Luis Muñoz Marín, he founded the Puerto Rican Casals Festival, which must rank as the greatest cultural event in the Antilles, and a formidable one even by world standards. In later years, Casals went on to form the Puerto Rico Symphony Orchestra and the Puerto Rico Conservatory of Music. On his death at the age of 97 in 1973, he considered himself a Puerto Rican; his compatriots consider him one of their national heroes.

Rhythm of the tropics

Salsa is what happens when Afro-Caribbean music meets big-band jazz. Its roots may be found in the early explorations of the late Puerto Rican Tito Puente and Cuban musicians in New York City clubs following World War II. After serving three years in the United States Navy, Puente studied percussion at the prestigious Juilliard School on New York's Upper West Side. He was soon playing and composing for top bandleaders such as Machito and Pupi Campo, and he quickly proceeded to establish his own orchestra.

LEFT: San Juan Group guitar lessons in Old San Juan.
RIGHT: drumming out a *bomba* beat.

In an interview in *Latin US* magazine, before his death in 2000 at age 77, Puente was asked to define salsa. "As you know, salsa in Spanish means 'sauce,' and we use it mostly as a condiment for our foods," he said. "Salsa in general is all our fast Latin music put together: the merengue, the rumba, the mambo, the cha-cha, the guaguancó, boogaloo, all of it is salsa… in Latin music, we

> Miguel A. Valenzuela Morales, better known as Miguelito, is one of the most popular reggaetón artists today and he's only 10 years old.

have many types of rhythms, like ballads (boleros), rancheros, tangos, and, of course, salsa."

The salsa band is usually composed of a lead vocalist and chorus, a piano, a bass, a horn section and a heavy assortment of percussion instruments (bongos, conga, maracas, *güiros*, timbales, claves, and the ever-present cowbell – a *jíbaro* touch). The overall effect is mesmerizing; the rhythm contagious. It is highly danceable music and you will hear it everywhere.

Salsa (the center of which is now thought to have shifted *back* to Puerto Rico from New York) has firmly placed the island on the map of popular music, with more and more young *salseros* getting in on the act every day – and not just in Puerto Rico.

"It's totally unexpected to see Belgians, Swedes, Finns and Danes swing to the Latin Beat... the bands there are playing more salsa than we are," said Puente.

A musical evolution

Music has played a crucial role in Puerto Rican society and culture for as long as there have been Puerto Ricans. During Spanish rule, the *danza* was the chief form of entertainment for the *criollo* aristocracy; it reached its high point in the late 19th century when Juan Morel Campos and other masters gave it a popularity that resounded back to Spain. This highly stylized tradition of music and its accompanying dance movements are preserved by several local ensembles in Puerto Rico. The *danza* is characterized by a string orchestra, woodwind, and a formal ambience. *La Borinqueña*, the Puerto Rican national anthem, is a *danza*.

A more popular and widely practiced Puerto Rican musical tradition is the *aguinaldo*, a song performed around the Christmas and Three Kings holiday, usually in the form of an *asalto*. The *asalto* is a charming tradition which dates back to the 19th century, and perhaps earlier. It goes along with the unrestrained partying of the holiday season. It is customary at an *asalto*

JUSTINO DÍAZ

Internationally renowned bass singer Justino Díaz first studied at the University of Puerto Rico. He made his operatic debut in 1957 as Ben in Menotti's *The Telephone*, and later studied with Frederick Jager and at the New England Conservatory of Music in Boston.

After winning the Metropolitan Opera Auditions of the Air, he made his debut at the Metropolitan Opera House of New York as Monterone in *Rigoletto* in 1963, beginning a long-term association with that house. He has sung 30 roles and given nearly 300 performances there.

In 1966, he starred in the role of Antony in Samuel Barber's *Antony and Cleopatra* on the occasion of the opening of the new opera house. In the same year, he made his Salzburg debut as Escamillo in *Carmen*.

In 1971, he created another new role at the inauguration of another opera house, this time as Francesco in Ginastera's *Beatrix Cenci* at the Kennedy Center Opera House in Washington DC. His London Covent Garden debut was also as Escamillo, in 1976, and his La Scala debut was as Asdrubale in Rossini's *La Pietra del Paragone* in 1982. He also appeared in the Zeffirelli film of Verdi's *Otello* in 1986.

On March 29, 2003, Justino Díaz retired after 40 years in the arts. Díaz and fellow Puerto Rican pianist Elías López Soba are the current artistic and musical directors of the Casals Festival.

to feast on *lechón asado* (roast suckling pig), *arroz con pollo* (chicken with rice), *gandules* (pigeon peas), and *palos de ron* (well, okay, so they have some rum). Following the feast, a group of noisy celebrants stumbles from house to house, waking the residents and singing *aguinaldos*. The members of each household are expected to join the *asalto* as it moves throughout the surrounding neighborhood.

The décima

The *décima* is arguably the most appealing form of traditional Puerto Rican music. It is the vehicle through which the *jíbaro* expresses his joys and

Star performers

In Puerto Rico, salsa is king, but who is the King of Salsa? No one can agree, but lists generally include Willie Colón, Rubén Blades, the late Héctor Lavoe, El Gran Combo de Puerto Rico, and the Fania All-Stars. Puerto Rico's biggest salsa star is Gilberto Santa Rosa, affectionately known as "Gilbertito." In addition to salsa, merengue groups from the nearby Dominican Republic have become very popular, and some locals, led by Olga Tañón, Elvis Crespo, and Melina León, have been able to cash in on the fast-paced merengue sound. Local salsa musicians in Cuba and Puerto Rico

frustrations; it is the poetry of the Puerto Rican soul. Instrumentation for the *décima* consists of three-, four-, and six-stringed instruments (called appropriately the *tres, cuatro* and *seis*).

The trademark of the *décima* is verbal improvisation. Often, two singers will alternate stanzas, trying to outboast each other with rhyming tales of luscious fruit, pretty women, or physical prowess. The verbal jousting is significantly fueled by the audience. The similarity between the traditional *décima* and the more modern verbal dueling of today's rap DJs is striking.

compete in playing the most infectious melodies, but it is said that the latter are more avant-garde in their approach.

Willie Colón and his band have produced some of the most inspired salsa music to date. The album *Siembra*, a collaboration with Rubén Blades in 1978, is one of the hottest classics. The songs on *Siembra* show the rhythmic complexity which lies at the core of salsa, as well as the thematic motifs which tie all of salsa together. Like the *plena* singers of old, today's salsa vocalists often tell a story filled with satire or a social commentary.

Whatever the individual's taste, salsa continues to be one of the hottest forms of popular music in the world today. ❑

LEFT: street band in Old San Juan.
ABOVE: Puerto Rican folk music is almost inevitably accompanied by lively dance.

A LAND OF FANTASTIC FESTIVALS

Puerto Ricans express their zest for life through a succession of exuberant celebrations. Many have their origins in the island's strong Catholicism

No matter where or when you go, Puerto Ricans always seem to be celebrating something – be it a saint's feast day or a cultural tradition. First and foremost are the *fiestas patronales*, or patron saint festivals, during which each town honors the area's patron saint. Incredibly, there are 78 of these, beginning on January 6 and continuing straight through December 12, and the festivities at each last 10 days. So, in theory, you can party your way around the island nonstop.

And this isn't even taking into consideration the *other* festivals, which all celebrate something, no matter how insignificant it may seem.

In April, for instance, Juana Díaz hosts the Maví Festival, which honors *maví*, a fermented drink made from the bark of the ironwood tree.

With farming being a dominant occupation, harvest festivals abound. Yauco and Maricao both have Coffee Harvest Festivals in February, while the picturesque western town of San Germán marks the end of the island's sugar harvest in April with an appropriate celebration.

If you have to choose, three of the best festivals are the Carnival in Ponce (February), where the *vejigante* masks were first created, the Loíza's *fiesta* of Santiago Apóstol (July), and the Hatillo Masks Festival (December). All feature music, dancing, ornate masks and costumes, games, religious processions, shows, parades, drink, and food, food, food. It's very difficult not to join in the dancing, and easy to forget about the diet.

ABOVE: an essential element of *any* festival is music and dance. Folk dances include the *bomba*, of pure African origin, and the *plena*, which blends elements from the island's many cultures.

BELOW: a Puerto Rican waves a national flag at a festival remembering the Holy Innocents in Hatillo. The Holy Innocents Day commemorates the biblical story of King Herod.

LEFT: Yauco and Maricao have both had a flourishing coffee industry since the nineteenth century, so it's not suprising that the island would honor this lucrative export with a festival.

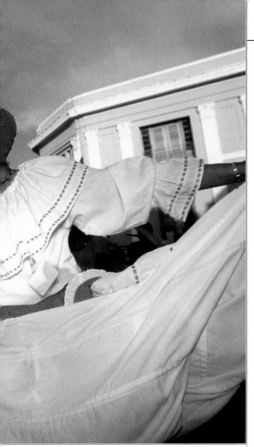

THE CATHOLIC CONNECTION

With all the colorful costumes and riotous behavior, it is easy to forget that many of Puerto Rico's festivals – particularly the *fiestas patronales* – have religious roots. Religious candle processions with statues, or *santos*, often kick things off, and many Masses are held throughout each festival. Christmas is celebrated here with more fervor than anywhere else in the world. Festivities go on until January 6, the Festival de Los Tres Reyes (Epiphany). Carnival is also big news – the week before the start of Lent is filled with festivals. Easter or Semana Santa is the most important Catholic festival.

Puerto Rico is strongly Catholic, with many convents, monasteries, and even one or two shrines where the Virgin Mary has appeared to the faithful. But this Catholicism has, over the years, been blended – like everything else in Puerto Rico – with animist elements of African and Taíno origin. Some of the elements are simple superstition: at midnight during the San Juan Bautista festival on June 24, thousands fill the beaches and walk backward into the sea (or nearest body of water – even a pool will do!) three times to renew good luck for the coming year. Beach parties, together with the usual dancing and music, round off the occasion.

Above: parades feature costumed marchers, bands, floats – and generally anyone who wants to tag along.

Top: Carnival fun in the capital San Juan.
Right: garishly dressed masked *vejigantes* roam the streets during the island's *fiestas patronales* to chase away evil spirits.

THE LANGUAGE OF PUERTO RICO

Although English and Spanish are both designated "official" languages, it's Español that rules the heart – and tongue – of most Puerto Ricans

Even before Columbus's fleet "discovered" the island in 1493, Puerto Rico was in a state of cultural unrest. Invading Carib tribes from South America were threatening the native Arawaks, as they had many other cultures throughout the Caribbean. When the local Arawaks met the invading Caribs, what language was created? The Arawak name for the island, Borikén, is still used (*La Borinqueña* is the Puerto Rican national anthem), and the Caribs live on in the word Caribbean. Many Puerto Rican municipalities go by their pre-Columbian names, for example Caguas, Arecibo, Mayagüez, Yauco and Guaynabo. The Arawaks feared the god Juracán, while we fear hurricanes. And the *hamacas* in which the early Indians slept are just as popular today under the name of hammocks.

Obliteration of the Arawaks

If the Arawaks welcomed the Spaniards as a strategy to ward off the Caribs, they miscalculated. A wave of Spaniards swept across the island. Eventually there came battle and disease, which obliterated the native Arawak population. Then came sex, producing the first Puerto Ricans and the first people who could claim to speak a truly Puerto Rican Spanish. The Spanish of the earliest Puerto Ricans, like that of their modern descendants, can be said to reflect either a pronunciational sloppiness or an Arawak love of diphthongs. For example, Spanish words which end in *ado* are pronounced as if the *d* were silent. Humacao is an Arawak name, but *pescao* will get you fish anywhere on the island. A good stew is an *asopao*, but if your *fiao* (credit) isn't good enough, you won't be served one in any restaurant.

MANUEL ALONSO

Manuel A. Alonso was a poet, journalist, and author. Born in San Juan in 1822, he later studied medicine at the University of Barcelona. His *El Gíbaro* collection of verses examined the impoverished lives of farmers in Puerto Rico and also some of the island's local customs.

He established a medical office in Caguas, Puerto Rico, in 1848. Working alongside other respected writers, he published the *Album Puertorriqueño*, only the second anthology of poems to be published in his home country. Alonso joined the Liberal Reform movement and directed its publication, *El Agente* (The Agent). He died in San Juan in 1889.

Puerto Rico's first Africans were brought as slaves, mostly from West-Central Africa. They brought with them another language; they also had many musical instruments, including the drums, and countless customs which have found their way into the lives of everyone.

The *baquine*, a festival of mourning for the death of a child, is a ritual of African origin, and is the scene of a great deal of rum, dancing, and *lechón asado* (roast suckling pig). By the mid-19th century, Africans made up a fifth of the population, and such customs penetrated society.

Integration of the races has worked smoothly in Puerto Rico, and it is said that *él que no tiene*

1849, his book *El Gíbaro* was published in Barcelona, and in it there are invaluable accounts of a *jíbaro* wedding, dances and cockfights, Christmas celebrations, and the arrival of the magic lantern in the hills. Equally important is the portrait of mid-19th-century *jíbaro* speech patterns. In Alonso's verses we can hear the *jíbaro* dialect in its purest form. He mentions foods such as *lechón asado*, *toytiyas* (tortillas) and *maví* (a drink made from tree bark).

Quirks and oddities

For all the eccentricities of the Puerto Rican tongue, it is important to remember that the

dinga tiene mandinga, a phrase which attributes some amount of African ancestry to virtually all Puerto Ricans. The Mandinga were one of the more populous of the West African tribes, brought to Puerto Rico to harvest sugar cane, coffee, and tobacco.

The farmers of those crops, black, white, and *mestizo*, gradually became the Puerto Rican *jíbaros*. The most famous record of the *jíbaro* was written by Manuel A. Alonso, a doctor whose writings fit into the Latin American literary movement known as *costumbrismo*. In

language of the island is Spanish, albeit a Spanish heavily influenced by other nationalities, and that Puerto Rican Spanish shares many oddities with the Spanish of its Caribbean neighbors – such as *seseo*, by which *s* sounds are muted, and sometimes disappear altogether, at the end of syllables.

Matches are *loh fohforoh* rather than *los fósforos* and *graciah* means thanks. *Yeismo* is another confusing variation; this involves pronouncing the Spanish *ll* and *y* sounds as English *j*s, so as to render a word like *Luquillo*, the island's most popular beach, as "Look here, Joe."

Those who live in Puerto Rico also practice an important non-verbal language in everyday dealings. For example, wrinkling the nose

LEFT: English spoken – high school students celebrate the end of term with hugs. **ABOVE:** all is well in Arroyo. **RIGHT:** reading the day's news.

usually means, "What is that?" Both hands raised palms front means "Wait a minute," and when an individual tweaks his or her cheek it means "I like that." A movement akin to washing of the hands means "It's done."

Spanish spoken here

The granting of United States citizenship to Puerto Ricans in 1917 signaled the advent of English as the first Germanic language to become part of the Puerto Rican dialect. The startling result of this last infusion is Spanglish, a colloquial Spanish which may be as familiar to a North American as it is to a Spaniard. Spanglish consists not only of a shared vocabulary but also of the terse sentence construction characteristic of English. The first penetration of English into Puerto Rican Spanish seems to have come from English labels on consumer products.

> *Check out* Taíno: Pre-Columbian Art and Culture from the Caribbean, *The Monacelli Press, co-published with El Museo del Barrio. It is the first English-language publication on the fascinating legacy of Taíno art and culture.*

Indeed, men still sit at bars nursing *un scotch* while their children look on, chewing *chicles*. The introduction of American commerce was no less confounding in other ways. When the first American cash registers were introduced in San Juan's grocery and department stores, a whole generation stood paralyzed at checkout counters when the "No Sale" tab, marking the end of the transaction, flipped up. *No sale* in Spanish translates as "Do not leave."

Spanglish truly entered its heyday only with the mass migration of Puerto Ricans to the United States in the 1940s. This exodus created a generation of so-called *Nuyoricans*, who returned to their native island with the baffling customs and speech patterns developed on the streets of New York. Or they would send letters home with news, and, if they had no money, they would send the letter *ciodí* (cash on delivery).

Letters to the Cordillera would have to be transported by *un trok*. Perhaps there would

LET'S SPEAK SPANGLISH

Many terms used in the Latin world are now derived from modern English. Here are a few examples:

Parquear is used instead of the Spanish *estacionar*, coming from the English word "park"

Bye bye is used instead of the Spanish *adiós*

The verb *bulear* is derived from the English verb to bully

The verb *charlar* means to chat or make small talk

Troca is used for "pickup truck" instead of the standard Spanish *camioneta*

Computadora, derived from the English word "computer," is now used even in standard Spanish, despite the original Spanish term for computer, which was *ordenador*

"Hasta you later" is a corruption of the Spanish *hasta luego*, which means "until later"

The adjective *serioso* denotes the English "serious" instead of the Spanish *serio*

Norsa comes from the English word "nurse", rather than the standard Spanish *enfermera*

The word *actualmente*, meaning "currently," is very frequently misused to replace both the English terms "actually" and "in fact." The official Spanish term for "actually" is *de hecho*

Marketa is an often used word derived from the English word "market" (as used in supermarket) instead of the standard Spanish word *mercado*

be bad news, that a son had been *bosteado* by the *policías* for dealing in *las drogas*. More often the letters would just contain idle chatter, or discussions of the decisions of the world *líderes*, or of how a brother had won a pool game by sinking the important eight ball in the corner *poquete*.

Puerto Ricans love pool, but if Puerto Rico and the Spanglish language have an official sport it has to be *el béisbol*, or baseball. Everyone knows that Roberto Clemente (from Carolina) and Orlando Cepeda (from Santurce) were Puerto Rico's greatest hitters of *jonrones* and *dobles* (home-runs and doubles).

Rican will ask a visitor is "*¿Habla español?*" If the visitor responds positively, then he or she will be welcomed into the fold graciously.

Taíno talk

The island's language has been considerably enriched by that of the ancestral Taínos, including the following words and phrases:

canoa canoe
burén ceramic grill
coa gardening instrument (hoe)
barbacoa barbecue
tibes rough stone
areyto ceremonial dance

Most Puerto Ricans would say their ballplayers were *wilson*, meaning "very good." Some things have remained little changed, though. Dollars are sometimes called *dolares*, but more often *pesos*. Quarters are *pesetas*, nickels *vellones,* and pennies *centavos*.

Language means more to the people of Puerto Rico than just about anything else. Most Puerto Ricans fear the loss of their language through the influence of other cultures, especially if the island were to become a state of America. One of the first questions a Puerto

guasábara war or fight
bija a red pigment
higüera a tree whose fruit (the gourds) are used for utensils and musical instruments
jicotea water turtle
anón fruit tree
guanábana fruit
quenepa fruit
guayacán a tree with very hard wood
batata sweet potato
maní peanut

Having such a rich and vibrant oral tradition, Puerto Ricans love good conversation, and, with at least four linguistic families from which to draw, enjoy a speech that is at once cryptic and colorful. ❏

LEFT: poster advertising a Don Quixote musical in Ponce's La Perla Theater.
ABOVE: street talk in Yabucoa.

A SPORTING LIFE

Baseball, basketball, and volleyball fire the Puerto Ricans'
competitive spirit, but there is plenty for the visitor
to do on and off the island's tropical waters

When the first ball was thrown in the Taíno *batú*, sport was born in Puerto Rico. All that remains of this early interest in sport are the ruins of the Taíno game courts south of Arecibo at the Caguana Ceremonial Ballpark and the Tibes Indian Ceremonial Park in Ponce, where early people played a game much like soccer.

Today, baseball games have replaced the Taíno diversion. The 20th century brought a wealth of action to Puerto Rico, but it all started with the US's national pastime, which became the island's most popular sport. This is not surprising, since the climate enables baseball to be played virtually every day of the year.

The amateur leagues set up their schedules so that there are games on most days. The Winter League slates its games from October to January. Teams represent Manatí, Bayamón, Caguas, Carolina, Ponce, and Mayagüez.

In February, the Caribbean Series is held, with teams representing Puerto Rico, the

> With 23 golf courses located throughout the island and six more underway, Puerto Rico is considered the golf capital of the Caribbean.

Dominican Republic, Venezuela, and Mexico. The game has produced such luminaries as Roberto Clemente, Orlando Cepeda, and Rubén Gómez, with current stars including Iván "Pudge" Rodríguez, Carlos Delgado, Carlos Beltrán, Bernie Williams, and Jorge Posada.

LEFT: ready for some hoop action. **RIGHT:** the Trump International Golf Club in Río Grande is superb.

Hoop dreams

Although baseball has been the sport most identified with Puerto Rico, since the 1990s basketball has ranked a close second. This sport draws much interest because of the island team's success in international competitions such as the Olympics and the Pan-American Games. Puerto Rican teams have even given the powerful US entries a run for their money. The Superior Basketball League fields 12 teams in San Germán, Guayama, Santurce, Arecibo, Guaynabo, Caguas, Carolina, Humacao, Mayagüez, Ponce, Quebradillas, and Bayamón. The season runs through spring and summer, adjusted annually to accommodate the island basketball team's international participation in the Olympics, Pan-American Games, and other events. Most basketball games in Puerto Rico are played in indoor coliseums.

Puerto Rico has produced a large group of champion boxers, tennis players, golfers – and even a horse that won the Kentucky Derby, Bold Forbes. Horse-racing draws great interest, even though there is only one race track, Camarero in Canóvanas. Offtrack betting agencies in every town are usually full on racing days, which are every day except Tuesday and Saturday.

Puerto Rico's boxers have won gold medals in international competition. More than 50 professional pugilists have held champion status in every weight category except heavyweight. Three-time world champions include Wilfredo Gómez, Wilfredo Benítez, and Felix "Tito" Trinidad.

The Net Set

Tennis courts abound on the island, and the public may use hotel and resort facilities for a fee. A few internationally known tennis players have emerged from the local courts, such as Charlie Pasarell and Gigi Fernández. The Baldrich Tennis Club in Hato Rey provides 10 regulation courts for use at a nominal cost.

THE HIGHS OF SKYDIVING

For those thrill seekers who thrive on the adrenaline rush of extreme sports, Puerto Rico has it all. From skydiving to rock climbing, there is something for you.

The northern town of Arecibo is known for skydiving. You can jump from more than 10,500ft (3,200 meters) and freefall at more than 100mph (160kph) while enjoying a scenic view of Arecibo, from the mountains to the sea. While you can skydive any time of year, the Xtreme Divers professional school hosts the annual Puerto Rico Freefall Festival, which attracts thousands of divers and spectators each year.

Golf is a natural for the island, with championship courses mainly found at the resorts. Public courses are available at reasonable rates in Punta Borinquen and Aguirre, with a public driving range in Bayamón and a golf academy and range in San Juan. All hotel courses are available at higher rates. Puerto Rico's most famous golfer is Juan "Chichi" Rodríguez, who has his own golf resort, El Legado, in Guayama.

Watersports of all types feature, naturally, and boating marinas are at Isla Grande, Boca de Cangrejos, Fajardo, Ponce, and Mayagüez. Surfing has become a way of life in areas like Rincón, where international events have been held. Windsurfing is a natural choice for the waters of the Atlantic and the Caribbean. On any given day, the colorful sails flash by. Ocean kayaking has gained popularity in recent times, with kayaks for rent on the placid Condado Lagoon. On the beaches and in the parks, racquetball, volleyball, soccer, and even touch football attract large crowds.

Anglers can indulge in all types of fishing, although deep-sea fishing is particularly good, with billfish plentiful. Marlin as heavy as 500lbs (227kg) have been reeled in.

Something different

For a country that is considered *machista*, Puerto Rico's fascination with women's volleyball is notable. Some sports writers suggest it may be

legged pub crawls that include anyone who's managed to raise a horse in his backyard.

The Puerto Rican *pasofino* horse, descended from the first Andalusian horses to be brought by the Spaniards, is said to be the only breed born with a Lipizzaner-style gait. Even a complete

> Punta Borinquen in Aguadilla is part of the military golf legacy on the island. With the ocean in the background, this course was played by Dwight Eisenhower when he was a general and later as President of the United States.

the short shorts the players wear, but whatever the cause, the semi-pro leagues fill arenas all over the island. Even the high-school levels get a great deal of media attention, sometimes nudging the baseball and basketball news to less prominent sports pages.

In four-legged sports, a favorite weekend activity is *cabalgatas*. Derived from the Spanish word for horse – *caballo* – these are trail rides that can range from elegant *paseos* on fine US$50,000 *pasofino* horses accompanied by catering vans along the way, right through to raucous four-

beginner will generally feel comfortable astride one of these small-boned and gentle horses.

Sports bars provide a full complement of National Football League games on TV during the season. Shannan's Pub in Guaynabo shows all of Sunday's games. And cable TV covers college and pro games weekly during the season.

The grand San Blas Half-Marathon, held in the southern Coamo area every year, draws hundreds of contestants from around the world and attracts thousands of spectators.

Unquestionably, the islanders' interest in a wide variety of sports is growing at a fast pace. And it's a far cry from the Taíno games of ancient times: modern technology promises new dimensions to the already booming field. ❏

LEFT: surfing is very popular throughout the island. **ABOVE:** sailing away. **RIGHT:** New York Mets star Carlos Beltrán hails from Puerto Rico.

PLACES

A detailed guide to the entire island, with
principal sites clearly cross-referenced
by number to the maps

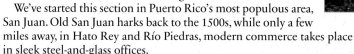

Puerto Rico? That's beaches, right, and *paradores*, and old Spanish forts tossed in with a few frosty rum drinks? Well, yes and no. You won't want to miss Old San Juan's colorful streets, or the chance to stand on El Morro's walls, looking out into the Atlantic at the ghosts of 16th-century British invaders, and you shouldn't leave without tasting a *piña colada* – but there are far more places to see and understand than those fringed with surf and sand.

We've started this section in Puerto Rico's most populous area, San Juan. Old San Juan harks back to the 1500s, while only a few miles away, in Hato Rey and Río Piedras, modern commerce takes place in sleek steel-and-glass offices.

If metropolitan San Juan is the most populated area of the island, then the northeast is the most geographically diverse. Its range of terrain, from beaches to rainforest to secluded islands, is staggering. Here, too, you'll find most of the island's best beaches and some of the finest yachting.

As you head west from San Juan exploration of the northern part of the island reveals one of the largest cave networks in the Western Hemisphere, as well as the oddly scaled karst mountain region. Limestone formations rise above the island's most historic cities – Arecibo, Lares, and San Sebastián.

The western reaches of Puerto Rico feature beautiful beaches, surfers' paradises and towns worth discovering, such as metropolitan Mayagüez and architecturally rich San Germán. In the south of the island, you'll realize fully the relaxed pace of life in Puerto Rico. There's Ponce, a pearl of a city on the coast, but if you're tired of the urban hustle you'll never be at a loss to find a quiet place to sit in the sun.

The heart of the island is the Cordillera Central. Here, the Ruta Panorámica will take the adventurous driver from one end of the range to the other, affording spectacular views. But don't let the island's boundaries stop your explorations: off its shores lie three other islands with charms all of their own – Vieques, Culebra, and Mona. ❑

PRECEDING PAGES: mountains in the mist in the Cordillera Central; ancient and modern at the Old Casino in San Juan; boats moored in the port of Naguabo.
LEFT: pastel-hued Old San Juan. **ABOVE:** Playa Las Palmas, Punta la Galiena.
RIGHT: view from the Ruta Panorámica.

A T L A N T I C

Playa Pu

Areopuerto Rafael
Hernández

Pta Borinquen

Bahía de
Aguadilla

AGUADILLA
Aguadilla

Pta
Higüero
Centro Punta

Rincón

Córcega

Pta Cadena

Bahía
de Añasco

Pta Algarrobo

Bahía de
Mayagüez

Pta Guanajibo

Bahía Bramadero

Joyuda

Pta Ostiones
Puerto Real

Pta Boca Prieta

Pta Guaniquilla

Bahía de Boquerón

Pta Melones
El Combate

Pta Aguila
Bahía Salinas

Pta Jagüey

Pta Tocón

Pta Jacinto
Aguacate
Jobos   Isabela

San Antonio
Feliciano

Centro
Palmar

Coloso
Cuba
Capá
Hebrinas

Aguada

115

2

Cadena
Tres
Hermanos

La

Añasco
Joseña
Maní

Mayagüez

Finca
La Cerza

Sábalos
Rosario

Cerrillos
Conde Avila

San Agustín

Cabo
Rojo

Lajas

102

Boquerón

Llanos

100

Refugio de Vida
Silvestre de Boquerón

Corozo

Bosque Estatal
de Boquerón
La Parguera

Isla
Guayacán

Isla
Magueyes

Parguera

116

Pta Brea

Mora
Quebradillas

San Antonio

112

Cordillera Jaicoa

Bosque Estatal
de Guajataca

San Sebastián

111

109

Perchas

Las Marías

Montañas de Uroyán

Las Vegas

Hormigueros

La Plata

San Germán
120
2

Bosque Estatal
Maricao

Maricao

Bosque Estatal
de Susúa

La Pica

Liborio
Negrón Torres
128

Palomas

La Plata

Laguna
de Guánica

Guánica

Bosque Estatal
de Guánica

Salinas

Bosque Estatal
de Guánica

Cayos de
Caña Gorda

Ensenada

Playa de
Tamarindo

Cayo
María Langa

Pta
Peñón
Camuy

Piedra
Gorda

La Casa
de Piedra

Lake
Guajataca

Lares

Tabonuco
124

Prieto

Angeles

Pta
Hatillo

La Pica

Matojillo

Bayaney

Parque Nacional
Cavernas del
Río Camuy

Grande
de Añasco

105

105

119

Mt Guarionex

Mt Jimamón

129

111

Rafael
Capó

Camuy

San Pedro

Lechuga

Los
Rabanos

Indiera
Alta

Santo
Domingo

Mariao

Villa Perez

939

Monte Guilarte
1205

889

Bosque Estatal
de Guilarte

Bosque Estatal
de Guilarte
1044

1205

10

Adjuntas

Marueño

Tallaboa
Alta

Tallaboa

Guayanilla
2

Indios
Playa de
Guayanilla

22

Arecibo

Cueva del Indio

La Marina   San Luis

San Luis

Dominguito

22

Bajadero

Arecibo
Observatory

Bosque Estatal
de Río Abajo

988

Utuado

111

Lago
Caonillas

140

Jayuya

Vivi
Arriba

Cerro de Punta
(Punta)

1338

Cerro
Maravilla
1188

Guaraguao

1079

Maragüez

Corral Viejo

139

Pta
Las Tunas

Palmas
Altas

Pta
Manatí

Barceloneta

Imbery

Allende

Montaña

Dos Bocas
Lago
Dos Bocas

Lago
988

10

La Pica

Los Tres Picachos
1205

Coabey

Cienaga

Margarita

Guaraguao

10

Santo
Domingo

Juana Díaz

52

Aguilita

Ponce

132

1

Boca
Chica

Pta
Cuchara

Pta
Carenero

Pta
Cabullones

Cayo Morrillito

Cayo Berberia

Caja
de Mue

C A R I B B E A N

Dominican Republic

Manatí

149

Grande de Manatí

Florida

Montebello

149

Baran

La Cordillera

Cerro Gordo

149

Bosque Es
de Toro N

Villa

Lago
Toa

Guay

14

Pta
Boquillas

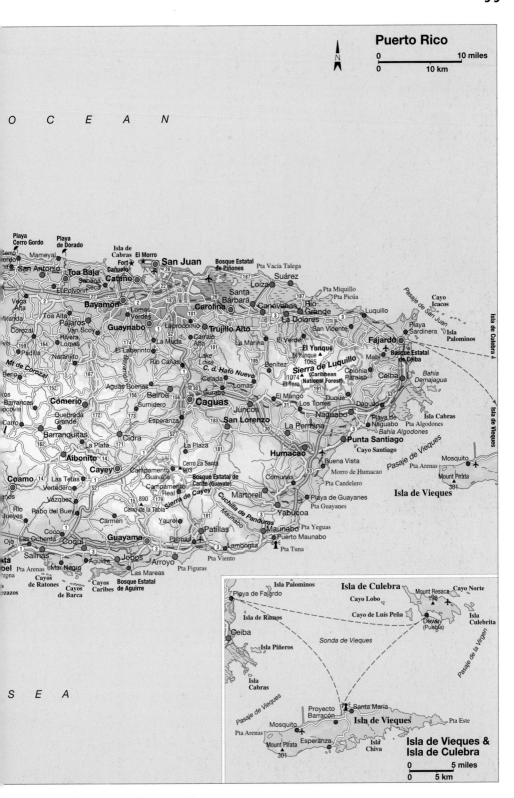

Puerto Rico

0   10 miles
0   10 km

O C E A N

Playa Cerro Gordo
Playa de Dorado
Mameyal
Isla de Cabras
El Morro
San Juan
Fort Cañuelo
Bosque Estatal de Piñones
Pta Vacía Talega
San Antonio
Toa Baja
Cataño
Sabana Seca
El Polvorin
Suárez
Loíza
Pta Miquillo
Pta Picúa
Pta Vacía Talega
Pasaje de San Juan
Cayo Icacos
Vega Alta
Bayamón
Lomas Verdes
Santa Bárbara
Carolina
Canóvanas
Río Grande
La Dolores
Luquillo
Playa Sardinera
Isla Palominos
Toa Alta
Pajaros
Van Scoy
Rivera
Lomas
Guaynabo
Leprocomio
Carraíso
Trujillo Alto
La Muda
San Vicente
Fajardo
Bosque Estatal de Ceiba
Corozal
El Laberinto
La Marina
El Verde
El Yunque
El Yunque 1065
Mabí
Bahía Demajagua
Naranjito
Río Cañas
Lake Loíza
El Toro 1074
Benítez
185
Sierra de Luquillo (Caribbean National Forest)
Colonia Paraíso
Ceiba
Isla Cabras
Mt de Corozal
Berio
Aguas Buenas
C. d. Hato Nuevo
Celada
Gurabo
Lomas
El Mango
191
Duque
Daguao
Playa de Naguabo
Pta Algodones
Comerío
Sumidero
Caguas
Bairoa
El Torres
Naguabo
Bahía Algodones
Quebrada Grande
Esperanza
Juncos
La Perrina
Punta Santiago
Isla Cabras
Barranquitas
Cidra
San Lorenzo
Cayo Santiago
Mosquito
La Plata
La Plaza
Humacao
Buena Vista
Pta Arenas
Mount Pirata
Aibonito
Cerro La Santa
Campamento Guavate
Bosque Estatal de Carite (Guavate)
Morro de Humacao
Pasaje de Vieques
Pta Candelero
301
Coamo
Las Tetas
Cayey
Campamento Real
Martorell
Comunas
Isla de Vieques
Vertedero
Vázquez
Cerro de la Tabla
Sierra de Cayey
Cuchilla de Pandures
Playa de Guayanes
Pta Guayanes
Yabucoa
Rabo del Buey
Carmen
Patillas
Maunabo
Pta Yeguas
Coco
Yaurel
Palmas
Maunabo
Puerto Maunabo
Las Ochenta
Coquí
Guayama
Lamboglia
Pta Tuna
Salinas
Aguirre
Jobos
Arroyo
Pta Viento
Mar Negro
Las Mareas
Pta Figuras
Cayos de Ratones
Cayos de Barca
Cayos Caribes
Bosque Estatal de Aguirre

S E A

Isla de Vieques & Isla de Culebra

Playa de Fajardo
Isla Palominos
Isla de Culebra
Mount Resaca 198
Cayo Norte
Cayo Lobo
Isla de Ramos
Cayo de Luís Peña
Deway (Puabla)
Isla Culebrita
Ceiba
Isla Piñeros
Sonda de Vieques
Pasaje de la Virgen
Isla Cabras
Pasaje de Vieques
Proyecto Barracón
Santa María
Mosquito
Isla de Vieques
Pta Este
Pta Arenas
Esperanza
Isla Chiva
Mount Pirata 301

0   5 miles
0   5 km

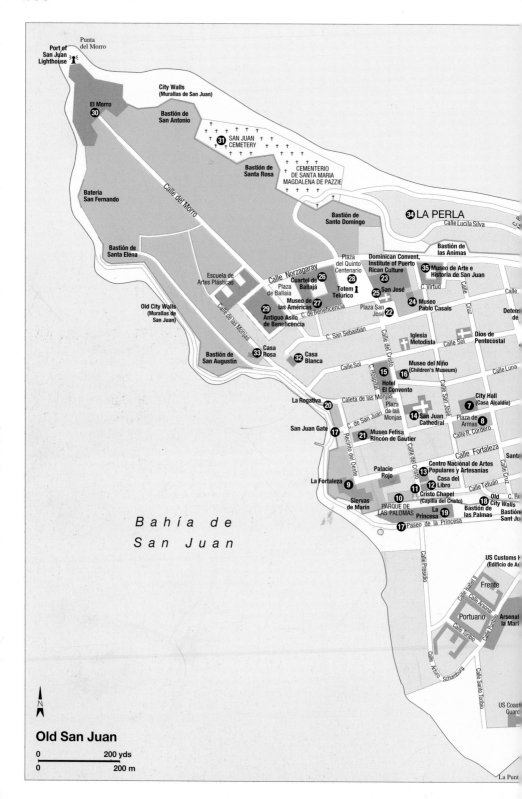

Port of San Juan Lighthouse

Punta del Morro

City Walls (Murallas de San Juan)

El Morro
30

Bastión de San Antonio

SAN JUAN CEMETERY
31

CEMENTERIO DE SANTA MARIA MAGDALENA DE PAZZIE

Bastión de Santa Rosa

Calle del Morro

Batería San Fernando

Bastión de Santo Domingo

34 LA PERLA

Calle Lucila Silva

Bastión de las Ánimas

Bastión de Santa Elena

Calle Norzagaray

Plaza del Quinto Centenario

Dominican Convent, Institute of Puerto Rican Culture
23

35 Museo de Arte e Historia de San Juan

Escuela de Artes Plásticas

Quartel de Ballajá
26

28

C. Virtud

Calle

Plaza de Ballaia

Totem Telúrico

25 San José

Calle Cruz

Old City Walls (Murallas de San Juan)

Museo de las Américas
29

27

24 Museo Pablo Casals

Detens de

Antiguo Asilo de Beneficencia

C. de Beneficencia

Plaza San José
22

C. San Sebastián

Calle del Cristo

Iglesia Metodista

Calle Sol

Dios de Pentecostal

Bastión de San Augustín

33 Casa Rosa

32 Casa Blanca

Calle Sol

C. Hospital

Museo del Niño (Children's Museum)

Calle Luna

La Rogativa

20

Caleta de las Monjas

15

16

Calle San José

City Hall (Casa Alcaldía)
7

Hotel El Convento

San Juan Gate
17

Recinto del Oeste

C. de San Juan

Plaza de las Monjas

21 Museo Felisa Rincón de Gautier

14 San Juan Cathedral

Plaza de Armas
8

Calle R. Cordero

Palacio Rojo

Centro Nacional de Artes Populares y Artesanías
13

Calle Fortaleza

Santa

Calle Cruz

La Fortaleza
9

11

Casa del Libro
12

Calle Tetuán

Cristo Chapel (Capilla del Cristo)

Old City Walls
18

C. Re

Siervas de Marín

10

La Princesa
19

Bastión de las Palmas

Bastión Sant Ju

PARQUE DE LAS PALOMAS

17 Paseo de la Princesa

Bahía de San Juan

US Customs H (Edificio de Ad

Calle Gabel II

Calle Arsenal

Frente

Calle Presidio

Portuario

Arsenal la Mari

Calle Toribio

Calle Badillo

Calle Arturo Schomburg

Calle Santo Toribio

US Coast Guard

Old San Juan

0   200 yds
0   200 m

La Punt

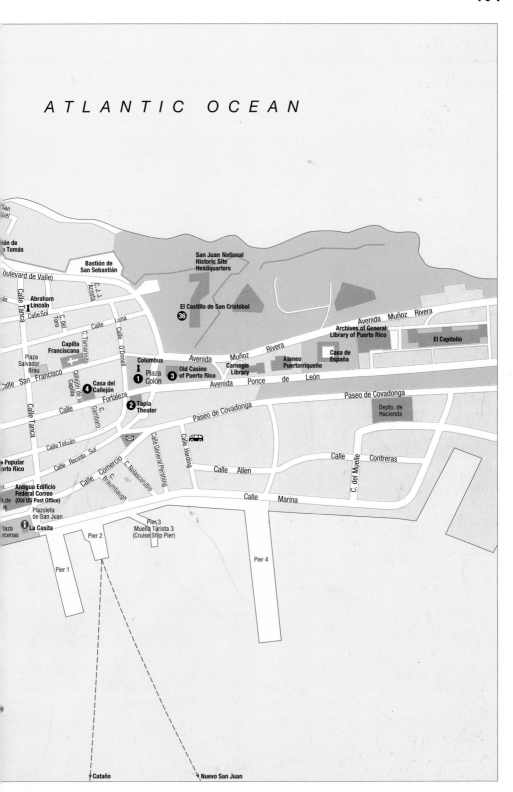

ATLANTIC OCEAN

San Juan National
Historic Site
Headquarters

Bastión de
San Sebastián

Boulevard de Valle)

C. J. J. Acosta

Abraham
Lincoln

Calle Sol

Calle Tanca

C. del Toro

El Castillo de San Cristóbal

36

Calle Luna

C. Tamarindo

Calle O'Donell

Capilla
Franciscana

Plaza
Salvador
Brau

Calle San Francisco

Callejón de la Capilla

Casa del
Callejón

4

Columbus

Plaza
Colón

1

Old Casino
of Puerto Rico

3

Carnegie
Library

Ateneo
Puertorriqueño

Archives of General
Library of Puerto Rico

Avenida Muñoz Rivera

Casa de
España

El Capitolio

Avenida Muñoz Rivera

Avenida Ponce de León

Paseo de Covadonga

Fortaleza

Tapia
Theater

2

Calle Gambaro

Calle

Paseo de Covadonga

Depto. de
Hacienda

Calle Tanca

Calle Tetuán

Calle Recinto Sur

C. Nolascoribio

Calle General Pershing

Calle Harding

Calle Comercio

C. Braumbaugh

Calle Allen

Calle

Contreras

C. del Muelle

Popular
Puerto Rico

Antigua Edificio
Federal Correo
(Old US Post Office)

Plazoleta
de San Juan

Plaza
rcenas

La Casita

1

Pier 1

Pier 2

Pier 3
Muella Turista 3
(Cruise Ship Pier)

Pier 4

Calle Marina

Cataño

Nuevo San Juan

OLD SAN JUAN

There's a wealth of architectural treasures in this oldest of American cities. Fortunately, many of them aren't swamped by the hordes of cruise-ship tourists

Old San Juan, walled within the island capital, is the oldest city under the US flag and the second-oldest European settlement in the Americas. Built by Spanish colonists in 1521, it exhibits magnificent colonial fortresses such as El Morro, San Cristóbal and La Fortaleza, superb examples of 16th- and 17th-century colonial architecture with blue cobblestoned streets.

No matter how much history is crammed within the *adoquín*-lined streets of Old San Juan, it is something altogether more spiritual that attracts Puerto Ricans and visitors alike to San Juan. There is something that traps travellers and forces them to move at the city's pace. If you've rushed through Old San Juan, you certainly have not been there. Get a good pair of walking shoes and ramble; a car is as much a liability as it is an asset here.

The 7-mile (11km) square city was declared a World Heritage Site by Unesco in 1983. A cultural center, fine dining and shopping district, and nightlife center, the islet is also home to almost 450,000 people.

Old San Juan has an endless supply of undiscovered attractions to enjoy. These are what lead second-time visitors to call for a taxi to Old San Juan as soon as they step off the plane at Luis Muñoz Marín International Airport.

Into the city

As Puerto Rico's Spanish history begins with Columbus, an exploration of Old San Juan could naturally begin in the **Plaza Colón ❶**, or Columbus Square. Built in the 17th century as Plaza Santiago, it was first named after the patron saint of Spanish soldiers, Saint James. In front of the quadrangle lay the Puerta de Santiago and the walls surrounding the city, most of which were demolished in the 19th century. For the 400th anniversary of the discovery of Puerto Rico, a statue of Christopher Columbus was commissioned in 1893, and it was unveiled at the remodeled *plaza* in 1894.

Main attractions
PLAZA COLÓN
TAPIA THEATER
LA FORTALEZA
CALLE DEL CRISTO
SAN JUAN CATHEDRAL
MUSEO DEL NIÑO
EL MORRO
EL CASTILLO DE SAN CRISTÓBAL

LEFT: colonial style in Old San Juan.
BELOW: cruise ship on the waterfront.

BELOW:
busy sidewalk in the Old City.

It is here that the high-speed, heavily trafficked Ponce de León and Muñoz Rivera avenues give way to the narrow grid that is Old San Juan. If you're without a car this will be your last stop on the municipal bus, or *público*. If you are driving, you should now start looking for a place to park.

Located at the southeastern corner , Plaza Colón is an ideal spot for fanning out on a walking tour of the city. The square itself offers a good introductory stroll.

On its south side is the **Tapia Theater** ❷ (tel: 787-721 0180; box office: Mon–Fri 9am–4pm). This neoclassical gem may be the oldest freestanding theater stage building that is still in use in the US territories. It takes the form of a horseshoe-shaped opera house and there are three tiers of wooden seats, providing enough space for 700 people. The theater has served as a cultural center since 1832, when construction finished on the public theater originally named the Teatro Municipal de San Juan.

Despite the fact that it had seen the likes of singers and performers such as Adelina Patti and Anna Pavlova, it fell into a period of neglect during the 1940s that nearly resulted in its demolition. Fortunately Felisa Rincón, then mayor of San Juan, saw the need to preserve this Puerto Rican treasure. The restorations were finished in 1949 and it was renamed after renowned local playwright Alejandro Tapia y Rivera. Soon the theatre was in full use once again. In 1975 and 2008 the building went through more extensive restorations, keeping in line with its original architectural glory and adding state-of-the-art technology.

Today the venue continues its traditional use by serving as host to ballets, concerts, operas, theatrical performances, and cultural events. It is also used for meetings and presentations.

Across the street from the theater on the plaza's eastern side is the **Old Casino of Puerto Rico** ❸. Built in 1917 in the style of a French mansion of the Louis XVI era, it sits on the spot of the old Puerta de Santiago, also referred to as Puerta de Tierra, and part of the walls surrounding the Old City. Built by an elite social club of the time,

the most glamorous events were cele-brated at the casino.

In 1941 it was appropriated by the US Armed Forces, only to be returned to local government a little over a dec-ade later, serving as the Education Department's Free School of Music and then a cultural center.

The casino went through extensive renovations from 1982, when it was restored to its original glory – with a copper copula, a ballroom with elabor-ate plasterwork and a 12ft (3.5-meter) chandelier – and now functions as the State Department Reception Center.

Calle Fortaleza

Ironically, if somewhat predictably, the path many tourists take into Old San Juan is the least characteristic of the city. **Calle Fortaleza** is, at least for three blocks, as cluttered with souvenir shops, jewelry shops, and shoe stores as any place in the city. Fortunately, Calle Fortaleza is just as crowded with archi-tectural wonders. The first right along the street is **Callejón de la Capilla**, a romantic, lantern-lit alleyway that arcs uphill to Calle San Francisco.

At the corner of Fortaleza and Calle-jón de la Capilla, the **Casa del Callejón** ④, an 18th-century residence, houses two charming museums – one dedi-cated to pharmacology and the other to the Puerto Rican family.

Located on the first floor of the build-ing, the **Museo de la Farmacia** (tel: 787-977 2700; Tue–Sat 8.30am–4.20pm) houses a valuable collection of crystal and porcelain flasks as well as furniture and other objects that were typical of drugstores in the mid-19th century. The second floor is home to the **Casa de la Familia Puertorriqueña** (tel: 787-977 2700; Tue–Sat 8.30am–4.20pm). This museum illustrates, with its decor and furnishings, the times and daily routines of domestic life for middle-class Puerto Rican families of the 19th century.

Continuing on Calle Fortaleza, you can turn right on Calle Tanca for a bit of relaxation in the sloping Plaza Sal-vador Brau, or make a left toward the piers of San Juan Port. Nearby at the waterfront, **Plazoleta de San Juan** teems with eager visitors who pur-chase souvenirs and folk art from the local artisans.

The Spanish flavor of Old San Juan's architecture is evident from any angle.

Old San Juan Dining

With so many places to go and things to do right in their own neighborhood, it's a wonder Old San Juan residents ever leave their walled haven. When it comes to food, most travel experts will tell you to take a cue from the locals.

For breakfast, there is one name that comes up over and over again – **La Bombonera**. This landmark establishment opened its doors to the public in 1903 and is a favorite for locals and tourists alike. The stained-glass windows serve to tempt passers-by with freshly baked pastries. It is incredibly popular in the mornings and stays open for lunch and dinner.

Just down the street is **Café Mallorca** (300 San Fran-cisco; tel: 787-724 4607). Operated by the owners of La Bombonera, it has the same ages-old atmosphere. Open for breakfast and lunch, the bakery serves delicious treats, sandwiches and heavier Puerto Rican fare.

There are plenty of lunch spots, but once again there is one restaurant on most people's list of favorites. **El Jibarito** is a mecca for the masses that seek popular Puerto Rican staples like rice and beans, roast pork, fried plaintains and more. This cozy establishment also offers an outdoor café space.

Known for its "mojito" chicken breast and succulent sea-food, **Mojito's** (323 Recinto Sur Street; tel: 787-723 7539; daily noon–10pm) is a quaint locale that packs a lunch crowd. Their classic Cuban cocktail with fresh mint is excellent.

Old San Juan is a thriving nightlife spot and people pour into the city from all over the island, but there are plenty of restaurants to go around. **El Burén** (tel: 787-977 5023; Mon–Fri 5.30–11.30pm, Sat–Sun noon–11.30pm) in front of El Convento Hotel on Cristo Street, offers Puerto Rican and other Caribbean dishes. But the signature food is pizza – famous here for its fresh ingredients. Just up the street is **Bodega Chic** (tel: 787-725 7370; daily 6–11pm, Thur–Sat until mid-night). This French-Algerian bistro has the locals trying to keep it a secret. Fortunately, word of mouth has made the place known to tourists, and the food lives up to the hype.

Fortaleza Street has seen a boom in fashionable restau-rants, and one place that always attracts the dinner crowd is **The Parrot Club**, a colorful restaurant with a modern take on Puerto Rican and Latin cuisine.

So, no need to leave the city walls, then…

The City Hall, or Casa Alcaldía, was built in stages from 1604 to 1789 and underwent extensive alterations in 1841. Free English-language Old City tours can be arranged by appointment (tel: 787-977 4825).

BELOW: a rainbow of facades.

Most ports which serve a large number of cruise ships end up looking rather like jungles of cranes and heavy machinery. San Juan, which takes more cruise traffic than any other port in the Caribbean, is an exception. The port not only benefits from the tastefulness of its more utilitarian maritime buildings (the pink, mock-colonial **US Customs House ❺** is a good example of this) but has a beautiful cityscape, too.

The waterfront has become even more attractive with its **Frente Portuario** complex. This Mediterranean-style mega-project offers 200 condo apartments across three buildings, the vast 240-room Sheraton Hotel and Casino, two office towers, a 603-space parking garage, and a large amount of retail space.

Frente Portuario, designed to blend in with the rest of Old San Juan, features picturesque cobblestone-like paved boulevards lined with wrought-iron lamps and red-tiled roofs. Visitors can browse through art galleries, eateries, and boutiques.

The government has already spent $100 million on renovating half a dozen cruise-ship ports along the waterfront. Some of the world's largest cruise ships, including Royal Caribbean Line's *Monarch of the Seas* and its twin sister, *Sovereign of the Seas*, regularly call here. From Pier 2 you can also take the ferry to Cataño, home of the Bacardi rum distillery. At 50 cents a passenger, this ferry is truly one of Puerto Rico's great bargains.

Oasis of shade

Plaza de Hostos is an oasis of shade in a square full of *adoquines*. Named for the 19th-century scholar, it provides a haven for sunburned tourists and locals alike; the square must be the dominoes capital of the Caribbean. Looming over the plaza is the original office of the **Banco Popular de Puerto Rico ❻**, which has to be one of the great modern architectural triumphs of the Caribbean region. This brawny, 10-story edifice, built in the mid-1930s, is a fine example of Art Deco. Heavy cameo eagles brood over the impressive main entrance, which is lettered in sans-serif gilt intaglio. Elongated windows with prominent pastel mullions run the full

height of a faintly apsidal facade. The bank presents various exhibits of historical interest during the year.

The area is particularly fortunate in its culinary offerings. Calle Fortaleza has a number of first-rate restaurants, ranging from Dragonfly (Asian Latino) to Tantra (Indian).

Whether approaching uphill on Calle Cruz from Plaza de Hostos, or via Calle Fortaleza from Plaza Colón, almost all travelers pass through the workaday heart of Old San Juan, centering around the **City Hall** (Casa Alcaldía) ❼ (tel: 787-724 7171; www.sanjuancapital.com; Mon–Fri 8am–4pm, closed pub. hols) and the adjacent **Plaza de Armas** ❽. Construction began in 1602 and was completed in 1789. The building, of neoclassical design, was remodeled in the 1840s to replicate the facade of the City Hall in Madrid, with two towers overlooking the plaza. Casa Alcaldía is currently home to the office of the mayor, is open to the public, and has periodic exhibitions. There is also a visitor information center.

The plaza, originally known as Plaza Mayor, is no less historic. Built in 1521, it was the first square in the newly established city. It also served, in the days before soldiers were permanently billeted in San Juan, as the training field for Spanish soldiers sent out from Europe to defend the island – hence its current name. Stone paving of the plaza began in 1840 and was completely remodeled in the late 1980s.

Anchoring the plaza is the Fuente de las Cuatro Estaciones, the Fountain of the Four Seasons. Each statue represents a different season.

Calle San Francisco is a friendly mix of tourist shops and government buildings, while the part of Calle Fortaleza just south of the plaza is an engaging few blocks of restaurants and department stores.

La Fortaleza

Calle Fortaleza grows more dignified as it approaches **La Fortaleza** ❾ itself (tel: 787-721 7000 ext. 2211; http://fortaleza. govpr.org; Mon–Fri, closed pub. hols). This chalk-white wonder of a fortress is the oldest continuously inhabited executive mansion in the Western Hemisphere. Its construction began in 1532

TIP

Guided tours of the public areas of La Fortaleza (in English every hour; in Spanish every half-hour) depart from the main gate on Calle Fortaleza.

BELOW: lovely Plaza de Armas.

Campeche paintings and a gold-and-silver altar can be seen through the Cristo Chapel's glass doors.

and was completed in 1540, and it serves to this day as the residence of the Governor of Puerto Rico. It is an architectural wonder, but strategically it was always inadequate. This was apparent even to the Spanish architects, who decided that the gnarled peninsula on which La Fortaleza was being built did not command enough of San Juan Bay to protect completely against invasion from the sea. Accordingly, construction of the massive fort at the tip of the San Juan Peninsula – **El Morro** – began in the 1540s. *(See page 117.)*

The 1588 sinking of the Spanish Armada made the West Indian possessions of the Spanish Crown more vulnerable than ever, with the result that even more Puerto Rican colonists clamored for greater fortification. By 1595, Queen Elizabeth I had dispatched Sir Francis Drake, whose ambitions included not only a great bounty of gold but all the Spanish lands of the New World as well. Drake arrived in San Juan in late November of that year. He stopped across the bay at Isla de Cabras, and launched several dozen ships from there. Ten would never go

RIGHT: children frolic with feathered friends in Parque de las Palomas.

back to England, and a total of 400 English sailors would rest forever beneath San Juan harbor. Drake's own cabin was torn apart by a mortar shell during the invasion.

Perhaps the Spanish grew complacent after the first thwarted invasion of their colonial capital, for in June 1598 the Earl of Cumberland was able to land a force of about 1,000 men in the area of Puerta de Tierra, and then march into San Juan. The 400 Spanish soldiers defending the city were suffering from tropical diseases but put up valiant resistance, enduring a 15-day siege inside El Morro before capitulating. The British flag flew over the walls of La Fortaleza. The British were hounded by Spanish colonists almost immediately, but it was less Spanish resistance than British *lack* of resistance to the same diseases that led them to give in. In a matter of several weeks after the invasion, Cumberland sailed for home, having lost over 400 men, to leave San Juan to recover in peace for another 27 years.

The year 1625 saw the final occupation of La Fortaleza during colonial times. A Dutch fleet under the com-

Architecture in the Old City

From an architectural standpoint, La Fortaleza really captures the essence of all of Old San Juan: it is an amazing blend of building styles through the ages, from its 16th-century core to its 19th-century facade. La Fortaleza and El Morro – both World Heritage Sites – are perhaps the most outstanding, but throughout the streets of the Old City are fine examples of medieval, Gothic, baroque, neoclassical and even Arabian architecture. Most buildings are in excellent condition, partly owing to the painstaking efforts of those who restored them (who worked from many original plans and used, whenever possible, original materials, like *ausubo*, or ironwood, beams) and partly because Old San Juan's sandstone walls and fortresses prevented any modern expansion.

There are some 400 historically important structures in this part of the Puerto Rican capital city, some of which are considered to be the finest examples of Spanish colonial architecture anywhere in the New World. Those of particular note include San Juan Cathedral, with a baroque facade but a medieval core; San José Church, the only truly Gothic structure under the United States flag; and the Dominican Convent, a 16th-century white building that now houses the Institute of Puerto Rican Culture.

mand of Boudewijn Hendrikszoon swiftly moved into San Juan Bay and set up a beachhead between El Morro and La Fortaleza. The Dutch burned much of the city to the ground, including a large portion of La Fortaleza. Reconstruction began in 1640; the building was expanded in 1800 and 1846.

Romantic road

Calle del Cristo (Christ's Street) is the most alluring of Old San Juan's thoroughfares, an intoxicating avenue of sights and sounds, of romance and history. Running from a point high above San Juan Bay, Calle del Cristo arches to an even higher perch above San Juan's Atlantic shore, where El Morro looks sternly out to sea. It can claim Old San Juan's most popular park, underrated museum, and famous chapel.

This adventure in *adoquines* begins at the **Parque de las Palomas** (Pigeon Park) ⑩, a part of the city walls which thousands of pigeons have made their home. Fabulous views of San Juan Bay and the distant suburbs of Bayamón and Guaynabo make Parque de las Palomas a popular spot for lovers and an even more popular spot for any aspiring ones.

Building with love

Love almost certainly played a decisive part in the construction of the quaint **Cristo Chapel** or Capilla del Cristo ⑪ (Tue 10am–4pm; free). Romantic legend has it that, during an 18th-century horse race, one of two competing riders failed to make a left turn onto Calle Tetuán and fell over cliffs, seemingly to his death. When he survived, astounded locals constructed a chapel to commemorate Christ's intercession.

Others claim that the race was really a duel over a comely young woman between two chivalrous *enamorados*. One fell to his death, and the chapel was built both to commemorate the tragedy and to block off Calle del Cristo to prevent such a mishap from ever occurring again.

The peninsula stretching below the Cristo Chapel is known as **La Puntilla**. Today it accommodates the **Arsenal de la Marina** (tel: 787-721 1839; times vary; free), a former Spanish naval base that now houses the Plastic Arts

TIP

You can get many discounts and special offers on historic site tours, folklore shows, lodgings, meals, and more by joining Puerto Rico's LeLoLai VIP program for a small fee. Phone 787-721 2400 ext. 2715 for more information.

BELOW: strolling down Calle del Cristo.

Divisions of the Institute of Puerto Rican Culture. This complex houses offices and ample gallery space where diverse art exhibits are held year-round. The gardens and patio are also used for cultural activities.

A short walk up Calle del Cristo on the right is one of Puerto Rico's most enchanting and least-known museums. The **Casa del Libro** ⑫ (tel: 787-723 0354; www.lacasadellibro.org; Tue–Sat 11am–4.30pm, closed pub. hols; free) is a breezy, parqueted sanctuary which is dedicated to the history of books and printing. Within its walls are nearly 5,000 rare sketches, illustration, and ancient manuscripts, as well as work by local artists. Two of the museum's most prized possessions are royal mandates, signed in 1493 by Ferdinand and Isabella of Spain, concerning the provisioning of Columbus's fleet for his second voyage, which resulted in the discovery of Puerto Rico. Another precious work is one of only six known copies of the first printing of the Third Part of the *Summa* of St Thomas Aquinas, dating from 1477.

In front of San Juan Cathedral stands a gnarled tree – a living gesture of international friendship from dozens of North and South American nations.

BELOW: the much-photographed cupolas of San Juan Cathedral.

Next door, the **Centro Nacional de Artes Populares y Artesanías** or Popular Arts and Crafts Center ⑬ (Mon–Sat 9am–5pm; free), run by the Institute of Puerto Rican Culture (www.icp.gobierno.pr), houses a collection of paintings from the 18th century to the present. Island crafts are for sale at the shop inside.

If you build up an appetite – whether for food or shopping – exploring this oldest and best-known street of the Old City, don't worry: half a dozen eateries crowd this end of Calle del Cristo. And there are some wonderful art galleries and outlet stores (Coach, Ralph Lauren) along the way.

A cathedral and a convent

Ascending Calle del Cristo, even the most skeptical travelers will begin to see what they came to San Juan for. On the right, usually bathed in sunlight in the afternoon, is **San Juan Cathedral** ⑭ (daily 8.30am–4pm; donation), a fabulous beige-and-white structure that must count among the most important houses of worship in the West. It was built in 1540 and carefully restored in

the 19th and 20th centuries, and the beauty of its exterior is immediately perceptible. Three tiers of white pilasters and arches mount to a simple cross at the cathedral's pinnacle. The three brick-red and white cupolas are among San Juan's most photogenic sights.

The cathedral continues to function; Mass is held, along with many other religious activities. It is also a very popular venue for weddings, and has held funeral services for prominent local figures.

Among its highlights are **Ponce de León's marble tomb**, with an understated virgin warrior glancing down at the body and the red script of the epitaph, and the glittering blue statue of **La Virgen de Providencia**, Puerto Rico's patroness, located nearby. A relic of St Pius, a Roman martyr, is in a glass case containing a macabre plaster figure of the saint, behind the altar. There's another such effigy, of a prostrate Jesus, in the **Chapel of Souls in Purgatory**, which is in the cathedral's right nave.

Directly across Calle del Cristo is **Hotel El Convento 🖐**, established in 1651 as the first Carmelite convent in the Americas. It housed the nuns for 252 years until closing a few days before Christmas in 1903. Vacant for a decade, the abandoned building served as a retail store, a dance hall, and, for the next 40 years, a flophouse without running water, sanitary facilities, or electricity. Opened in 1962 as El Convento Hotel, it offered a tranquil, European-style alternative to the glitzy hotels lining the Condado strip. It was restored in 1996 and turned into a four-star, 100-room luxury hotel with a casino – much to the anger of the nuns, who argued that slot machines were a sacrilege to the memory of their sisters buried underneath. Though few of the fixtures are originals, the decor fits in harmoniously with the concept of a nunnery-turned-hotel and serves as a fine example of restoration of Spanish colonial architecture and design.

Museum magic for kids

Next door and across the street from the San Juan Cathedral is the **Museo del Niño 🖐** (tel: 787-722 3791; www. museodelninopr.org; Tue–Thur 9am– 3.30pm, Fri 9am–5pm, Sat–Sun 12.30–

BELOW: the San Juan-based Don Rey cigar company holds the Guinness World Record for the longest cigar in the world.

History aside, San Juan natives view their city as a place to have fun.

BELOW: modern sculpture in an ancient city: dramatic lines of La Rogativa.

5pm; charge), which has interactive exhibits and covers topics such as dinosaurs, space, music, and the human body, complete with a giant replica of a human heart. The 300-year-old colonial home opened its museum doors to the general public in 1993. Three floors of exhibits also include an opportunity to talk to youth in other countries on a short-wave radio, a miniature town square, and an extensive explanation of the benefits of recycling. The Children's Museum is a non-profit organization involved in preserving the island's cultural heritage and presenting subjects in a rich and interesting way for children.

One block away from El Convento, the **Center for Advanced Studies** – built in 1842 as a religious school for young men – houses a fine library of the Caribbean and Puerto Rico. Besides its academic value, the center can be a haven for weary tourists and locals.

Steps and statues

Across Cristo from San Juan Cathedral, between the fork of two of San Juan's oldest and most pleasant cobblestoned streets, lies the lush **Plazuela de las Monjas** (Nuns' Square), a perfect spot for an urban picnic. The square looks out not only on the cathedral and El Convento but on the **Casa Cabildo**, San Juan's original City Hall, which now houses an interior-design company.

A walk down **Caleta de San Juan** will take you to the massive wooden **San Juan Gate** ⓱, built in the 1700s and the only one of three original portals remaining. Sailors weary from their voyages used to moor their ships in San Juan Bay, ferry themselves ashore, enter through the gate, and walk to prayer services via Caleta de San Juan, which describes a conveniently straight line between the gates and the main altar of the cathedral.

Through the gate is **Paseo de la Princesa**, a romantic bayfront promenade that skirts the **Old City Walls** ⓲, or *murallas*. Built of sandstone from 1635 to 1641, it measures up to 20ft (6 meters) in thickness and at one time completely surrounded the colonial city, guarding it against enemy attacks. Along the *paseo* – an immaculate, landscaped pedestrian boulevard facing the

sea – are statues, a large fountain, and kiosk vendors selling everything from cotton candy to *guarapo de caña* (sugarcane juice). Various family activities, such as concerts and children's theater, are scheduled here on many weekends. The old **La Princesa** ⓭ jail (Mon–Sat 9am–4pm; free), midway along the promenade, now houses the Tourism Company offices, an art gallery, and a museum featuring the actual jail cells used centuries ago.

Continuing up Recinto del Oeste, past more examples of fine colonial architecture, you reach a modern sculpture, **La Rogativa** ⓴, showing the Bishop of San Juan followed by three torch-bearing women, which commemorates the failure of an English siege of the city in 1797. The legend runs that General Sir Ralph Abercrombie led a fleet of British ships to take San Juan in a rapid, all-out assault by land and sea. When this plan failed, Abercrombie ordered a naval blockade, which lasted two weeks, while the residents of San Juan began to suffer from dysentery, losing hope of the arrival of Spanish reinforcements from the inland settlements. The governor called for a *rogativa*, or divine entreaty, to the saints Ursula and Catherine. All the women of San Juan marched through the town carrying torches, to the loud ringing of tocsins. Abercrombie, believing reinforcements had arrived, quit San Juan, never to return.

Flamboyant fun

A short walk back down Recinto del Oeste brings you to the **Museo Felisa Rincón de Gautier** ㉑ (tel: 787-723 1897 or 787-724 7239; www.museofelisa rincon.com; Mon–Fri 9am–3.45pm; free). This little museum is the former home of Felisa Rincón de Gautier, or "Dona Fela," one of San Juan's most popular mayors, who led the city from 1946 to 1968 and was noted for her flamboyant style. The home-turned-museum contains many items belonging to the late Dona Fela, including her impressive collection of hand fans – as well as a film clip from the 1950s which shows the mayor bringing a plane-load of snow to the island from New York so that the children of San Juan could have a snowball fight.

From Paseo de la Princesa the waters of San Juan Bay look enticing – but they are considered too polluted here for swimming. The more adventurous locals and visitors, however, do often swim to the right of the big pier outside the San Juan Gate.

BELOW: the Paseo de la Princesa offers great views.

TIP

If your feet need a break, consider a ride on a *calesa* (horse-drawn carriage) reminiscent of old colonial days. The carriages are based just off Pier 1 at the San Juan Harbor front. Night rides are particularly enchanting.

The walk back to the cathedral on **Caleta de las Monjas** is full of surprises, chief among them the "step streets" leading up to the left toward calles Sol and San Sebastián. At the top of the first, **Escalinata de las Monjas**, is the old Palace of the Bishop of San Juan. The second, **Calle Hospital**, is a favorite of artists and photographers.

With all the historical legacy San Juan offers, it's easy to forget to view the city as its natives view it: a place to have fun. **Calle San Sebastián** is perhaps the pre-eminent place in the Old City in which to do just that. Perpendicular to the top of Calle del Cristo, it's a place of museums and old homes whose many bars and spacious plaza make it a mecca for *sanjuanero* youth.

Plaza San José ㉒ is the focal point of the street, paved with rosy Spanish conglomerate around a statue of Ponce de León made from English cannons melted down after the first invasion. The plaza draws strolling locals on warm weekend evenings, and fun-loving tourists throughout the year. Live concerts of traditional music often take place here.

San Juan's **Dominican Convent** ㉓ (Mon–Sat 9am–5pm) dominates the plaza. Built in 1523, this mammoth, white, elegantly domed structure has seen as much history as any building on the island, having housed both English and Dutch occupying forces over the centuries.

The convent now houses the craft and book store of the **Institute of Puerto Rican Culture** (tel: 787-724 0700; http://icp.gobierno.pr), the body which, more than any other, has been responsible for the renaissance in Puerto Rican scholarship and art over the past several years. Under its auspices the parts of the convent not used for office space have been converted to cultural use. A beautiful indoor patio is the scene of many concerts and plays, and it now serves as the focus for the magnificent San Juan Museum of History and Art. The old convent library has been restored to its original 16th-century decor.

Museum spin-offs

A complex of museums has sprung up around the Dominican Convent. The **Museo Pablo Casals** ㉔ (Tue–Sat 9.30am–4.45pm; charge), which abuts the convent, is a petite, gray, two-story townhouse storing memorabilia of the legendary cellist who moved to Puerto Rico in 1956 and lived here until his death in 1973. It includes manuscripts, instruments, texts of his speeches to the United Nations, and cassettes of his music which can be heard on request. A Casals arts festival takes place every year. (*See page 77.*)

Another interesting visit to consider in the Dominican Convent area is the **Museo del Indio** (tel: 787-724 5477; Tue–Sat 9am–4pm; free) on Calle San José, which concentrates on the indigenous cultures of Puerto Rico.

Next to the Convent is the stunning and unusual **San José Church** ㉕. Built shortly after the convent in the 1530s, San José is the second-oldest church in the Western Hemisphere; just San Juan Cathedral, a half-block

BELOW:
Ponce de León stands proudly on Plaza San José.

down the street, is older. The Gothic architecture of the structure is a true rarity; only the Spanish arrived in the New World early enough to build Gothic churches, and just a handful exist today. The interior of San José certainly has far more charm than that of the nearby cathedral.

A wooden crucifix of the mid-16th century, donated by Ponce de León, is one of the highlights, as is the 15th-century altar brought from Cádiz. In addition, the great Puerto Rican painter José Campeche is buried here.

Military architecture

Across from the Plaza San José is the **Cuartel de Ballajá**  (www.ballaja.com) or Ballajá Infantry Barracks Building, constructed by the Spanish Army between 1854 and 1864. The structure is one of the most impressive constructed by Spain in the New World and it stands as the last example of monumental military architecture by the Spanish monarchy in the Americas.

Located on a lot of approximately 3 acres (1.2 hectares), it occupies six city blocks that were expropriated and demolished in 1853. Used until 1898 as infantry barracks and permanent housing for approximately 1,000 troops, it consisted of rooms for officers, soldiers and their families, storage, kitchens, dining rooms, jail cells, and stables for horses. The ascending vaulted Gothic ceilings above the main staircase are unique in Puerto Rico, and its vast interior patio is a striking example of 19th-century architectural prowess.

After the change of sovereignty, the Americans also used the facilities as barracks until 1939. Then it became the Rodríguez Hospital. In 1986 renovation work began. The three-story structure was the centerpiece of the restoration of Old San Juan in time for the 500th anniversary in 1992 of Columbus's arrival in the New World. Today it is a cultural center that renders tribute to Puerto Rico's rich cultural heritage.

Ballajá's first floor houses the music school Fundación Dr Francisco López Cruz (tel: 787-722 4959), the dance school and cultural space Paulette Beauchamp/DanzActiva (tel: 787-775 9438), publisher Terranova Editores (tel: 787-

After Ponce de León's death in Cuba in 1521, his body was brought to Puerto Rico and laid to rest in San José Church, where his descendants worshipped. Later, in 1908, his remains were moved to San Juan Cathedral.

BELOW: taking a break in the shade.

725 7711), the art and paper store Taller Ballajá, and the Institute of Puerto Rican Culture's exhibition halls.

On Ballajá's second floor is the **Museo de las Américas**  (tel: 787-724 5052; www.museolasamericas.org; Tue–Sun 10am–4pm; free), which provides an overview of cultural development in the New World. Among its colorful exhibits of crafts in the Americas are a replica of a country chapel and examples of Haitian voodoo and *santos*. The permanent exhibits include artifacts and samples of the arts and crafts pertaining to daily life, such as clothes, tools, musical instruments, religious objects, etc. There is also a room dedicated to African heritage and a special exhibits on the Indian in the Americas. The temporary exhibits change throughout the year.

The third floor is home to the Puerto Rico Academy of the Spanish Language (tel: 787-721 6070) and the State Office of Historic Conservation (tel: 787-721 3737).

Directly in front is the three-level **Plaza del Quinto Centenario** ㉘, which looks out over the Atlantic.

Adoquines are blocks of slag, from the lowland smelting mills of Spain's 16th-century empire. The cobblestones were brought over by the Spanish as ballast for their ships.

BELOW: the informative Museo de las Américas.

Dominating this plaza, at the center of an eight-pointed pavement design, is the controversial **Totem Telúrico**, a terracotta (some say phallic) sculpture by local artist Jaime Suárez that symbolizes the blending of Taíno, African, and Spanish cultures. Nearby is a fountain with 100 jets of water; it is supposed to symbolize five centuries of Puerto Rican history.

Old Home for the Poor

Across the plaza from the Cuartel de Ballajá, along unmarked Calle de Beneficencia, is the stately **Antiguo Asilo de Beneficencia** or Old Home for the Poor ㉙ (galleries: Wed–Sun 9am–4.30pm; free). The building, constructed in the 1840s to house the destitute, today serves as headquarters for the Institute of Puerto Rican Culture.

Climb the stairs, go through an ornate foyer and enter the room immediately to your left. Here you'll find an impressive exhibit on the Taíno artifacts. On your right is a small exhibit of Puerto Rican religious statues. Two huge interior courtyards are used for various cultural activities;

surrounding them are the institute's main administration offices.

The Spanish colonists considered San Juan chiefly as a military stronghold, and held military architecture as their first priority. It is not surprising, then, that contemporary *sanjuaneros* are proudest of the breathtaking forts, unique in the Western world, that their antecedents left them.

El Morro

El Castillo San Felipe del Morro, simply known as **El Morro** ❸ (tel: 787-729 6777; www.nps.gov/archive/saju/morro.html; daily 9am–5pm; charge), features a maze of secret access tunnels, dungeons, lookouts, ramps, barracks, and vaults. Declared a World Heritage Site by the United Nations, El Morro falls under the auspices of the US National Park Service. Free tours in English and Spanish are given daily.

This, the larger of the city's two forts, commands San Juan Bay with six levels of gun emplacements and walls that tower 140ft (43 meters) over the Atlantic. Its guns were capable of aiming at any ship within El Morro's field of vision, no matter the distance, and the walls themselves, connected with the system that encircles Old San Juan, are 20ft (6 meters) thick.

The fort's first battery was completed in the 1540s, but it was not until 1589, when Juan Bautista Antonelli arrived with a team of other Spanish military engineers to begin raising a true bulwark along the edge of the peninsula, that the fort was completed. When Sir Francis Drake attacked in 1595 he was roundly repulsed, but Cumberland's land attack from the Condado succeeded in piercing El Morro's still vulnerable rear approach.

The English held the fort for three months, until dysentery took the lives of nearly half their men. It would be the last time El Morro would fall, even holding out against the Dutch siege of 1625 and the American gunnery fire which rained upon it during the Spanish-American War of 1898.

Today, visitors appreciate El Morro (which means "headland" in Spanish) more for its breathtaking views and architecture than for the protection it gives them. The approach to the fort is

The lovely rounded garitas, or sentry boxes, that line the walls of San Juan's forts serve as Puerto Rico's official symbol.

BELOW: San Juan Cemetery glimpsed through El Morro's stone walls.

over a vast, 27-acre (11-hectare) park-land, once the former drill square for the soldiers and currently a haven for kite-flyers and strolling lovers. A gravel path through the green leads over a moat and into the massive structure, crossing El Morro's main courtyard surrounded by beautiful yellow walls and white archways. Here you will discover a souvenir shop and a museum, both of which are useful in orienting the traveler to the fort's layout and long history.

The massive archway facing over San Juan Bay on the west side of the court-yard is the entrance to what looks like the longest skateboard run in the world: a huge, stone, step-flanked ramp leading to the lower ramparts. This is the most popular of the fort's various sections, affording views of the surf crashing below, and profiling the fort from the ocean side, as its invaders saw it.

Back on the upper level of El Morro, a left turn through the courtyard patio leads to another ramp, this one twist-ing rightward toward the **Port of San Juan Lighthouse**, which was destroyed by an American mortar

shell during the Spanish-American War but later restored.

San Juan Cemetery ㉛, considered by many to be the most picturesque resting place for old bones in the world, sits on a broad, grassy hummock of land tucked between El Morro's walls and the pounding surf. The cem-etery's highlight is a tiny, 19th-century circular chapel, set among the bleached-white gravestones. Abutting El Morro's grounds, the **Casa Blanca** ㉜ (tel: 787-725 1454; Tue–Sat 9am–noon, 1–4pm; charge) is the oldest house in Puerto Rico, having been built for Ponce de León in 1521. Used in the years preceding the construction of La Fortaleza as a shelter against the attacks of savage Carib tribes, it was owned by the conquistador's family until the late 18th century and is now a museum of 16th- and 17th-century family life, with an interesting ethno-graphic section.

The nearby **Casa Rosa** ㉝ (also referred to as Casa Rosada) is a lovely pink building overlooking the bay and serves as a day-care center for govern-ment employees' children.

La Perla

A glance down the beachfront from El Morro will show one of the most bizarre and colorful coastal cityscapes imaginable. One- and two-story shacks, seemingly piled one on top of another, crowd the coastline all the way from El Morro to San Cristóbal, running along the battlements which formerly connected the two castles. This is **La Perla** ㉞, the so-called "world's prettiest slum."

Set against the backdrop of an aquamarine Atlantic, it looks at first glance delightful, but even the tough-est of San Juan residents will warn tourists not to wander around here, as drugs, violence, and a general lawless-ness are rampant in this otherwise charming neighborhood.

Along Calle Norzagaray, the **Museo de Arte e Historia de San Juan** ㉟ (tel: 787-724 1875; Mon–Fri 8am–

A key shipping lane to the Panama Canal, San Juan is one of the biggest and best natu-ral harbors in the Caribbean.

BELOW:
Puerto Rico's most famous silhouette: El Morro fort in Old San Juan.

4pm; free) beckons visitors for a look. Its construction as the Plaza del Mercado, or farmers' market, from 1853 to 1857, served to align the streets and allowed for uniformity of facade for its surrounding structures. In 1979 it was converted into a museum. The galleries feature plastic art exhibits and the interior patio hosts cultural activities year-round.

El Castillo de San Cristóbal

Though overshadowed by its more famous neighbor to the west, **El Castillo de San Cristóbal** ㊱ (tel: 787-729 6777; daily 9am–5pm; charge) makes as fascinating a trip as El Morro. What El Morro achieved with brute force, San Cristóbal achieved with much more subtlety.

Sitting 150ft (45 meters) above the ocean waves, the fort reflects the best of 17th-century military architectural thought, and has a fascinating network of tunnels that was used both for transporting artillery and for ambushing luckless invaders.

San Cristóbal was completed in 1678 as a means of staving off land attacks on San Juan, like the English one under the Earl of Cumberland, made to capture El Morro in 1598. But the fort as it is known today is the product of the acumen of two Irishmen, "Wild Geese" who had fled from the Orange monarchy and were in the employ of the Spanish Army.

Alejandro O'Reilly and fellow Irishman Colonel Thomas O'Daly designed a system of battlements and sub-forts that ensured that no one could take El Castillo de San Cristóbal without taking all of its ramparts first. No one ever did. The first shot of the Spanish-American War was fired from San Cristóbal's walls.

Frequent guided tours explain how San Cristóbal's unique system of defense worked, and also point out some of the fort's big attractions, like the **"Devil's Sentry Box,"** a *garita* at the end of a long tunnel that runs to the waterline.

Views from the battlements are outstandingly spectacular, particularly in the direction *sanjuaneros* describe as "towards Puerto Rico": Condado, Hato Rey, and El Yunque. ❏

The atmospheric Plaza del Mercado has a great nightlife, with cafés and bars open until late.

LEFT: view of La Perla and El Morro from San Cristóbal.
BELOW: inside El Castillo de San Cristóbal.

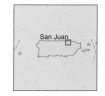

METROPOLITAN SAN JUAN

Condado, Ocean Park, and Isla Verde have
fine beaches, Santurce is a genuine marketplace,
Hato Rey is a major finance center, and Bayamón
has a maverick quality

I t's easy to try to relegate **Puerta de Tierra ❶** to the status of a sort of verdant buffer zone between San Juan's body and its soul, separating as it does the brawn of Santurce from the historical grandeur and romance of Old San Juan. Puerta de Tierra means "gateway of land," but Puerta de Tierra is a gateway in more ways than just the narrow literal sense.

Beachfront Capitol

Commanding a fabulous view of beach and water, straddled by Puerta de Tierra's two main thoroughfares, **El Capitolio ❷**, Puerto Rico's Capitol building, serves as the centerpiece to the whole peninsula. Constructed between 1925 and 1929, El Capitolio is a grand, white classical structure resembling the Capitol building in Washington, on a rather smaller scale and with wonderful ocean views. The large rotunda features four corner sections done in Venetian mosaic with gold, silver, and bronze, depicting some of the most important events in Puerto Rico's history. In the very center of the dome is a lovely stained-glass rendering of Puerto Rico's seal. Near the main entrance is the original Constitution of Puerto Rico, signed in 1952 and brought back to the island in 1992 after spending nearly five years in a Washington restoration laboratory.

Nearby are a number of buildings which, though less imposing, are no less beautiful. The ornate **Casa de**

España ❸, just down the hill toward Old San Juan from El Capitolio, is a blue-tiled, four-towered edifice built in 1935 and paid for by the Spanish expatriate community. Once a popular gathering spot for local men, it now has a restaurant and is the site of cultural events. Of interest inside are the tiled painting of Don Quixote and the Salón de Los Espejos (Hall of Mirrors) with its painted wooden ceiling.

Down Avenida Ponce de León is the lovely **Archives and General Library of Puerto Rico** (open by appointment,

Main attractions
EL CAPITOLIO
PARQUE LUIS MUÑOZ RIVERA
CONDADO
OCEAN PARK
ISLA VERDE
RÍO PIEDRAS/BOTANICAL GARDEN
CATAÑO
BAYAMÓN

PRECEDING PAGES:
view of Condado.
LEFT: the imposing
El Capitolio.
BELOW: El Parque
Luis Muñoz Rivera.

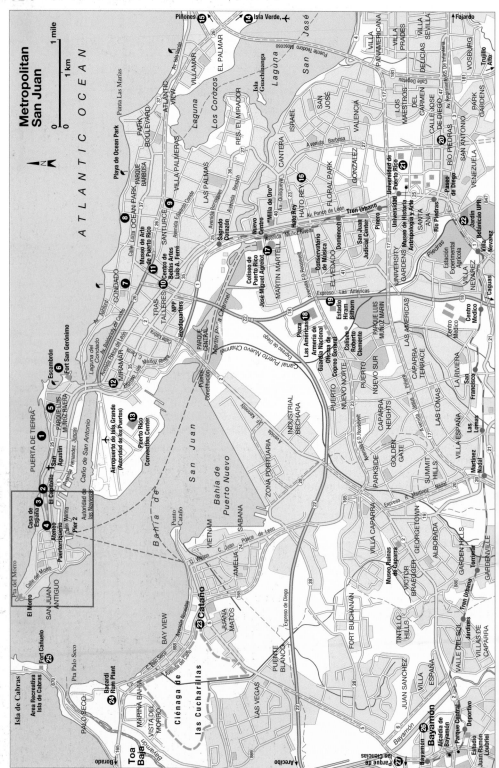

Metropolitan San Juan

ATLANTIC OCEAN

tel: 787-724 0700). Pedestals and pilasters support a graceful pediment and throw a skeleton of white against a lovely sun-washed yellow. Now run by the Institute of Puerto Rican Culture, the General Library lives up to the standards the Institute has set for its other buildings, with tessellation of red stone, chandeliers, and fine furniture. There's also a small chapel on the first floor. If this seems out of place in a library, it is because the building, constructed in 1877 as the last major Spanish architectural effort on the island, was originally designed as a hospital.

Another landmark along the boulevard is the **Ateneo Puertorriqueño ❹** (tel: 787-721 3877), which promotes cultural activity through conferences, lectures, films, and the like. Next door is the **Carnegie Library** (tel: 787-722 4739), established by the Carnegie Foundation and now run by the Department of Education. Further east, **Parque Luis Muñoz Rivera ❺** was dedicated by Nobel Peace Prize winner and former Costa Rican president, Óscar Arias. The **Caribe Hilton** (*see Travel Tips, page 249*) sits on several acres of beautifully landscaped grass and sand, overlooking a little beach-lined cove that stretches to Condado. The hotel played an important role in the industrialization of the island, as the many companies that set up shop from the 1950s onwards used the Caribe Hilton as an initial base for their executives. The Caribe Hilton also has a historical asset in **Fort San Gerónimo ❻**, a small but crucial element of the old Spanish fortifications which stymied a British invasion of the region in 1797. The military museum inside (not always open, so call the hotel first, tel: 787-721 0303) is entertaining and worthwhile. Within view of the Hilton stands the Art Deco **Normandie Hotel**, which first opened in 1942 and was designed to resemble the famous French ocean liner of the same name.

Condado

Condado ❼ in Spanish means "county," and many Puerto Ricans still refer to the glittering strip of land between the Condado lagoon and the Atlantic Ocean as "*the* Condado." If the appellation is meant to convey anything rustic about this part of town, it grossly misses the mark. A trip across the Puente San Gerónimo from Puerta de Tierra takes one out of history and into the tourist zone, where gambling, dining, drinking, and dancing are the main activities of the evening. **Ashford Avenue**, Condado's main thoroughfare, looks as though it is trying to run for election as the sixth borough of New York City, or perhaps as an annex of Miami Beach. In a large measure, it succeeds. Its lengthy oceanfront is lined with chic boutiques, banks, restaurants, and – most conspicuously – hotels.

Quality hotels

Hotels are of varying quality in Condado, but the town's lodgings seldom dip far below the "luxury" rating. The casinos aren't exclusive: non-hotel patrons are welcome at the tables. Restaurants, both hotel-affiliated and otherwise, tend to be of good quality. However, there's a price to pay for

The Condado beaches are said to be the best in the city. Snorkeling is good, and a wide range of watersports equipment can be hired. But be warned that it is not advisable to walk along the beaches at night.

BELOW:
the San Gerónimo fort looks out onto the Atlantic and the Condado hotels.

Hot stuff: spicy Caribbean sauces are a good buy and a tasty – albeit temporary – reminder of a trip to Puerto Rico.

BELOW: the Museo de Arte de Puerto Rico in Santurce mixes old and new harmoniously.

quality in Condado, and it is a high one. Some of the restaurants in town are almost legendary – for both their food and their prices – but they are definitely worth it for the experience. The Condado area is constantly changing: old hotels are being knocked down and replaced by newer, bigger, more modern ones, or a public park. The venerable Condado Beach Hotel, constructed by the Vanderbilt family in 1919, is currently under renovation along with La Concha hotel.

To go to the beach in Condado implies more than taking the sun and riding the waves. People-watching is the chief popular pastime, and there is certainly a fine variety of types to watch, enjoying the warm, unpolluted water and the gentle waves. The Condado beaches are mostly pockets of sand tucked behind the major hotels, and, although all beaches are public – none of the beachfront is privately owned – they are less accessible. The big hotels aren't going to go out of their way to show anyone the easy route to the beach, but the determined visitor, of course, will usually find the way. El

Escambrón, next to the Normandie, is a family-oriented exception.

Ocean Park

Heading east on Ashford Avenue, past the Marriott Hotel and the Radisson Ambassador, you approach **Ocean Park 8**, the most popular beach in the area, where sunbathers, dogs, kite-boarders, children and beautiful people coexist in happy harmony. From here, the high-rises give way to residential houses, and the beaches become less crowded. This is one of the more scenic of San Juan's beachfront panoramas, with views stretching from the palm-lined point at Boca de Cangrejos to the bright white high-rise wall of Ashford Avenue's hotels.

After a swim and a wander along one of the longest and most varied stretches of beaches on Puerto Rico's north coast, you may like to retire to **Kasalta**, an oasis of fine (and reasonably priced) native and Spanish cuisine in a desert of kitsch. In this famous cafeteria, which is also a bakery and delicatessen, you'll find all the San Juan newspapers, a range of Puerto Rican

delicacies unmatched anywhere on the island, and a fresh cup of local coffee that will electrify you.

South of Condado

A knot of highways and main roads, **Santurce** ❾ connects the more touristy and more picturesque areas of the metropolis. It can't claim a seacoast; in fact, one could almost define the area as the set of neighborhoods one encounters moving south from more fashionable Condado and Ocean Park. It hasn't the history of Old San Juan, having been founded only about a century ago as a fashionable suburb. But Santurce does have its own appeal, making it well worth a visit.

Santurce is considered by most to be the heart of San Juan, and not just in the sense that it's the source of the city's main traffic arteries, but it survives as a true marketplace. The quaintest manifestation of this ethic is in the **Plaza del Mercado** on Calle Canals, where vendors sell fruits and vegetables and on Friday evenings the neighboring streets come alive with music and dancing.

While many *sanjuaneros* come to work in Santurce, a surprising proportion come to eat, too, at the many elegant restaurants, and the appealing little *fondas*, as low on price as they are on pretentiousness. The arts thrive in Santurce as well, and the construction in 1981 of the attractive **Centro de Bellas Artes Luis A. Ferré** ❿, (box office tel: 787-620 4444; www.cba.gobierno.pr) at the corner of avenidas Ponce de Léon and de Diego, has brought the neighborhood a share in San Juan's cultural wealth with a 1,800-seat Festival Hall, 760-seat Drama Hall, 210-seat Experimental Theater and the new, 1,300-seat Symphony Hall.

Further along Avenida de Diego is the US$60-million-plus, state-of-the-art **Museo de Arte de Puerto Rico** ⓫ (tel: 787-977 6277 ext. 2230/2261 for guided tours; www.mapr.org; Tue–Sat 10am–5pm, Wed until 8pm, Sun 11am–6pm; charge), which traces the history of Puerto Rican art from José Campeche to the present. The facade of the former hospital has been retained and its graceful columns are echoed in the modern construction behind. The museum has

TIP

If you fancy seeing an art-house film while in Puerto Rico, your best bet is in Santurce. Try the Metro 1, 2, 3, or the Fine Arts Cinema – all on Avenida Ponce de León.

LEFT: friendly smile.

El Parque Luis Muñoz Rivera

The Parque Luis Muñoz Rivera is a 27-acre (11-hectare) recreational and national park located in Puerta de Tierra. Named in honor of Puerto Rican statesman Luis Muñoz Rivera, it displays his statue.

In 1919, land was set aside to create a sizeable park for the locals of San Juan. It once composed part of the third line of defense for the city. The powder house built in 1769 (El Polvorín) which supplied Fort San Jerónimo (Condado) is still located in park grounds.

The east side of the park is bordered by the building of the Puerto Rican Supreme Court, designed by architect Toro Ferrer. Northward lies the public beach of Escambrón, the Parque del Tercer Milenio and the Sixto Escobar Stadium, former home of the San Juan Senators and Santurce Crabbers baseball teams. Designed by Bennett, Parsons & Frost of Chicago in 1924, construction work began in 1928.

The *barrio* of Santurce suffered from the harsh economic climate in the 1970s and its middle class moved to the suburbs. By the 1980s, the area was almost a ghost town. Thankfully the 1990s saw a much-needed renovation program. The park was restored by architects Otto Reyes Casanova in 1990, and by Andrés Mignucci in 2003. It's now a great place to relax after braving the bustle of the city, and where the kids can let off steam.

a lovely sculpture garden, a fine collection of prints, and revolving exhibitions featuring international and local artists. The restaurant, **Pikayo**, is one of the city's best, offering exotic Creole cuisine, but it is an expensive treat. *(See Travel Tips, page 258.)*

On the western edge of Santurce, closest to Old San Juan, is **Miramar ⑫**, one of the most appealing suburbs in the metropolitan area, now that the red-light district has been cleaned up, with lovely tree-lined avenues of pretty modern residences. Miramar's crowning jewel is the **Puerto Rico Convention Center ⑬** (tel: 787-641 7722; www.prconvention.com), inaugurated in 2005. Within the 600,000-sq-ft (56,000-sq-meter) state-of-the-art center is a large exhibition space with a modern wave-shaped roof, and a hotel is set to open by December 2009.

Airport beach

Almost everyone arrives in Puerto Rico at Luis Muñoz Marín International Airport on **Isla Verde ⑭**. Technically part of the municipality of Carolina, this San Juan suburb takes on a look of affluence that few areas as close to such booming noise, annoying traffic snarls, and transient lifestyle possess – big, chalk-white blocks of high-income apartment houses choke one of the most beautiful beachfronts on the island, giving Isla Verde one of the most Miami-Beachesque aspects this side of… well, Miami Beach.

Isla Verde is very rich, but a bit dull. The usual airport businesses – car-rental agencies, vinyl cocktail lounges, and the like – have overrun the place, and suburbs separate the area from the historical charms of the older parts of San Juan, while water separates it from the allure of Piñones. An array of fine hotels just west of the airport include the Wyndham El San Juan, the Ritz-Carlton and the InterContinental San Juan Resort. Along with these giants stand Embassy Suites, Hampton Inn, and some smaller hostels. Along Avenida Isla Verde, the many low-priced guesthouses, restaurants, fast-food emporia, the cock-fighting arena, and garish stores give the area a honky-tonk look.

The golden sandy beach at Isla Verde stretches for over a mile to the north of

In the narrow strip of land beyond Isla Verde, between the sea and the airport, is Avenida Boca de Cangrejos, where many quioscos – semi-permanent shacks – sell barbecued specialties including fish and cod-and-plantain fritters.

BELOW:
Puerto Rico's version of Miami Beach, Isla Verde.

the airport. To the east are the lovely coral reefs at **Boca de Cangrejos**, and farther on the surf is formidable, especially in winter, rolling into the area known as **Piñones** , a popular hangout for young locals, especially on weekends, when a twisting road along 5 miles (8km) of beaches becomes the site of an ongoing party, and roadside kiosks sell raw oysters, seasoned pork and *coco frío*. On this wild piece of coastline, hotels have not yet begun to encroach on and replace the natural mangrove forest where visitors can go for a 6-mile (10km) bicycle ride *(see page 140)*.

Hato Rey

It's odd that, in so many of the great cities of the world, financial brawn and bohemian asceticism have shared the same neighborhoods. Opposites attract: New York City's arty districts of Tribeca and SoHo rub shoulders with Wall Street; the City of London is surrounded by universities and art galleries. San Juan follows this rule to an unusual degree. Here, **Hato Rey** ⑯, the undisputed business and high-finance capital of the Caribbean,

abuts – and often intermingles with – **Río Piedras**, the home of the University of Puerto Rico.

The Golden Mile

Most of the money in the Antilles is filtered through a group of institutions clustered on a section of Avenida Luis Muñoz Rivera in Hato Rey known as **Milla de Oro** (The Golden Mile). Though Operation Bootstrap certainly contributed to Puerto Rico's importance as a financial center, the recent emergence of Hato Rey as a mecca for banks and corporations owes a great deal to a long-standing commitment to banking.

Everyone who visits San Juan should head down to Hato Rey, if only to see the intriguing modern architecture. Particularly interesting is the **Banco de Santander Building** with its reflecting plate-glass arching from an austere concrete shaft. Hato Rey is also home to the headquarters of the **Banco Popular de Puerto Rico**, which is the island's oldest and largest bank. Law and order is carried out at the **San Juan Judicial Center**, where visitors may want to witness a criminal court

BELOW: shooting pool.

case – Puerto Rican style. Enrique Adsuar González, a respected commentator on local custom, has mentioned that the sight of Hato Rey businessmen walking the streets in Wall Street-cut woollen winter suits in 90-degree weather is one of the great ironies of contemporary Puerto Rican life.

Culinary capital

Hato Rey has also become something of a culinary capital, if in a modest and basic way. One can't expect gourmet food in restaurants which cater solely to men who will lose their jobs if they go for an extra course, but solid Puerto Rican fare is to be had here for prices one wouldn't mind paying in the Cordillera.

The district's majestic 18,000-seat **Coliseo de Puerto Rico José Miguel Agrelot** ⓱ (tel: 877-265 4736; www. coliseodepuertorico.com; Mon–Fri 10am–5pm), which opened in 2004, hosts a wide variety of major sports and entertainment events – everything from a Rolling Stones concert to pro sport.

Puerto Rico's first mass-transit light-rail system, the US$2-billion

Urban Train or Tren Urbano (tel: 787-729 8714, 866-900 1284; daily 5.30am–11.30pm) operates a direct service to the Coliseo de Puerto Rico from any of its 16 stations. The 10-mile (16km) train connects the areas of Santurce, Hato Rey, Río Piedras, Guaynabo, and Bayamón, and is an inexpensive and fun way to get around the metropolitan area.

The entire route, from the first stop at Sagrado Corazón University in Santurce to the edge of Bayamón's town center, takes about half an hour. The trains run every eight minutes during rush hour and every 12 minutes at other times. Following the Sagrado Corazón stop, the train makes three stops in Hato Rey, the first in front of the Coliseo de Puerto Rico. There are also six stops in Río Piedras, including one at the University of Puerto Rico (*see opposite*), and another at Paseo de Diego, a great place for bargain shopping.

A mile west of the business district on Route 23 (Avenida Franklin Delano Roosevelt) are some of Puerto Rico's more high-profile structures. The first,

on the north side of the highway, is **Plaza Las Américas**  (www.plazalas americas.net; Mon–Sat 9am–9pm, Sun 11am–5pm), the largest shopping mall in the Caribbean. Locals flock here to stroll amid its fountains and flowered walks and to buy everything from *guayaberas* (traditional Puerto Rican shirts) to guava juice.

The mega shopping center includes flagship stores Macy's, Sears, and JC Penney, and others such as Brookstone and Borders Bookstore. Across the highway to the south is the **Estadio Hiram Bithorn** , a state-of-the-art stadium, which is the site for a variety of sporting and cultural events – including the start of the baseball season in November each year. Neighboring **Coliseo Roberto Clemente** also hosts a number of major events, sporting and otherwise.

Río Piedras

Perhaps Hato Rey only maintains its humanity due to the humanizing influence of the university town of **Río Piedras**  to the south. Within the shortest of walks, concrete and plate-glass give way to cobbled paths and flower gardens. With 25,000 students and distinguished faculty from all parts of the world, the **Universidad de Puerto Rico (UPR)**  is certainly unique in the American university community. Among those who've taught here have been Juan Ramón Jiménez, Pablo Casals, and Arturo Morales Carrión. At the intellectual heart of the university on Avenida Ponce de Léon is the **Museo de Historia**, **Antropología y Arte** (tel: 787-764 0000 ext. 2452; Mon–Fri 9am–4pm, Wed–Thur until 9pm, Sun 11.30am–4pm; free guided tours by appointment). Important exhibits include Francisco Oller's masterpiece *El Velorio* (The Wake) and the only Egyptian collection in the Caribbean. Hurricane Georges in 1998 and Urban Train construction work in 2000 caused structural damage to the permanent collection gallery. Renovation work at the museum, designed by architect Henry Klumb, will restore the gallery by the fall of 2009. The octagonal clock-tower, which soars out of the palms at one side of the campus, has become something of a symbol for Río Piedras.

More than 700 cruise ships arrive every year at the Port of San Juan, the busiest ocean terminal in the West Indies.

LEFT: the university clock-tower.
BELOW: Hato Rey's Coliseo de Puerto Rico, where the big names come to perform.

The Botanical Garden

The highlight of any visit to Río Piedras must be the **Jardín Botánico** (Botanical Garden) ㉒ at UPR's Agricultural Experimental Station (tel: 787-763 4408), a mile south of the university and reached by following the signs after turning off at the intersection of Avenida Muñoz Rivera and Route 847. Hundreds of varieties of tropical and semi-tropical plants, including many from Australia and Africa, make up this extensive park. The gardens comprise 200 acres (80 hectares) and it's hard to imagine a botanical garden landscaped as imaginatively or as subtly as this one. Ponds, lilies, ferns, and ubiquitous *yautía* compete for attention with an exceptional orchid garden.

Río Piedras is not, however, all ivory towers and ivied lanes. Its **Paseo de Diego** is the largest pedestrian market in San Juan, with all the haggling frenzy of an Arab *souk*.

Heading west on Avenida Franklin Delano Roosevelt, past Plaza Las Américas, stop at La Ceiba in **Puerto Nuevo**, a bakery or *panadería* offering coffee, sandwiches, pastries, and delicacies imported from Spain. Further up the road, **Fort Buchanan** billets elements of the US Army, which hosts a number of community activities throughout the year, including Pee Wee Football.

Cataño

Crossing from Old San Juan on the Cataño ferry allows excellent views of windswept San Juan Bay. **Cataño** ㉓ itself is by no means a picturesque town, but it does have a pleasant enough beachfront area and unrivaled views of the Old City.

It also has rum. In the most remote corners of the world, people know the name Bacardi. That they automatically associate it with Puerto Rico is all the more surprising, considering that Bacardi isn't the island's only rum, or even its best. Yet few tourists visit Puerto Rico without making a pilgrimage to the sprawling **Bacardi Rum Plant** ㉔ (www.casabacardi.org; guided tours Mon–Sat 8.30am–4.15pm, Sun 10am–3.45pm; free), five minutes west on Route 165. From the distillery – which has a capacity of 100,000 gallons

TIP

If you're planning to go by ferry to Cataño for a tour of the Bacardi distillery, bear in mind that there is a short taxi ride from the ferry port to the plant.

RIGHT: learning how to mix the perfect rum cocktail at the Bacardi Rum Plant.

"Legend of the Bat"

The next time you pick up a bottle of Bacardi rum, take note of the bat pictured on the label. When Don Facundo Bacardí experimented with the rum-making process in his tiny shed in Cuba back in the 1800s, colonies of fruit bats hung over his head and watched the strange proceedings with interest.

The wine merchant and importer ended up inventing a whole new process, distilled his very first bottle of rum and never looked back. For the Bacardí family, the bat became a symbol of good luck, prosperity, and tradition – and was made the Bacardi corporate symbol in 1862. Business was so good that Don Facundo quickly expanded it; by 1936 the family had decided to open a distillery in Puerto Rico.

In 1959, Fidel Castro came to power in Cuba. Shortly after, the Communists confiscated the family's extensive holdings – worth an estimated $76 million at the time – and the Bacardís were forced to shift production to Puerto Rico, Bermuda, the Bahamas, and elsewhere.

Today, Bacardi is truly a global empire, with plants in more than a dozen countries. Through a web of companies that include Bacardi Corporation, Bacardi & Company, Bacardi Limited, and half a dozen others, the empire now accounts for 75 percent of US, and 50 percent of all the world's, rum consumption.

(454,000 liters) a day and is the largest rum distillery in the world – you are taken from the waiting area/outdoor pavillion by trolley to the Bacardi Visitor Center, and back to the pavilion in the spacious grounds with a view across the bay, where complimentary drinks are waiting.

Seafood center

Just north of Cataño, at the end of a pine-flecked spit of land, is **Isla de Cabras**, now a recreational area and hangout for local fishermen. The island originally housed the long-range artillery of **Fort Cañuelo** ㉕, built in 1608. In later centuries it served as a leper colony. Cabras also boasts a beautiful – but unswimmable – beach. Hedonists should head further west on Route 165 to **Punta Salinas**, which is flanked by two pretty beaches.

South of Cabras and bathed in the warm aroma of Bacardi's molasses, **Palo Seco** offers an almost unbroken string of seafood restaurants, parallel to the ocean, many named after local pirate Roberto Cofresí.

Cowboy town

To the south of Cataño is **Bayamón** ㉖, whose inhabitants are referred to as *vaqueros* or "cowboys." This is due to a sort of maverick quality that has put the city in friendly opposition to others on the island.

Founded in 1509 by a group of settlers led by Ponce de León, Bayamón labors under the stereotype of a sort of glorified shopping mall. It is a place where the antiquated *fincas* and plantations of an older Puerto Rico are set in sharp juxtaposition to some of the most innovative civic architecture.

Bayamón has been fastidious about retaining its regional customs and cuisine. Along almost every road leading into the city are *bayamoneses*, food vendors selling roast chicken, bread, and the most legendary of all local treats – the *chicharrón*, deep-fried pork rinds or crackling in cholestrol-hiking, molar-cracking hunks. (Male visitors should know that *chicharrón* has a connotation which makes it inadvisable to ask a local woman if she'd like a taste.)

The first sight of Bayamón is the eight-story **Alcaldía de Bayamón**, which spans five lanes of highway. Built in 1978 of concrete, glass and steel, it is the only building so suspended in the entire Caribbean.

Across the highway is the **Estadio Juan Ramón Loubriel**, an attractive baseball stadium. Nearby, the **Parque Central** is also dedicated to recreation, with historical and cultural displays and in the placid **Paseo Barbosa**, numerous shops are ranged about the restored 19th-century house of Barbosa.

Bayamón native Francisco Oller was Puerto Rico's greatest artist; his work is at the **Museo Francisco Oller** in the Old Alcaldía at 2 Calle Degetau (tel: 787-787 8620; Mon–Fri 8am–4pm; free). And not far from here, on Route 167, is the **Parque de las Ciencias** ㉗ (tel: 787-740 6868; Wed–Fri 9am–4pm, Sat–Sun and pub. hols 10am–6pm; charge). Much more than just a science museum, this is a major complex of seven themed museums and a zoo. ❏

Every December the Bacardi Artisans Fair is held on the distillery grounds; more than 125 Puerto Rican artisans exhibit and sell the best of their work, and much other family-style entertainment is on offer.

BELOW: antique locomotive in Bayamón's Parque Central.

RUM:
HOLDING ITS OWN IN
THE SPIRITS WORLD

As Puerto Rico is the world's leading producer of rum, it's no surprise that's the national drink – but few realize its versatility and broad range of flavors

It is Christopher Columbus who can be thanked for the fine Caribbean rums today, because he happened to bring some sugar cane with him on his second voyage to the New World in 1493. It wasn't long before large cane plantations sprang up to meet the growing world demand for sugar. But the Spanish settlers discovered that sugar wasn't the only profitable substance produced from cane when they found that its by-product, molasses, fermented naturally.

Not satisfied with the flavor and proof of this "molasses wine," the Spaniards distilled it, filtering out impurities and increasing the concentration of alcohol. Rum was born.

There are four essential steps in the making of rum: fermentation, distillation, aging, and blending. Aging is most commonly done in used bourbon barrels made of white American oak. Puerto Rican law states that rum must age untouched for at least one year; there are, in fact, rigid standards for every step of the rum-making process.

Puerto Rican rum is distinguished from other Caribbean rums by its light body and smooth flavor. Its premium-aged rum competes admirably in the upper end of the spirits world and is said to have a broader range of flavors than single malt Scotch.

ABOVE: the island is full of inviting places to relax and sample the national drink in some of its many guises. Flavored rums are tasty and can be paired with in much the same way as vodka. Brands include Bacardi Apple, Bacardi Coco, Don Q Limón, and Don Q Passion.

RIGHT: A drink of many colors. Rum can be a light, dry white (a replacement for gin or vodka in cocktails), smooth amber (often mixed with cola), or mellow gold ("on the rocks").

ABOVE: Spanish settlers planted sugar cane on the island in 1515, later discovering how to turn a sugar by-product, molasses, into rum.

BELOW: Stainless-steel stills produce the cleanest rum and are most widely used. Premium-age rums are distilled in copper to bring out more aroma and flavor.

RIGHT: Caribbean classic. Reputedly invented in Puerto Rico, the *piña colada* remains a favorite rum libation. It's made with cream of coconut, white rum, and pineapple juice.

THE ROLLS-ROYCE OF RUMS?

If you think rum is only good for fancy cocktails, think again. Gold, premium-aged rums can, at the very least, be a suitable substitute for whiskey: consumed straight or on the rocks. At their best, gold – or *añejos* – rums rank right up there with the finest cognac. There is more than one *añejo* out there, of course – Bacardi has its "Gold Reserve"; Serrallés has "El Dorado." But many rum connoisseurs point to Ron del Barrilito, who *only* makes premium-aged rums, as a real leader in the field with its unblended three-year-old Two-Star and blended six- to 10-year-old Three-Star – both coming in at 86 percent proof. Only 10 minutes away from the ultra-modern Bacardi facility in San Juan, Barrilito rum is produced on a 200-year-old family farm called Hacienda Santa Ana. Instead of using white American oak bourbon barrels for aging like most rums, Pedro Fernández – who developed Ron del Barrilito – used only sherry casks, and this practice continues to this day. So put away those paper umbrellas and get out your snifter: these are rums to be savored.

THE NORTHEAST

Loíza is a center of authentic African culture,
El Yunque is a protected rainforest, Luquillo
is arguably the island's finest beach, and Icacos
is the most popular cay

San Juan

I f someone arriving in Puerto Rico with the inexcusable intention of spending only a few days here were to hire a guide and ask to be shown as much as possible of the island, he or she would be driven directly east from San Juan. It is not that the northeastern corner of the island contains all the island's attractions; that would be impossible. It is only that the variety of landscapes and societies – none of them farther than 45 minutes from San Juan – is astonishing. The ease with which one can move from one landscape to another, which bears no resemblance to the previous one, will make even the crassest traveler feel that he or she is cheating.

Route 187: road of contrasts

Nowhere are the island's contrasts more shocking than on Route 187 just east of San Juan. Here, the highway that links the metropolis with the Caribbean's most modern international airport passes over a bridge and heads for **Boca de Cangrejos** ("Crabmouth") ❶, as exotic a spot as one will find within 20 minutes of any major city in the world. Perhaps at first appearance it is Puerto Rico at its most typically Latin American (read "Third World"), but the ricketiness is deceptive. The flocks of sheep and herds of cows in the area belong to the residents of nearby settlements around the *municipio* of Loíza. The shacks on the beach are not residences by any stretch of the

imagination, rather seaside food emporia. Boca de Cangrejos is where *sanjuaneros* retreat for a *coco frío* – ice-cold coconut milk, which is served in its own shell.

Grove diggers

Long beaches under luxuriant pine groves are what draw visitors to Boca de Cangrejos. Surfers are the most devoted of such partisans, and can be seen riding the waves at the part called **Aviones** (Airplanes) for the flights from Isla Verde that roar over all day.

Main attractions
BOCA DE CONGREJOS
PIÑONES
LOÍZA
EL YUNQUE
LUQUILLO
FAJARDO
EL FARO
ICACOS

PRECEDING PAGES:
the oppressive
Torrecilla Baja.
LEFT: El Yunque.
BELOW: riding the
surf in Luquillo.

El Yunque's flora and fauna are spectacular. Fifty varieties of fern, more than 20 kinds of orchid, and some 240 types of tree are just some of the fantastic flora to be found here, as well as over 30 species of amphibian and reptile.

It's advisable to stay away from **Piñones** ❷ when the beach is deserted, which seldom happens. A 6-mile (10km) bike trail goes from end to end and is extremely popular with the locals, especially because most of the seaside route is dotted with kiosks serving cold drinks. Bikes can be rented in Boca de Cangrejos.

Piñones grows more eerie, rustic, and beautiful as one moves further eastwards. At its farthest point from San Juan is **Vacia Talega Beach**, a breathtaking finger of rock capped by palms and carved into strange formations by eons of surf.

Beyond the swamps

Few towns in Puerto Rico balance natural beauty and cultural achievement as gracefully or as charmingly as Loíza Aldea. Just 6 miles (10km) east of metropolitan San Juan, predominantly Afro-Puerto Rican **Loíza** ❸ (population 32,500) has maintained its separateness from the capital thanks to a cluster of natural barriers.

Puerto Rico's largest mangrove swamp, the massive and mysterious woodland of **Torrecilla Baja** ❹, sits smack between the two communities, and can be traversed via the coastal Route 187, which goes through Piñones and crosses the **Río Grande de Loíza**, the island's widest, roughest, and only navigable river.

Loíza is arguably among the purest centers of true African culture in the Western world. It was settled in the 16th century by black slaves sent by the Spanish Crown to mine a rich gold deposit in the area. When the gold ran out they became cane-cutters and, when slavery was abolished in 1873, many black residents turned to this agricultural economy.

They learned Spanish and became Catholics, but in the subsequent fusion of African culture with Spanish and Indian, the African certainly won out – although the town's Church of St Patrick/Holy Spirit is the oldest in continuous use on the island, dating from 1670.

Such influence is most visible during the Fiesta de Santiago Apóstol, when the people of Loíza gather to praise Saint James, patron of the

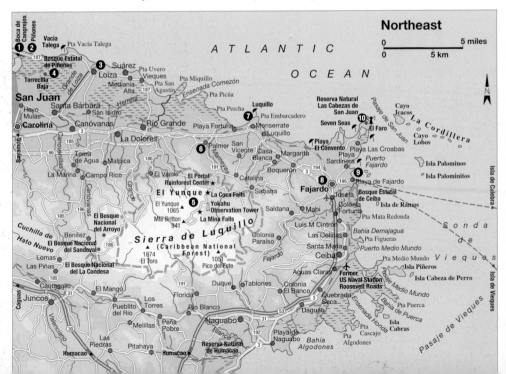

town. The week-long celebration commences each July 25, when citizens dress in ceremonial costumes strikingly and significantly similar to those of the Yoruba tribe of West Africa, from whom many Puerto Ricans are descended.

Participants include masqueraders, ghouls, and *viejos* (old men), and the making of costumes for the ceremonial rites is ordered by a social hierarchy which is quite alien to the rest of Latin America.

The most distinctive festival attire, however, belongs to the *vejigantes*, most of them young men, who dress in garish costumes and parade through the streets. Their religious purpose is generally taken to be that of frightening the lapsed back into the Christian faith, though they can be just as much a source of celebration and mirth.

Most true *vejigante* masks are fashioned from coconuts or from other gourds and carved into grimaces like those of the most sinister jack-o'-lanterns. Sometimes aluminum foil is used to make a mask's teeth appear even more eerie.

El Yunque rainforest

As you continue east, a turn-off at the town of Palmer points toward El Yunque, the rainforest that attracts many visitors to the island.

The only tropical rainforest in the USDA National Forest system, and the only part of Puerto Rico administered by the US Department of Agriculture, the **Caribbean National Forest**, known to practically everybody as **El Yunque ❺** – named after the good Taíno spirit Yukiyú – is home to all the mystery and wonder that comes in the color green. These 28,000 acres (11,000 hectares) of bucking mountain at the highest part of the Sierra de Luquillo offer one of the island's most extreme climates, and the most extreme of its ecosystems as well (tel: 787-888 1880; www.fs.fed.us/r8/caribbean; daily 7.30am–6pm).

Showers and towers

To begin with, there is the rain. The massive, low-lying, purplish-black clouds one sees moving across the Atlantic onto Puerto Rico's northeast coast dump most of their cargo when

Literally millions of the tiny coquí *tree frogs – which have become somewhat of a Puerto Rican "symbol" – make El Yunque their home. They are nocturnal and endemic to the island; their distinctive cry of "koh-kee" gave them their name.*

BELOW: the impenetrable El Yunque rainforest.

they hit the northern flank of the Sierra de Luquillo, with the result that this is far and away the rainiest section of the island.

El Yunque gets upward of 240 inches (600cm) of rain annually – put in more alarming terms, this is 100 billion gallons per year. However, rain does not bother the hundreds of different animal species that make El Yunque their home, among them 26 endemic to the island. Puerto Rico's most familiar animals are here, like the mellifluous tree frog known as the *coquí*. And more exotic ones are here as well, like the colorful but endangered Puerto Rican parrot, and the rare Puerto Rican boa, the island's largest snake, which can grow up to 7ft (2 meters) long.

Hurricane Hugo

Looking out at all the palm trees, ferns and other plant life crowding the road, it's hard to believe that Hurricane Hugo nearly wiped out this paradise on September 18, 1989. The storm's 200mph (320kph) winds left a path of destruction extending from the eastern fringes of San Juan to the offshore islands of Vieques and Culebra. Yet Hugo may have done El Yunque a favor. Ecologists say that the hurricane has removed the canopy of darkness created by taller trees, giving smaller plant life a chance to flourish.

Driving rain

However alluring the upper reaches of El Yunque, most people will see it only by automobile. The most popular and varied route leads south from the town of **Palmer** ❻, known in Spanish as Mameyes, along Route 191. Palmer is a tiny, haunting town, one which seems all the more so for its striking contrast to the 45-minute drive from San Juan, which carries you through glittering, modern industrial and commercial landscapes. Nonetheless, Palmer is admirably uncommercialized and untouristy for a park entrance.

Route 191 used to lead straight through the forest to Naguabo, but a landslide which damaged roads on the southern edge of the forest about 20 years ago has never been cleared; a gate now blocks access to the dam-

BELOW: learn all about the forest environment at El Portal Rainforest Center.

aged part of the road at Km 13.5. But despite the damage, and despite the fact that Puerto Rico's hiking enthusiasts will tell you that you have to get up *into* the woods to appreciate them, Route 191 provides a sterling introduction to the forest.

Another good introduction – which really should be a required pre-hike stop – is provided at the new **El Portal Rainforest Center** (tel: 787-888 1810; daily; charge) within the forest. Here, visitors can learn about the unique beauty and history of El Yunque and the forest environment through interpretive displays, discussions, and a 15-minute documentary film. Patios provide a place to relax and admire the superb view.

Attractive falls

Rising gradually, Route 191 hits one of El Yunque's premier attractions at a bend in the road not far into the forest. **La Coca Falls**, at Km 8.2, is a blurry cascade of ice-gray river rushing down a wall of beautiful moss-covered stones. Though the forest service claims most of the water in El

Yunque to be perfectly potable, and although you'll almost certainly see people drinking from the stream, do exercise caution here, as anywhere in the mountains, because Puerto Rico has a number of river snails which produce "*schisto*" (*schistosoma*), a bacterium causing the highly dangerous liver disease bilharzia.

El Yunque's second great waterfall, **La Mina**, is just off the road a mile (1.5km) ahead. Unfortunately, it's invisible from Route 191 and can be reached most easily from the Palo Colorado Recreation Site at Km 12. On your way there, you will pass the **Palma de Sierra Visitors' Center**, which also houses a food concession.

Highland hoofing

Over the years, landslides on Route 191 have left El Yunque much less accessible by car. Of the many hiking attractions of the place, a few are especially recommended.

The **Tradewinds National Recreation Trail** connects with El Toro to form the island's longest nature trail, at about 4 miles (6.5km). Commencing a

El Yunque's gift shop sells interesting curios.

LEFT: many trails criss-cross El Yunque.

The Many Faces of the Forest

One would think that a forest is full of pretty much the same types of tree, but in fact a place like El Yunque – with an intensity characteristic of Puerto Rico's sub-climates – offers a startling diversity of vegetation and "forest types." Most widespread is the Tabonuco forest, which ranges around the warmer, drier parts of El Yunque at altitudes of under 2,000ft (600 meters).

Higher up is the Colorado forest, which is mossy and more humid than the Tabonuco. Although taking up less than a fifth of El Yunque's territory, the reserve's palm forest is the "rainforest" that gives the area its reputation. Perhaps this is because its beauty is so unexpected and almost unnatural; perhaps it's because Route 191, which most tourists take through El Yunque, never gets above 2,500ft (760 meters), where the palm forest stops.

Sierra palms, which account for most of the sub-climate's vegetation, can grow in very slippery and unstable soil. Thus they can be found in the most dramatic locations: half-submerged in river beds or jutting from cliffsides. Areas above the palm forest are even more bizarre and fascinating. This cloud forest with moss-covered dwarf trees represents less than 1,000 acres (400 hectares) and gets the full brunt of the island's sometimes intense weather.

The view from El Yunque's Yokahu Tower is spectacular: Luquillo and Fajardo in the foreground, the islands of Vieques and Culebra far off on the horizon, and the lush rainforested peaks of El Yunque all around.

BELOW:
a bird's-eye view
from the tower.

few hundred yards beyond the gate on Route 191, it tends to be rather a trail out of the forest, bypassing all of El Yunque's "big" attractions, but it does have the advantage of going through all the major ecosystems and vegetation types of the forest. The **Big Tree Trail**, leaving from the first parking lot along Route 191, gives a good bird's-eye view of La Mina Falls before meeting the road again at the Palo Colorado Recreation Area.

Perhaps most spectacular of all is the **El Yunque Trail**, which you may access from **Caimitillo Trail** (Route 191 Km 12) for three of the most spectacular vistas in the forest. To get to **Los Picachos Lookout Tower**, continue along El Yunque Trail. When you get to the junction with the Mount Britton Trail, a left will take you to Mount Britton Tower. A right turn will keep you on El Yunque Trail where you will encounter another right which will bring you to Los Picachos Trail. A left turn just before reaching Los Picachos leads you to the lookout tower at **Pico El Yunque** and the fabulous vistas at the remote **El Yunque Rock**.

The best beach

While it's true that there's plenty to see in Puerto Rico's northeast, few visitors get to see any of the area's attractions without first making at least a day's detour to what many consider is the island's finest beach. Shimmering **Luquillo** ❼ is just 35 minutes east of San Juan on either Route 66 or Route 3, which, in travelers' terms, is about the same time it would take to get to lovely but arduous El Yunque, or Fajardo's mob scene (*see opposite*), and about half the time it would take to get to Humacao. (*See page 153.*) The only liability of a trip to palm-fringed Luquillo is that it can get very crowded, especially at weekends.

Mountains to the sea

Even those not terribly enthusiastic about beaches will find it hard to ignore Luquillo's appeal. This beautiful, bleached-white town is tucked cozily between dark Atlantic waters and Puerto Rico's most imposing mountain chain, the Sierra de Luquillo, from which the town draws its name. There are few more dramatic

sights on the island than that of the whitecaps of the shoreline glistening in summer sunlight while the peaks of the El Yunque rainforest just inland are suffused in purple thunder clouds. Occasionally, some of the rain intended for the forest does fall on Luquillo, and there are times when the beach is under heavy cloud cover.

On the eastern end of the beach is Mar Sin Barreras (sea without barriers), a park specially constructed for people with physical impairments. Personnel are on hand to help disabled visitors enjoy one of Puerto Rico's best strands.

Luquillo is also the premier beach-side food emporium in Puerto Rico – a seemingly endless string of *friquitines*, or kiosks sells delectably rich local seafood specialties.

Two-faced town

To some, the town of **Fajardo** ❽, the next sizeable destination beyond Luquillo, is merely an overcluttered dockfront town, ranking third behind Brindisi in Italy and Hyannis in Massachusetts in the "Grim Ferry Ports of the World" rating. To others it is an eminently glamorous resort, a charming community, gateway to a handful of fabulous islands and home to some of the finest sailing in the Caribbean.

The first major town along Puerto Rico's northeast coast, Fajardo remains a mecca for yachting enthusiasts. Originally a small fishing and agricultural village, in the late 1700s it became a popular supply port for many pirate and contraband vessels.

The town itself, a hodge-podge of clothing, furniture, and video stores, will appear somewhat unprepossessing to most visitors compared with the area's natural attractions – the calm, clear waters and cays and coral reefs of Vieques Sound. **Playa de Fajardo** ❾, a waterfront community at the east end of the town, is the docking-place for the ferries headed to Culebra, Vieques, and a small island marina nearby. Next to the ferry terminal is the pink stucco **US Post Office/Customs House** and one of Fajardo's few hotels.

Just north of Fajardo, two condominium high-rises, architectural anomalies here, loom over the small fishing village of **Playa Sardinera**. Hundreds

Don't let the Puerto Rican nickname for the residents of Fajardo – cariduros, meaning "the hard-faced ones" – put you off; the people here are very friendly.

BELOW: beach near Luquillo.

TIP

A tour of Las Cabezas de San Juan is well worthwhile. There are four each day (three in the morning and one in the afternoon) and there is an admission charge of $7 for adults and $4 for children.

of fancy motorboats and yachts of all descriptions crowd the two waterfront marinas nearby. Local fishermen line the beach in the middle of the village with boats and tents; they supply the half-dozen expensive seafood restaurants in the town.

A road over the hill passes a comfortable guesthouse and the lavish **El Conquistador Resort & Golden Door Spa**. With 918 rooms and more than 2,000 employees, El Conquistador is one of Puerto Rico's largest resorts. It's also one of the most expensive. First built in the 1960s, the resort was abandoned at one point and later turned into a Maharishi university that soon went bankrupt. Today it is spread among five distinct themed areas, with Moorish and Spanish architecture featured throughout. Guests can even take a ferry to Isla Palominas, not far offshore, where the hotel maintains its own private beach and grill.

The road continues on to **Playa Soroco**, a long, narrow stretch of crisp white-sand beach whose clean, shallow waters make it a favorite among locals. At the leftmost point of Soroco, a track leads to **Playa Escondido**, an isolated beach stretching for miles.

Nearby, right off Route 987, on Seven Seas Beach and Campground (tel: 787-863 8180) is the **Reserva Natural Las Cabezas de San Juan** ❿ (tel: 787-722 5882, or 787-860 2560 Sat–Sun; www.fideicomiso.org; groups: Wed–Thur, general public: Fri–Sun only by reservation; charge), an environmental paradise run by the Conservation Trust of Puerto Rico that encompasses 316 acres (128 hectares) of some of the Caribbean's most stunning landscape. Admission to the preserve is by guided tour only (*see left*).

Considering the preserve's natural beauty, it's surprising that so few tourists spend time here. One can observe nearly all of Puerto Rico's natural habitats – coral reefs, thalassia beds, sandy and rocky beaches, lagoons, a dry forest, and a mangrove forest.

Lighthouse views

Another important attraction at Cabezas de San Juan is the lighthouse, known simply as **El Faro**. Built in 1880, this pristine white neoclassical

BELOW: the luxury El Conquistador Resort.

structure with black trim is one of only two operational lighthouses on the island. The view from Las Cabezas de San Juan is head-spinning. As you look back toward the heart of Puerto Rico, El Yunque towers over the island. In the other direction a chain of cays ranges like enticing stepping stones to the islands of Culebra and Saint Thomas.

The dozens of cays and islands off Fajardo provide Puerto Rico's best boating. A protective reef stretching from Cabezas de San Juan to Culebra and beyond keeps the waters calm, while swift Atlantic tradewinds create perfect sailing conditions. You can charter a yacht from one of Fajardo's marinas, such as Puerto del Rey Marine, and spend the day sailing, sunbathing, and snorkeling.

Popular cays

Icacos, the largest and most popular cay, offers a narrow stretch of bone-white beach, making it a great spot for picnicking or even camping. Two rows of wooden posts from an abandoned dock march into the water, and, just beyond, a coral underworld descends to the sandy bottom 20ft (6 meters) below, providing all the action: elkhorn, staghorn, brain, star, and other corals host legions of underwater plant and animal life.

Other popular cays, somewhat less readily accessible, include **Culebrita**, **Cayo Lobos** (wolves), **Diablo** (devil), **Palominos** (doves) and **Palominitos** (take a wild guess). These and many smaller cays are ripe for underwater exploration among the coral, caverns, and tunnels.

Naval base

Just south of Fajardo is **Roosevelt Roads**, an area formerly leased by the military for one of the largest naval bases in the world. Occupying about a quarter of Puerto Rico's eastern coastline, this was the headquarters of the US Caribbean Naval Forces and a reserve training base. The land was turned over to the Puerto Rican government, to be followed by an environmental clean-up. The nearest town to Roosevelt Roads is **Ceiba**, which was founded in 1838.   ❏

> **TIP**
>
> Isla Palominos may be small, but it will astonish you with all the activities it has in store for you. There's snorkeling, horseback riding, volleyball, windsurfing, rafting, kayaking, and sailing.

BELOW: pretty plaza in Fajardo.

Ecotourism

Beyond the sun, the sand, and the water, Puerto Rico is an eden for ecotourism

Puerto Rico is full of natural wonders such as El Yunque National Forest, the Camuy River caves, the Guánica Biosphere Reserve and State Forest, wildlife and natural reserves, and bioluminescent lagoons, among others.

Located in the municipalities of Río Grande, Naguabo, Luquillo, Ceiba, Canóvanas, Las Piedras, Fajardo, and Juncos, El Yunque National Forest encompasses approximately 28,000 acres (11,000 hectares), where you can find a variety of plant and animal species.

It is home to more than 240 kinds of trees, 20 varieties of orchids, 50 species of ferns and a plethora of flowers. You can also find around 17 endemic species of birds, including the endangered Puerto Rican Parrot and the Puerto Rican Lizard-eating Cuckoo or *Pájaro Bobo*. The tiny *coquí* frog, which derives its name from its distinctive chirp and is a ¼–1 inch (6–25mm) in size, also lives in El Yunque, although it is found all over the island.

Whether you want to go bird watching or would simply like to enjoy the variety of plants, El Yunque has 13 hiking trails across the park. These trails are accessible to the public and can be accessed from the forest headquarters in Río Grande.

Visitors can also explore areas where crowds and tour buses cannot go. Several companies offer private guided ecotours of El Yunque day or night. Some companies hold special permits to be in the forest after 6pm.

Subtropical dry forest

Visitors can also find other types of forests throughout the island, such as the Guánica Biosphere Reserve and State Forest. A subtropical dry forest, it is home to around 700 plant species, of which 48 are endangered and 16 exist nowhere else in the world.

Approximately half of Puerto Rico's birds and nine of the 16 endemic bird species are also found there. The United Nations Educational, Scientific, and Cultural Organization, known as Unesco, declared it an International Biosphere Reserve back in 1981.

Caves to be explored

Puerto Rico also boasts an intricate system of caves called the Río Camuy Cave Park in Camuy. It is one of the largest cave systems and the third-largest underground river in the world.

The river runs through a network of caves, canyons, and sinkholes that date back to the most ancient times. There are guided tours available to the public, who can find stalactites, stalagmites, and multitudes of bats.

For those who seek a little more adventure, private companies offer expeditions to other caves that are not accessible to the public. Near the Camuy Cave Park, you can find Cueva del Infierno, which has around 2,000 caves, where you can find 13 species of bats, *coquí* frogs, crickets, and an unusual arachnid called the *guavá*, among many other species.

For those travelers who would like to enjoy the unique experience of seeing a bay glow at night thanks to microscopic organisms called dinoflagellates, Puerto Rico has several bioluminescent bays, also referred to as phosphorescent bays. It is one of the few places on the planet where you can enjoy this phenomenon almost every evening. However, the effect can only be seen properly in pitch darkness, so try not to go on the night of a full moon.

La Parguera Bioluminescent Bay, in the southwestern town of Lajas, is one of the most popular, although pollution has altered the ecology, thereby reducing the aforementioned dinoflagellate population. However, it can still be appreciated. Once you arrive at the area of La Parguera, you will find countless boating services that offer excursions to see the bay.

In the island municipality of Vieques, just off the coast of Fajardo, you can find the Puerto Mosquito Bioluminescent Bay Natural Reserve, considered to be one of the most spectacular in the world for its brightness. You can either take a kayak-guided tour of the bay or opt for an electric pontoon boat.

Puerto Rico also has a bioluminescent lagoon in Fajardo. This saltwater lagoon is brightest during August through October, though it can be appreciated throughout the year. Because it is an environmentally sensitive area, tour guides take you through the lagoon on kayaks rather than on polluting motor boats.

Thus, Puerto Rico is more than sand and sea. There are many fascinating ecological treasures just waiting to be discovered. The following is a list of contact details:

El Yunque National Forest
Located up Route 191 in Río Grande, it is open daily from 7.30am to 6pm.
Tel: 787-888 1880

Camuy River Caves
Located on Route 129, Km 9.8, it is open Wednesday through Sunday, from 8.30am to 5pm.
Tel: 787-898 3100

Guánica Biosphere Reserve and State Forest
Located on Route 333, Guánica, it is open daily from 9am to 5pm.
Tel: 787-821 5706

Cabo Rojo Wildlife Refuge & Salt Flats Interpretative Center
Located on Route 301 in Cabo Rojo, the visitor center is open Monday through Friday from 7.30am to 4pm, but the refuge is open seven days a week.
Tel: 787-851 7258

Cambalache State Forest
Located on Route 682 between Arecibo and Bar-celoneta, it is open Monday through Friday from 7.30am to 3pm. Tel: 787-878 7279.

Fajardo Bioluminescent Lagoon
Located in the heart of Las Cabezas de San Juan Natural Reserve, tours are offered between 6pm and 8pm and usually last around two hours.
Tel: 787-722 5882

Humacao Natural Reserve
Located on Route 3, it is open from Monday through Friday from 7.30am to 3.30pm and until 5.30pm on weekends and holidays.
Tel: 787-724 3647 or 787-724 3724

Caguas Botanical Gardens
Located in Caguas, it is open Thursday through Sunday from 10am to 4pm.
Tel: 787-653 8990

Jobos Bay National Estuarine Research Reserve
Located between the towns of Guayama and Salinas, it is open daily from 9.30am to 2.30pm.
Tel: 787-853 4617

Toro Negro State Forest
Located in Orocovis, it is open daily 6am to 6pm.
Tel: 787-867 3040.   ❑

LEFT: La Mina waterfall in El Yunque.
RIGHT: watch out for flash floods.

THE SOUTHEAST

Palmas del Mar is a busy resort, Cayo Santiago is strictly for the monkeys, there are quiet beaches near Punta Tuna, and towns such as Patillas and Arroyo are down to earth

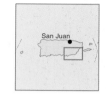

San Juan

The southeastern section of Puerto Rico – thought by many to be one of the prettiest parts of the island – has the interesting characteristic of having some of the most heavily developed, as well as some of the least developed, parts of the country. It is largely residential and quiet, blessed by the pleasant Caribbean tradewinds that blow steadily in this region all year, stabilizing the weather. During the "rainy" season, from about May to September, the southeast may get some 9 inches (23cm) of rain a month, while during the December to April "dry" season, monthly rainfall averages 3 to 5 inches (7 to 12cm).

A major town in the region is **Humacao ❶**, which, although a first-rate industrial center, does have its charms. Previously subsisting off agriculture, Humacao now aspires to being a first-rate resort town, which it is on the way to achieving: several tourist resorts, golf courses and beaches are among its attractions. The restored **Casa Roig Museum** (tel: 787-852 8380; Wed–Sun 10am–4pm; free), the former home of a wealthy sugar-cane landowner, is worth a visit if you are stopping in the town. It was designed by Antonín Nechodemo, a protégé – some say plagiarist – of Frank Lloyd Wright. Only a 45-minute drive from San Juan via Route 30, Humacao is within 2 miles (3km) of some of the most dazzling beachfront that Vieques Sound has to offer. Add to that its convenience

as a starting point for excursions in the southeast, and it earns its standing as a serious holiday resort.

Tour of the beaches

The best way to begin a beach tour of this part of the island is to head north to **Playa Humacao ❷**, probably the best-equipped public beach on the island. It boasts not only miles of bright sand and a handful of offshore cays, but also a veritable arcade of lockers, refreshment stands, and other amenities. The beach benefits from its size, drawing heavily

Main attractions
PLAYA HUMACAO
PALMAS DEL MAR
CAYO SANTIAGO
YABUCOA
PUNTA TUNA
PATILLAS
ARROYO
JOBOS BAY

PRECEDING PAGES:
the marina at
Palmas del Mar.
LEFT: horsing
around at the beach.
BELOW: chit-chat.

Brilliant red-blossomed flamboyán trees dot the southeastern countryside.

enough from local and tourist groups alike to ensure that there's always something going on, if only a pick-up volleyball game: join in.

Halfway down the eastern coast and a 10-minute drive south from Humacao is **Palmas del Mar ❸**, Puerto Rico's largest vacation resort. The self-appointed "New American Riviera," this 2,700-acre (1,100-hectare) holiday heaven comprises just about everything but a monorail: 20 tennis courts ("Is there a court available?" "No, sir, not 'til Thursday"), two gorgeous beachfront golf courses, riding stables, fine beaches, deep-sea fishing, 18 restaurants, numerous bars, a casino, a marina, and so on.

Monkey business

A little less than a mile off the coast of Playa Humacao lies a 39-acre (16-hectare) island that few people have had the opportunity to visit. This place, **Cayo Santiago ❹**, is home to approximately 700 rhesus monkeys. With a grant from Columbia University, the animals were brought from India to Puerto Rico in 1938 for research into primate behavior. Never before had

such a social troupe of monkeys been transported into the Western world and placed in semi-natural conditions. Despite the comfortable climate and undisturbed environment of Cayo Santiago, many experts remained skeptical on the question of whether the primates could survive and breed.

For two years, tuberculosis scourged the colony. Then, during World War II, grant money ran out and the monkeys faced the threat of starvation. Townspeople from Playa de Humacao helped the colony by regularly taking bananas, coconuts, and other foods out to the island for the duration of the war.

Today, the island is administered by the University of Puerto Rico, and scientists from the Caribbean Primate Research Center there spend many, many hours studying the behavioral patterns of these fascinating creatures.

Due to the ongoing research and possible health hazards (and the fact that rhesus monkeys can be very aggressive at times), visitors are not allowed on the island. However, there are various sightseeing boats that will take visitors relatively close to the

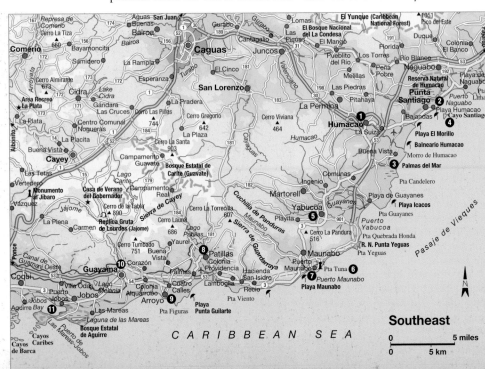

Southeast

0   5 miles

0   5 km

CARIBBEAN SEA

island, where they can snorkel and get a closer glimpse of the frisky primates. Check at the Palmas del Mar marina.

Sugar-cane center

From Humacao to **Yabucoa** ❺ (a native Indian term meaning "Place of the Yuca Trees"), rolling hills, semi-tropical forests, sugar-cane fields, and cow pastures highlight an exceedingly pleasant drive. Just before reaching Yabucoa – also known as "The Sugar Town" – Route 3 passes the **Roig Sugar Mill**, a rusty piece of antiquity, one of the few survivors of the southeast's agricultural economy that unfortunately has gone belly-up. Also of interest in the area is **Hacienda Lucía**, an old sugar plantation.

Yabucoa marks the beginning of an industrial circuit that continues southwestward. Taking advantage of low-wage labor and liberal tax laws, oil refineries, pharmaceutical companies, textile manufacturers, and industrial chemical plants border the smaller towns all the way down the coast.

Leaving Yabucoa, Route 30 to Route 901 takes you on a scenic drive south-ward (part of the Ruta Panorámica) through arid coastal headlands which form part of the Cuchilla de Panduras mountain range.

Ghost beach

A few miles away from town along the **Balneario Lucía** shore, abandoned sea-food restaurants indicate that, at one point, this spot was believed to have potential as a popular bathing retreat. Now, it's a ghost beach; few bother with it. Rows of planted coconut palm trees grow in awkwardly misshapen directions along the beach. The trunks of these trees are wrapped with sheet metal, apparently to prevent rats from climbing them.

The rats have joy-riding in mind, according to a native writer: "When there are no such bands, rats with a penchant for primitive piloting climb the trunks, nibble a hole in the coconuts, lap out the milk, crawl through the hole into the nut, gnaw off the stem and sit inside the shell as it makes its break-neck descent to the ground."

Route 901 curves upward into a series of hills overlooking rugged

The Festival del Azúcar (*Sugar Festival*) *is held in Yabucoa each May – one of half a dozen festivals held in the town throughout the year.*

BELOW: the Sheraton Hotel and Casino dominates the plush Palmas del Mar resort.

shoreline and an expanse of the Caribbean Sea, with the island of Vieques
visible in the distance.

The road descends to **Punta Tuna ⑥**,
where one of Puerto Rico's two active
lighthouses stands. Built in the 1890s by
Spain, the lighthouse is now run by the
US Coast Guard. Adjacent to Punta
Tuna, a little-known beach ranks among
the nicest on the southeastern coast.

Farther down the road, on the other
side of Punta Tuna, another good beach
arches for nearly a mile around tiny
Puerto Maunabo ⑦. Pack a picnic
before setting out from Yabucoa and
have a lunch break on one of the lovely
beaches; camping is also allowed here.

The Ruta Panorámica continues past
the town of Maunabo and winds up a
narrow road past cliffside houses and
damp verdure over the Cuchilla de
Panduras and back to Yabucoa.

Unspoiled corner

At first glance not much has happened
in the southeastern corner of Puerto
Rico since the sugar-cane industry
died. But in its isolation, it has acquired
a patina of respectability.

Patillas ⑧ is known as the Emerald
of the South for its rolling green hills
and agricultural base. "Patilla" is a word
for watermelon and reflects the fruit-
basket reputation of this town. Today,
remarkably enough, vineyards dot the
landscape, as a number of Patillan
farms, like Hacienda Córcega, have
planted grapes from North America
and are producing wine. **Carite Forest**
and **Charco Azul** natural pool are two
other attractions of the area.

Samuel Morse installed the first telegraph line in Puerto Rico in **Arroyo ⑨**
in 1859, and the **Old Customs House
Museum** (tel: 787-839 8096; Mon–Fri
9am–4pm; closed for lunch; free) holds
memorabilia of the event. From here,
train buffs can ride what was the only
working train in Puerto Rico until the
Tren Urbano started up in 2004. **Tren
del Sur de Arroyo** (daily, summer 9am–
4pm, winter Mon–Fri 8am–4.30pm,
Sat–Sun 9am–5pm; charge) takes visitors back and forth to **Guayama ⑩** in
transformed cane wagons on an hour-
long trip along old sugar rails through
cane fields and across two rivers.

Guayama has one of Puerto Rico's
best-preserved and lovely plazas, and the
church of **St Anthony of Padua** beside
it is the only neo-Romantic church on
the island. A clock painted on the right
tower points to 11.30, the exact time the
church was "baptized." The Art Deco
cinema still shows first-run films, while
Casa Cautiño's facade is a riot of neoclassical creole embellishments. The
house of a rich 19th-century family, it's
now a museum (Tue–Sat 9am–4.30pm,
Sun 10am–4.30pm; charge).

Jobos Bay ⑪ (Visitor Center on
Road 705; calling ahead is recommended, tel: 787-853 4617; Mon–Fri
7.30am–4pm, Sat–Sun 9am–3pm,
closed for lunch; charge), one of the
finest protected shallow-water areas on
the island, is close by. Popular with ich-
thyologists (fish enthusiasts) and orni-
thologists, the reserve has several
species of rare Puerto Rican birds, and
fish are well served by the bay's healthy
quantity of micro-organisms. ❑

American Landing at Guánica

During the Spanish-American War, American forces under the com-
mand of General Nelson A. Miles landed at Guánica near Ponce on
July 26, 1898. The landing surprised the United States War Department
no less than the Spanish, as Miles had been instructed to land near San
Juan (the War Department learned of the landing through an Associated
Press release).

However, en route to Puerto Rico, Miles concluded that a San Juan
landing was vulnerable to attack by small boats, and so changed
plans. Ponce, said at the time to be the largest city in Puerto Rico, was
connected with San Juan by a 70-mile (110km) military road, well
defended by the Spanish at Coamo and Aibonito.

In order to flank this position, American Major General John R.
Brooke landed at Arroyo, just east of Guayama, intending to move on
Cayey, which is northwest of Guayama, along the road from Ponce to
San Juan. General Brooke occupied Guayama on August 5, 1898, after
slight opposition, in the Battle of Guayama. On August 9, the Battle of
Guamani took place north of Guayama.

A more significant battle, the Battle of Abonito Pass, was halted on
the morning of August 13 upon notification of the armistice between
the United states and Spain.

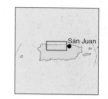

THE NORTH

Dorado has upscale attractions, Playa de Vega Baja is a popular beach, Arecibo has a renowned observatory, and San Sebastián is a good base for exploring the remarkable karst country

Driving west from San Juan on Route 2, as the landscape opens up a bit and the first hills begin to rise, first-time visitors may begin to feel they have left the metropolis and are about to penetrate Puerto Rico's fabled countryside. That is, until you hit sprawling, congested Bayamón; then you begin to wonder if the big cities will ever stop. They stop in **Dorado** ❶, 10 miles (16km) west of San Juan, the first town which can claim to be out from under its shadow.

Dorado's a pleasant, quiet, unassuming little town. You'll miss it if you stay on the highway, and may have to look twice for it even if you take the detour on Route 165, which leaves Route 2 and runs north across emerald marshlands before looping back to it.

Hospitable hamlet

The friendly little town of **Toa Baja** ❷ signals the turn-off. If Dorado is unassuming, Toa Baja is positively diffident, though it is full of charms which belie the quiet. Dividing Toa Baja from Dorado itself is the sluggish **Río de la Plata**, whose grassy banks and meandering course would remind you of some of the more timeless parts of rural England were it not for the clay river bed which has turned the stream's waters a rugged brick red.

Dorado follows Route 165 loosely on both sides. No cross-streets slow traffic enough to draw attention to the small main plaza by the roadside, and the town's businesses are admirably free of gaudy billboards and other "Welcome to..." bric-a-brac. "Urban" Dorado is just clean, slow-paced and friendly, and a disproportionate number of its business establishments – bakeries, bars, juice stands – have camaraderie as their *raison d'être*.

Dorado was first a *barrio* of Toa Baja. It grew and in 1831 established its own town center called the "new pueblo." On November 22, 1842, Jacinto López Martínez, the Sergeant at Arms for the ward of Dorado, petitioned the Spanish

Main attractions
DORADO
PLAYA DE VEGA BAJA
LAGUNA TORTUGUERO
ARECIBO
KARST COUNTRY
LARES
RÍO CAMUY CAVE PARK
SAN SEBASTIÁN

PRECEDING PAGES: waves pounding the north-coast shore. **LEFT:** Manatí. **BELOW:** cheerful northerner.

Governor of Puerto Rico, Santiago Méndez Vigo, to establish the municipality of Dorado. The governor authorized the founding of the town pending the construction of public works, including an administrative building and a church near the town square. In 1848, the construction of the public works were completed and López Martínez became the first mayor of Dorado. In 1902, after the US invasion, Dorado was again appended to Toa Baja, but some decades later it changed back.

Two sites that stand out are the **Santuario del Cristo de la Reconciliación**, whose temple holds the third-largest statue of Jesus Christ in the Caribbean, and **La Casa del Rey** (tel: 787-796 5740), a former Spanish garrison. Both were built in 1823 and are the oldest buildings in Dorado. The church statue, at 25ft (7.6 meters), was created by Puerto Rican sculptor Sonny Rodríguez.

Right on Méndez Vigo and next to City Hall, La Casa del Rey was originally built as a Spanish guard station and consisted of a main hall and office, and a small prison cell. It was aban-

The Casa del Rey in Dorado dates back to the founding of the city.

doned after 1898 and in the 1950s it was purchased as a home. Always accessible to visitors and friends alike, it was only fitting that it be restored in 1978 by the Institute of Puerto Rican Culture to become a museum. It exhibits mid-19th-century furniture and fixtures.

Another stop on the downtown trail is the **Museo de Arte e Historia de Dorado** (tel: 787-796 5740; Mon–Fri 8am–3.30pm, Sat 9am–3.30pm). Located on Méndez Vigo at Juan Francisco, the building has three galleries holding exhibits of art, archeological artifacts and a presentation on the history of Dorado.

The **Plaza de Recreo** houses a remarkable landmark, a statue showing three life-sized figures: Spanish, African, and Taíno. This is the **Monumento a las Raíces**, sculpted by Dorado native Salvador Rivera Cardona.

Not all culture

But Dorado is not all culture. Its beaches are inviting and easily accessible via the buses that leave from near the town plaza. A mile northwest of town, through a spinney of mangroves and a bone-

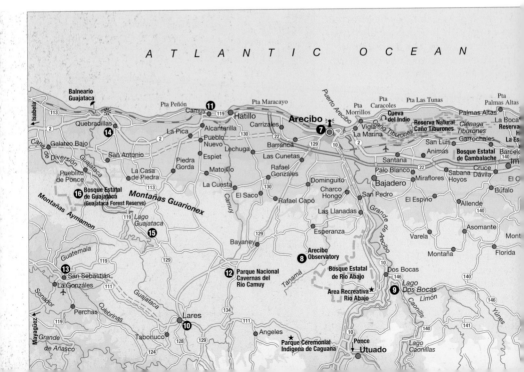

white graveyard on Route 693, is the irresistibly lovely beach at **Playa Dorado-Sardinera**, and also nearby is **El Ojo del Buey** (The Ox's Eye), a seaside recreational area that takes its name from a large rock bearing an amazing resemblance to the head of an ox.

In May of 2006 Dorado's fabled luxury hotel, the Hyatt Dorado Beach, closed its doors. Its sister hotel, the Hyatt Cerromar, was shuttered in 2004, and converted into timeshare units. Real-estate investment company Caribbean Property Group and local developers Prisa Group – who through a joint venture purchased the Dorado properties for an undisclosed amount – announced in July 2008 that they would undergo a multimillion-dollar redevelopment, and are slated to operate under the flags Ritz-Carlton and Fairmont Hotels & Resorts, respectively.

The 297-room Dorado Beach hotel, built on the site of a grapefruit plantation, originally opened its doors in 1958 as one of Laurance Rockefeller's Rockresorts. In its heyday the hotel, once owned by Clara Livingston, Puerto Rico's first woman pilot and head of the Air Civil Defense, welcomed celebrities and dignitaries from around the world. Dorado Beach's four championship golf courses, at one time administered by Juan "Chichi" Rodríguez, remain open for business to club members and guests.

Popular beachfront

Further west, a fast, 35-minute drive from San Juan on routes 2 and 686, **Playa de Vega Baja ❸** is one of the most popular of San Juan's metropolitan beachfronts, and is dotted with cabins belonging to the local residents. It benefits not only from spectacular juxtapositions of sand and sea, but also from lush and unusual surrounding countryside. The beach itself draws most attention for its weird and haunting rock formations, which are actually a string of coral islands running parallel to the seashore for 2,500ft (760 meters), from the palm-lined cove of **Boca del Cibuco** to craggy **Punta Puerto Nuevo**. This odd, almost unique formation has sheltered most of the beach, while causing its western end to resemble at times a sort of preternaturally large jacuzzi.

The nickname for those who live in Vega Baja is melaomelao, meaning "molasses-molasses," because of the large quantities of molasses produced here.

BELOW: a bronze in the town square honors Dorado's Indian, African, and Spanish heritage.

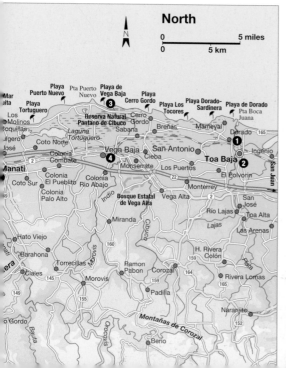

TIP

An interesting detour from Arecibo is to take the coast road (Route 681) past Mar Chiquita to another headland, Punta Caracoles, on which is the Cueva del Indio (Indian Cave). A short walk leads to the hole in the cliff, inside which are some (supposedly) pre-Columbian drawings.

BELOW: Playa Mar Chiquita is a good swimming beach.

The Cibuco, of one of the rivers that cross such fertile land, is a variation of the name "Sebuco," a chief or *cacique* Taíno Indian of the region. These "cells" of Taíno indians were known to settle in the vicinity of the rivers. Even though the Cibuco River is still prone to floods due to heavy seasonal rains, it fosters a rich diversity of ocean life and reefs.

The nearby town of **Vega Baja** ❹ has grown into a fairly modern and uniform Puerto Rican municipality. The town does have a sense of humor about its reputation as something of a hokey place. An official town bulletin offers not only the usual information on town history and famous residents but also a tongue-in-cheek roster of *Personajes típicos de Vega Baja*. These include the tallest man, the drunk, the beggar, and the basketball fan. A town that can parody itself so remorselessly deserves a visit, but not so much as the surrounding countryside does. Vega Baja sits in the middle of the fertile coastal flatlands west of San Juan. Visitors will be rewarded with long vistas over canefields and marshes, and an array of deciduous foliage:

most impressive in an island full of tropical trees.

Founded in 1776 by Antonio Viera as "Vega-baxa del Naranjal de Nuestra Señora del Rosario," the name was eventually shortened to Vega Baja.

Centuries before Spanish settlers first set foot on what is now Vega Baja, the area was populated by as many as four different indian civilizations from different ages in history. Relics of tribal civilizations from the vicinities of Vega Baja are considered among the most archeologically important in the area. Taíno carvings have been found on the exposed reefs in the vicinity of the Cibuco River. Among them, one depicts a face and others are shaped as fish, indicating these reefs were frequented for spear-fishing and other activities.

Because it lies 30 minutes from metropolitan San Juan, Vega Baja's population has increased rapidly as people move away from metropolitan centers to suburban refuges. The 2000 census showed the numbers at 61,000, and experts believe the numbers will continue to rise, not only in Vega Baja, but most towns surrounding San Juan.

The patron saint of Vega Baja is "Nuestra Señora del Rosario," and a feast is held each year on October 7 in her honor.

Further west along the coast, and accessible by Route 686, which runs near the bottom of it, is **Playa Tortuguero**, the largest and most palm-lined of the beaches. Half a mile inland, **Laguna Tortuguero**, while not officially a nature reserve, provides a haven for bird life. Though an old-time favorite for picnicking, boating, and fishing, the lake is now habitat to caimans, and its use for water-sports has consequently diminished.

Continuing west, the **Manatí ❺** area has produced most of the island's pineapple products. Here Puerto Rico's famous Lotus pineapple juice is canned under the supervision of the Land Administration. Vendors offer fresh pineapples along the road (Route 2). The sweet, Spanish Red variety goes into the 100 percent juice. No water is added. A short drive from town takes you to **Playa Mar Chiquita ❻**, an unusual beach in that the surf comes pounding through the high rocks to produce a most dramatic effect. The rocks enclose an oval lagoon that provides excellent swimming.

Manatí was founded in 1738 by Pedro Menéndez Valdés. It is believed to have been named after the manatee, a sea mammal popular in the region. Some say it was baptized after the Taíno-named river, the Manatuabón.

Some landmarks include the historic zone at the center of town, the Acropolis Sports Complex, and the Hacienda Marqués de la Esperanza ruins.

Arecibo

There are prettier cities on this island, but few are prettier to approach than **Arecibo ❼**. Route 2 takes a tortuous turn 48 miles (77km) west of San Juan and reveals the second capital city of Puerto Rico's north coast, backed by the blue Atlantic. Directly to the south of Arecibo lies karst country, with typical landscapes of pine and mahogany in the Río Abajo forest.

The western end of the expressway (PR 22) affords another dramatic perspective of the island's north coast, this one just west of Arecibo in Hatillo.

Arecibo's name comes from a local Indian chief called Jamaica Arecibo.

BELOW: the streets of Manatí.

The century-old Punta Morrillos lighthouse in Arecibo is now restored as a museum focusing on the city's heritage. For more details, call the Puerto Rico Tourism Company on 1-800-866-7827 or 721 6363.

BELOW:
the region is dotted with excellent golf courses and resorts.

Travelers are treated to a spectacular, unobstructed view of the Atlantic Ocean's crashing waves, fronted by acres of palm trees. This is Puerto Rico unspoiled. Navigation via the expressway obliges you to double back east to reach the town of Arecibo. However, it is not an unpleasant trip: Route 2 is packed with shopping malls and fast-food outlets, but in just a few miles you return to the town's historic area, all the while enjoying glimpses of the ocean to the north.

The coastal road, Route 681, is the road the expressway left behind. It meanders, meaning you won't get to Arecibo quickly, but you will enjoy the view from the cliffs. The drive runs from Palmas Altas through Islote, past Desvío Valdés and to Punta Caracoles (Seashell Point), site of **La Cueva del Indio** (Indian Cave; *see margin tip on page 164*).

The lighthouse and beyond

Further ahead, off Route 655 to your right at Punta Morrillos, you'll find the **Arecibo Lighthouse and Historical Park** (tel: 787-817 1936, 880 7540; www. arecibolighthouse.com; Mon–Fri and pub. hols 9am–6pm, Sun 10am–7pm; parking charge). The excursion is both fun and educational for children and adults alike. An expansive deck with a children's play area accompanies a restored museum that includes replicas of a Taíno Indian village, Christopher Columbus's ships and African slave quarters. A pirate's cave and a pirate's ship, together with a mini zoo, complete the facilities, along with the lighthouse itself, which was the last one built by the Spaniards, in 1898.

The reality of Arecibo is a bit more worldly than you would assume from its externally Arcadian aspect. It is one of the oldest Puerto Rican towns, and since its foundation in the 16th century has enjoyed one of the highest levels of prosperity on the island.

Operation Bootstrap, the project which was designed by Muñoz Marín and the US Congress to boost Puerto Rico into the industrial world, and Section 936, the American legislation that offered tax incentives to companies investing in Puerto Rico, accelerated Arecibo's advance in the business

world. Puerto Rico makes more pharmaceutical products than any other place in the world, and Arecibo is a hub for the island's pharmaceutical-manufacturing industry.

Oil for the wheels of life

Arecibo was a leader in the art of manufacturing products that have eased the country along the troubled road of life long before the pharmaceutical boom. The town still produces agricultural machinery, clothing, plastics, paper, and sporting goods. Ronrico, one of the greatest rums on the island (which is itself the rum capital of the world), was once the major industry in the town, and Arecibo is proud of its legacy from the island's rum trade.

Salubrious surroundings

For a town in its situation, Arecibo is center to a surprising variety of terrain. It forms a semi-peninsula pointing northeastward at the delta of two rivers: the **Río Grande de Arecibo** and the **Canal Perdomo**. The roads from San Juan hug the shoreline here, giving pleasant views of the city from afar.

Those roads were put here for a reason: to the east recede swamps of unmeasured depth and gloom. Be warned that the surrounding area is chock-a-block with mosquitoes in the wet season.

Arecibo itself disappoints some tourists who use the city as a way-station on their indefatigable search for all that is mundane and tacky on the island. It takes an intelligent and observant traveler to realize that Arecibo is one of the finer and more livable cities, not only on the island but also anywhere in the Caribbean. Its streets are broad, its citizens relatively well-off, and its shopping district has far more variety than one might expect from a city of only 100,000 inhabitants.

Moreover, Arecibo has cafés and theaters – not as commonplace as one might think in Puerto Rico – and its oldest building, a distinctive wooden structure, dates from 1884. **Calle Alejandro Salicrup**, at the tip of the semi-peninsular wedge, is one of the best thoroughfares on which to see such timbered architecture, which is as unique to Arecibo as the southwestern townhouse style is to San Germán. In a somewhat different

The radar/ radio-telescope at the Arecibo Observatory is equal in size to 13 football fields.

LEFT: the beach at Punta Las Tunas and the Punta Morrillos lighthouse in the background.
BELOW: Arecibo's Playa de Los Morrillos.

Arecibo Observatory

Hidden among the mountains, where the stars shine undimmed by city lights, sits the most sensitive radio telescope on Earth

The Arecibo Ionospheric Observatory is so huge that you can spot it from a jumbo jet at 33,000ft (10,000 meters). Yet on the ground, first-time visitors will need a detailed road map to find its guarded entrance. Located at the end of winding Route 625, in the heart of Puerto Rico's karst country, the observatory has been the focus of numerous astronomical breakthroughs over the years, ranging from Alexander Wolszcan's 1992 discovery of planets outside our own solar system to NASA's $100-million Search for Extraterrestrial Intelligence.

In 1993, the Arecibo Observatory "dish" gained world prominence when two American astronomers, Russell A. Hulse and Joseph H. Taylor Jr, won the Nobel Prize for Physics for work done using the powerful facility.

The observatory owes its existence largely to Puerto Rico's political status as a United States Commonwealth and to the island's geographic position 17° north of the equator. That makes it ideal for the observation of planets, quasars, pulsars, and other cosmic phenomena. The telescope is so sensitive that it can listen to emissions from places 13 billion light years away.

The Arecibo Observatory is funded by an annual $7.5 million grant from the National Science Foundation, though its day-to-day affairs are managed by Cornell University in Ithaca, New York.

The observatory counts some 140 full-time employees among its staff, and has hosted more than 200 visiting scientists from countries as diverse as Argentina, Bulgaria, Brazil, and Russia. Note that no military experiments of any kind are conducted here, and, despite the presence of security guards, there's absolutely nothing secretive about this place.

The "dish" itself, suspended over a huge natural sinkhole, is by far the largest of its kind in the world. Spanning 1,000ft (300 meters) in diameter, it covers 20 acres (8 hectares) and is composed of nearly 40,000 perforated aluminum mesh panels, each measuring 3ft by 6ft (1 by 2 meters). A 900-ton platform is suspended 425ft (130 meters) over the dish by 12 cables strung from three reinforced concrete towers.

Underneath the dish lies a jungle of ferns, orchids, and begonias. In fact, until recently tourists could get only as far as a viewing platform high above the site.

The dish itself is off-limits, and visitors were limited to a five-minute audio tape describing the facility and a display area explaining the telescope's construction together with some current scientific results.

However, this situation was remedied when Cornell University built a $2-million visitors' center (tel: 787-878 2612; www.naic.edu; Wed–Fri noon–4pm, Sat–Sun and most pub. hols 9am–4pm, students and groups: Wed–Fri from 10am), including a 120-seat auditorium, a 4,000-sq-ft (370-sq-meter) scientific museum, a gift shop, and a trail leading to a viewing platform from which the telescope can be seen at close range.

The observatory has featured in the movie *Contact*, in which Jodie Foster plays an astronomer searching for extraterrestrial life, the James Bond film *Goldeneye*, as well as the sci-fi television show *The X Files*. ❑

LEFT: the dish at the Arecibo Observatory is hidden in a natural sinkhole and is off-limits to visitors.

vein, the **San Felipe Cathedral**, between calles José de Diego and Gonzalo Marín, has an unusual cupola and is the second-largest cathedral built by the Spaniards in Puerto Rico.

The **Alcaldía** (Town Hall), tucked in at the intersection of calles José de Diego, Romero-Barceló and Juarregui, is among the prettier offices in Puerto Rico, and its inhabitants are among the friendliest and most receptive. Nearby, at No. 7 Gonzalo Marín, is **Casa Ulanga** (tel: 787-880 6079, 787-878 8044), Arecibo's cultural center. Built in 1854 by Spaniard Francisco Ulanga, Casa Ulanga was the city's first three-story building. Over time it served as a center for banking and business with stints as a jail, courthouse and town hall.

Formerly the Plaza Mayor, the **Plaza Luis Muñoz Rivera** is another of Puerto Rico's beautiful plazas, with a cathedral facing over an idiosyncratically landscaped park surrounded by wrought-iron railings and multicolored Spanish colonial architecture. The plaza has undergone an astounding number of transformations in the past 100 years. In the mid-1890s, it was burned to ashes during a fire that consumed much of the city. In 1899, a hurricane and the ensuing surf, which was not far short of a tidal wave, pounded it into disrepair.

Arecibo was one of the first of the Puerto Rican cities to jump off the Spanish imperial bandwagon and to honor its own native heroes. The monument in memory of Queen Isabella II of Spain, which for so long stood in the middle of the plaza, was replaced in 1927 with an obelisk honoring local hero and politician Luis Muñoz Marín.

The waterfront drive is quite lovely, with views of the lighthouse and the Atlantic coast, although the *malecón* (boardwalk) is somewhat sad. The **Museo de Arte e Historia** (tel: 787-879 4403; Mon–Sat 9am–4.30pm; free) on calles Juan Rosado and Santiago Iglesias, is a former transportation center, and displays old postcards of early Arecibo. Built in 1919, it was once used as a warehouse to store rum, and was painstakingly restored and re-inaugurated in 2006.

TIP

Make sure to stop in at the Heladería de Lares (Lares Ice-Cream Parlor), a famous ice-cream store located in front of the town square of Lares. Founded in 1968 by Salvador Barreto, it has an array of over 1,000 flavors ranging from the traditional (vanilla, chocolate) to the exotic (rum, avocado, corn).

BELOW:
Arecibo, one of the oldest, and most prosperous, towns in Puerto Rico.

Star attraction

Anyone who has ever taken sixth-grade science should have some familiarity with Arecibo. On one of those big, full-page spreads that fill up space in astronomy textbooks, the **Arecibo Observatory** ❽ is generally featured prominently. A complicated trip 20 miles (32km) south of the town of Arecibo into the karst country will bring you to this mammoth complex. From downtown Arecibo, follow de Diego to Route 129. Bear left on Route 651 and follow it for the 4 miles (6km) before it becomes 635. Travel about the same distance until you come to a T-intersection, at which you will turn right (onto Route 626) and travel a few hundred yards before making a left turn onto 625, at the end of which is the renowned observatory. *(For further details of this, one of the most important research observatories in the Americas, see page 168.)*

The karst country

Puerto Rico is one of those places blessed to an almost unfair extent with an enormous variety of beautiful land-scapes. But such places are legion, and what do you give in Puerto Rico to the tourist who has everything? The answer is not hard to find: the dark-green sector of the island's northwest where the land rises in regular green-and-white hillocks and appears to be boiling – the intriguing area known as the karst country.

Limestone sinkholes

Karst is the name for one of the world's oddest rock formations and can occur only under the most fortuitous circumstances. Some geologists claim there are only two other places on earth where rock formations resemble those of Puerto Rico: one just across the Mona Passage in the Dominican Republic, and one in the former Yugoslavia.

Karst is formed when water sinks into limestone and erodes larger and larger basins, known as "sinkholes." Many erosions create many sinkholes, until one is left with peaks of land only where the land has not sunk with the erosion of limestone: these are *mogotes*, or karstic hillocks, which resemble each other in size and shape to a striking extent, given the randomness of

TIP

If you have the time, take advantage of the 2-hour free launch trips on Lago dos Bocas provided four times a day (7am, 10am, 2pm and 5pm) by the Public Works Department.

RIGHT:
Lake Caonillas, one of many nestled into the hills of the north.

The Karstic Forests

Puerto Rico's Department of Natural Resources has recognized the beauty and fragility of its unique karstic landscape. It has created four national forests in which it is protected: **Cambalache** (east of Arecibo, with plantations of eucalyptus, teak, and mahoe trees), **Guajataca** (west of Arecibo, offering some 25 miles/40km of hiking trails), **Río Abajo** (south of Arecibo, and home to 223 plant and 175 wildlife species; 70 trails criss-cross its 5,780 acres/2,300 hectares), and **Vega Alta** (west of Toa Baja).

Not all the karst country is limited to these forests; in fact, they are woefully small, comprising only about 4,000 acres (1,600 hectares) in total, with Río Abajo accounting for over half of these. All are ripe for hiking, yet the trails in the karst country never seem as crowded as those up El Yunque and other Puerto Rican mountains. Perhaps this is owing to the dangers involved with this sort of landscape. Sinkholes are not like potholes, but they can come as unexpectedly, especially in heavy brush.

Get a trail map from the visitors' center at whatever reserve you try. Otherwise, *The Other Puerto Rico* by Kathryn Robinson offers helpful advice, and one read of it will convince you that there's nowhere in Puerto Rico that's not worth risking a little danger to see.

the process that created them. All this leads you to realize that the highest point on the highest *mogote* in the karst country is certainly below the level which the limestone ground held in earlier days when the first drop of rain opened the first sinkhole.

It's hard to say where the karst country begins. Some say at Manatí, though there are two hills not 10 minutes' drive west of San Juan which look suspiciously karstic. From Manatí, they carry on as far west as Isabela, and are at their most spectacular a short drive (5 miles/8km) south of the major cities of Puerto Rico's northwest.

It's just as hard to say wherein their appeal lies. Part of it must be in the odd symmetry of the things – despite the fact that it's the holes, not the hills, which have undergone the change over eons.

These hills are impressive mountains only 100ft (30 meters) high – they are probably the grandest landscape within which humans can feel a sense of scale. They encompass a startling variety within their regularity; certain *mogotes* can look like the Arizona Desert tucked in for bed in the Black Forest.

Cars to karst

Arecibo is the capital of the karst country, and some fine drives can begin from there. The easiest to undertake is certainly Route 10 south to **Lago Dos Bocas ❾**. Taking Route 129 southwest to Lares is a pleasant jaunt, which never lets you stray into the Cordillera, as the Route 10 trip is prone to do; the 129 is flanked by *colmados* (grocery stores).

If you like karst a lot, though, head west on Route 2, turn left on Route 119, and follow the road to **Lago Guajataca** for perhaps the finest views of the water and limestone that made the whole unfathomable but evocative landscape possible.

Make it a point, if at all possible, of getting out to the karst country. The unique beauty is staggering, and is worth a visit by itself. Even more, though, the sight of karst will add another dimension to this tropical paradise too often labeled as a place for a "beach vacation."

Frontier town

If this tiny island has a frontier town, surely **Lares ❿** must be it. It sits at the

Puerto Ricans pride themselves on their friendliness and warmth.

LEFT: palms and more palms.
BELOW: bathing in Lago Dos Bocas.

A plaque that commemorates the 1868 revolution in Lares.

western edge of the Cordillera Central's main cluster of peaks, and rests at the southernmost spur of the karst country. Lares is as far from the sea as you can get in Puerto Rico, and to its west a placid corridor of plains runs just to the north of the hills of La Cadena and south of Route 111 and the sleepy Río Culebrinas.

Like many of the towns in this area, where plains meet uplands to produce eerily spectacular vistas, Lares is as scenic to approach as it is to leave. Arriving from the south on either Route 124 or Route 128, you are greeted by a tiny, close-packed community perched on a gentle rise across a valley and shadowed by rugged twin karstic *mogotes*. Emerging from the east on Route 111 from the karstic clusters of the Río Abajo Forest Reserve, you are taken by surprise at Lares's anomalous urbanity.

The town itself exudes much of the toylike ambience which you may well have perceived from afar. It's an attenuated cluster of little businesses, bars and shops snaking along two main one-way streets that run in opposite directions. In the central **Plaza de la Revolución** stands an imposing 19th-century Spanish colonial church, whose pale pastel facade and gracefully arched roof give it something of a Middle Eastern look.

If Lares has a stern side, pride rather than inhospitableness is its source. For as the scene of the "Grito de Lares," Puerto Rico's glorious and ill-fated revolt against Spanish colonial rule, the town is generally considered to be the birthplace of modern Puerto Rican political consciousness.

The Grito de Lares

The "Grito de Lares" ("Shout of Lares") was not merely a Puerto Rican historical event; its roots lay in the serious political grievances that were to sweep Spain's Caribbean colonies in the mid-19th century and result, some decades later, in their ultimate loss.

When, in 1867, native Puerto Rican guards demonstrated in protest at discrepancies between their own salaries and those of Spanish guards, many liberals were expelled from the island, including Ramón Emeterio Betances, a distinguished physician and certainly

the most prominent voice in Puerto Rican politics at the time. He went to New York, Santo Domingo, and Saint Thomas, where he rallied support for abolition and self-determination.

On September 23, 1868, hundreds of Emeterio Betances's followers seized Lares and began to march on nearby San Sebastián. There they were met by Spanish forces, and easily routed. Though Emeterio Betances was merely exiled to France, and the revolution came to nought, the "Grito de Lares" led Puerto Ricans to think differently of their land and their aspirations for it, and the spirit of that September day lives on – not only in the streets of Lares but also in the hearts and on the tongues of Puerto Ricans throughout the island.

Caves to be explored

Also significant, but in a rather different way, is the unspectacular town of **Camuy** ⓫, just far enough west of Arecibo and just far enough north of Route 2 to appear almost untouched by the life of modern Puerto Rico. What appeal Camuy has is more primordial – a bewildering maze of one-way streets that will never accommodate automobiles; a lifestyle tranquil to the point of torpor; a few vestiges of an older era, like shops that sell salves and incense for the appeasement of various saints; and, most primordial of all, one of the largest cave systems in the Western world.

Subterranean river

Most easily reached by driving due south on Route 129, the cave system is actually a series of karstic sinkholes connected by the 350ft (106-meter) deep **Río Camuy**, which burrows underground through soft limestone for much of its course from the Cordillera to the Atlantic. The largest of these entrances has been developed as a tourist attraction, with inducements of the "fun for the whole family" variety.

The **Parque Nacional Cavernas del Río Camuy** (Río Camuy Cave Park) ⓬ (tel: 787-898 3100; www.parquesnacionales pr.com/cavernas_acm.asp; Wed–Sun, pub. hols 8am–4pm, last trip at 3.45pm), which is managed by the Puerto Rico Land Administration, contains one of the most massive cave networks in the

The part of Río Camuy that runs underground forms the second-largest subterranean river in the world.

BELOW: Cueva Clara is specially lit for visitors.

Western Hemisphere. This 268-acre (106-hectare) complex includes three crater-like sinkholes and one cave. The Taínos considered these formations sacred; their artifacts have been found throughout the area. The park's main attraction is the 170ft (52-meter) high and 695ft (210-meter) long **Cueva Clara**, which is specially lit, and accessible only by trolley and in guided groups.

The cave is home to a unique species of fish that is completely blind. The entrance looks like a cathedral facade, with a broad row of toothy stalactites descending from the bushy hillside. Visitors will notice that inside the cave's overhang, the light becomes bluish, and a weird silence descends, broken only by the constant chirp of bats hanging from the ceiling and minute distant echoes. Could they be the far-off sounds of water dripping through yet undiscovered passages? They are indeed. Dozens of river cave systems lie beneath the spectacular karst landscape.

Leaving the cave park, you have two excellent choices for lunch not far away. The **Restaurante Las Cavernas** and the **Restaurante El Taíno**, both located along Route 129, pride themselves on traditional Puerto Rican cuisine, bilingual waiters, a family atmosphere, and fairly reasonable prices. At Las Cavernas, the house specialty is *arroz con guinea* (rice with guinea hen), served on a large plate with beans, and *amarillos* (fried bananas) for dessert.

And even more caves...

If you're an avid spelunker, there's still more for you to see: close to Río Camuy is the privately owned **Cueva de Camuy** (daily 9am–5pm, Sun until 8pm; charge) on Route 486. Although smaller and less interesting, it too has guided tours as well as family-centered activities that include a swimming pool and waterslide, amusements, a café, ponies, and go-karts.

Day-long caving and rappelling (abseiling down sinkholes) trips can be organized through Aventuras Tierra Adentro (tel: 787-766 0470), which include floating down underground rivers solely by the light of headlamps. Some 2,000 caves have been discovered in the karst region. They provide homes for 13 species of bat, the tiny

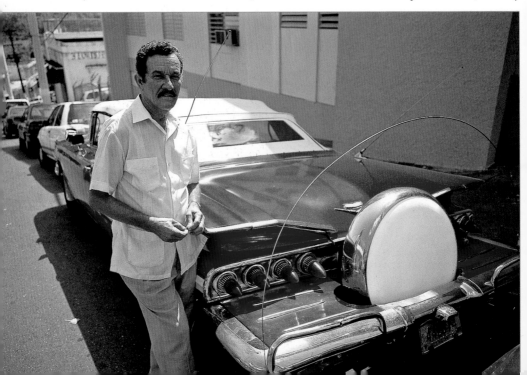

BELOW: ready for cruising: Lares man and his customized 1960s Chevy.

Map on pages 162–3

coquí, the *guavá* (an arachnid), crickets, and other species.

More caves are to be found near the town of **Hatillo**, on the north coast just east of Camuy, which produces most of the milk consumed on the island. But Hatillo's biggest attraction is in late December, when one of the most popular mask festivals in Puerto Rico is held here. Hundreds of people from around the island gather at the town's main square to enjoy the colorful festivities, which see locals dressing up with masks to enact King Herod's soldiers running after newborn boys, with murder on their minds.

San Sebastián and back to the coast

Of all the prosperous provincial towns of Puerto Rico's northwest, **San Sebastián** ⓭ stands out both as the most representative of the region and in the most noticeable contrast to the gloomy villages of the Cordillera Central which lie to the south and east.

Perhaps this is because it is the first of the towns which is truly out of the highlands and secure in its footing as part of the low-lying northwest. Perhaps, too, it has something to do with the cornucopia of food products which come from the region, for this is the heart of many of the island's oldest and most traditional food industries.

San Sebastián is surrounded by green and moist rolling grassland, and stood as one of Puerto Rico's sugar-boom towns in the cane industry's heyday. Now the area is given over to scattered dairy farming and various agricultural pursuits which used to be associated with other parts of the island.

Tobacco grows in many of the valleys, and coffee plants, once the preserve of Yauco and other towns in the island's arid southwest, can be seen growing on local hillsides.

With close to 40,000 residents, most of them living in the shady main streets that cluster about a lovely plaza, San Sebastián has more of an urban ambience than most of the northwest. The weekly Friday bazaar at Plaza Agropecuaria is a big attraction in town, as is the Hammock Festival in July.

Outside of the town, **Puente El Barandillo** is a hanging bridge over

Whitewashed holiday homes dot the northern coast.

BELOW: karstic country.

TIP

If you happen to be
in Quebradillas in the
week of October 24,
don't miss the town's
Fiestas del Pueblo,
which include a mara-
thon and live music.

Río Guatemala on Route 446, and a
great spot from which to begin exploring the karst region. There's also the
famous **Pozo de la Virgen**, a well that
is a religious shrine which attracts
thousands of devout Catholics every
year. To the north, Lago Guajataca has
nature walks and a couple of *paradores*
(country inns), as well as excellent fishing. And any drive into the countryside
will invariably lead to scenic delights.

Surprising town

Perhaps the single most stunning view
in all of Puerto Rico is the approach to
Quebradillas ⑭ heading west from
Arecibo on Route 2. As you drive up a
hill that curves to the left you will see
deep-blue sea and then a breathtaking
coastline of cliffs and rolling sea. Make
the approach slowly. On your right is a
miradero (lookout point) where you
can stop to take some incredible pictures. A little farther on, your first right
will take you down toward the beach
and a collection of Creole restaurants
as well as an old tunnel.

Quebradillas itself adds to the
appealing oddities you expect from

the towns west of Arecibo – spiritual-
ist herb shops, narrow streets, and
houses sloping towards the waterline
– with some geological oddities that
make it a town well worth going out
of your way for.

A short drive or walk northwest of
town, **Playa Guajataca**, described paradoxically by the local people as a "nice,
dangerous beach," is to be taken with
extreme care. Deep waters, white sands,
and raging surf make it a highly attractive proposition for surfers and bathers,
but highly dangerous for the average
swimmer, virtually anyone incapable of
swimming the English Channel. Even
expert swimmers and surfers should
exercise serious caution.

The **Río Guajataca** is another spot
that is as beautiful as it is forbidding,
and pocked with a cave system which,
although not completely charted,
appears to be quite as extensive and
awesome as that of the caves at Camuy.

Lakeside

Nearby **Lago Guajataca** ⑮, 7 miles
(11km) south on Route 113, is man-
made, as are the rest of Puerto Rico's
lakes, but offers a splendid natural
retreat, with two *paradores*, Vistamar
and El Guajataca, both situated on the
coast, serving as convenient bases for
hikes – the well-marked trails are easily
conquered by even the not-so-fit – into
the rolling **Montañas Aymamon** in
the **Guajataca Forest Reserve** ⑯,
located just to the west.

Both *paradores* are very good: El
Guajataca's rooms open onto the
Atlantic Ocean, and the dinners –
blending Creole and international
dishes – are remarkable; Vistamar, one
of Puerto Rico's largest *paradores*, features some beautiful gardens and the
opportunity to fish in the green waters
of the nearby river.

The lake itself is stocked with freshwater fish, and small electric boats are
available for rental most days. You can
climb to the top of the observation
tower here and see no other man-
made structure for miles.   ❑

BELOW: riding by.
RIGHT: beautiful
Toa Alta.

THE WEST

Aguada and Aguadilla are attractive seaside centers, Rincón has spectacular surf, Mayagüez mixes history and a world-class university, and San Germán is the island's second-oldest town

P uerto Rico's west coast, flagged by the Tourism Company as "Porta del Sol" (Gate of the Sun) is brimming with surfing, snorkeling, and diving beaches, among many other natural wonders. The region encompasses 17 municipalities: Quebradillas, Isabela, San Sebastián, Moca, Aguadilla, Aguada, Rincón, Añasco, Mayagüez, Las Marías, Maricao, Hormigueros, San Germán, Sábana Grande, Guánica, Lajas, and Cabo Rojo, which range from gracefully colonial to beach blanket bingo. When *sanjuaneros* need a break from the busy metropolitan area, they plan a weekend on the west coast.

Just two hours from the capital by car, Porta del Sol offers a variety of adventure options, but also a serenity that islanders flock to year-round. It is also "the destination" for some of the finest seafood in Puerto Rico.

The town of Isabela

Isabela ❶, along the north coast, is an amalgam of all the charms of this corner of Puerto Rico, with a cluster of brilliant whitewashed houses tumbling down the hills to some of the island's most renowned surfing and swimming beaches.

The Taíno chief Mabodamaca ruled the region of the "Guajataca" (the Taíno name for the northeastern region of Puerto Rico) where Isabela was originally founded in the 18th century. The first Spanish settlement arrived by the end of the 17th century or beginning of the 18th century in what today includes Isabela, Camuy, and Quebradillas. The original name, authorized by Governor José Antonio de Mendizábal y Azares in 1725, was San Antonio de La Tuna, in honor of Saint Anthony of Padua.

In 1818, the village obtained authorization from Governor Salvador Meléndez to transfer the population to a new location closer to the coast. It was rebaptized as Isabela, in honor of Queen Isabella of Castile.

Main attractions
ISABELA
AGUADA
AGUADILLA
RINCÓN
MAYAGÜEZ
CABO ROJO
BOQUERÓN
SAN GERMÁN

PRECEDING PAGES:
San Germán.
LEFT: pensive
Puerto Rican.
BELOW: Plaza Colón
in Mayagüez.

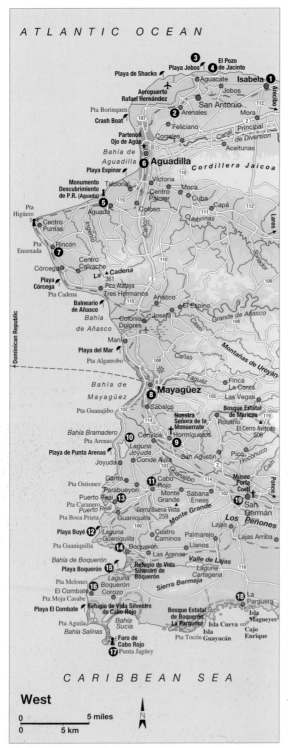

ATLANTIC OCEAN

West

| 0 | | 5 miles |
| 0 | 5 km | |

N

Today the city, like many Puerto Rican towns in the face of multiple factory closings, continues to soldier on, but is looking to tourism to fill the gap. Fortunately for Isabela, small farms still abound, providing much of the produce available at local markets. Isabela is also known for *queso de hoja* (leaf cheese), a delicious small-production white cheese that pulls apart in banana leaves and can be bought at local *panaderías* (bakeries) or at roadside stands. You may feel the occasional tremor here – Isabela is located on the Milwaukee Trench – but full-scale earthquakes are rare occurrences.

Breeding and beaches

Horse enthusiasts should not miss **Arenales ❷** to the southwest, where some fine *pasofino* stables have made Isabela a renowned equine breeding center. Most visitors to Isabela, however, come to ride waves, not steeds, and **Playa Jobos ❸**, just west of town on Route 466, is the place they head for. Beautiful cliffs frame many of the beaches. One of these is home to **El Pozo de Jacinto ❹**, a spurting well where waves meet cliff. The story goes that Jacinto was a farmer who had a favorite cow. He tied himself to the cow with a rope while he was pasturing his herd around the cliffs so he wouldn't lose her. Said bovine got too close to the edge and tumbled into the sea, taking poor, hapless Jacinto with him. Today, locals stand at the edge of the cliff and shout "*Jacinto! Dame la vaca!*" (Give me the cow!) as the spray comes up. It is said to bring good luck.

Nearby, **Playa de Shacks** is an all-purpose destination: diving, snorkeling, and swimming among underwater caves are favorite activities, while windsurfers and kiteboarders from around the world skim across the waves with their colorful sails and riders gallop horses along the beautiful sand.

Rival resorts

The two lovely seaside towns of **Aguada ❺** and **Aguadilla ❻** have a running rivalry over the exact spot of Columbus's first landing on Puerto Rico in 1493. **Parque de Colón**, a mile northwest of Aguada on Route 441, dead center of **Playa Espinar**, a 2,500ft (760-meter) stretch of golden beach, is Aguada's monument to its Columbus claim. Aguadilla's believed site is at **Parque El Parterre**, where a freshwater spring gives historical backing to the belief that Columbus and his sailors stopped here for refreshment on their second voyage of discovery to the West Indies.

Aguadilla, the home of **Ramey Air-force Base**, is the more prosperous of the towns. The base is no longer in service, but **Rafael Hernández Air-port** is operated from there and has the longest runway, at 11,000ft (3,350 meters), in the Caribbean. The airport is mainly used for domestic flights, but direct flights from Canada, North America, and Europe are increasing, and it is hoped they will bring more tourism and more prosperity to the region. In the meantime, the Coast Guard and National Guard offices are still based there.

The town's windswept, palm tree-studded, 18-hole golf course is the cheapest on the island, and there are a dozen pretty little beaches tucked among the coves that form Aguadilla's northwest border. **Crash Boat Beach** (Route 2 to Route 107 to Route 458) is one of the best known and best serviced; it is frequented by ebullient locals at the weekends, when you can go for a look at how Puerto Ricans celebrate the natural gifts of their island.

International waves

Rincón ❼, southwest of Aguadilla, has become an escape destination for locals and visitors over the past 10 years. A peninsula that becomes the western-most point of the island and is separated from the rest by green mountains, Rincón's relative isolation makes it seem like an island unto itself. And its community, made up of farmers and fisher-men who have lived there for generations and tow-headed gringos there for the surf and the ecology, creates a friendly, if schizophrenic, environment more like the tiny islands of the Eastern Caribbean than bustling Puerto Rico. *Rincón* means corner in Spanish and is an apt moniker for the town, but it actually got its name

Whale-watchers are becoming increasingly attracted to the Rincón shores; a bit farther out is a wintering place for humpback whales. (See page 186.)

BELOW: Crash Boat Beach in Aguadilla.

from a Spanish aristocrat called Rincón who deeded this hillside village to the laborers who worked for him. That generosity of spirit is evident in the unhurried smiles of the inhabitants.

A big attraction in Rincón has nothing to do with the surf: the Horned Dorset Primavera Hotel (see page 252) here is considered one of the best hotels in the whole of the Caribbean (tel: 787-823 4030).

Rincón beaches

Visitors mostly come for the beaches. The Atlantic north side of the point is the Caribbean's stellar surf strip. The south side is a dead-flat bathing beach with excellent snorkeling, particularly at Steps. The coral and the colorful small fish that live off it are particularly fine. Winter tends to be high season, because of the waves and whales *(see page 186)*, but more and more families and couples are coming in the low season for the romantic sunsets, photo opportunities at the **Punta Higüero Lighthouse** – recently restored and set in a charming strolling park overlooking the sea and Domes Beach – and lower off-season prices.

Favorite activities include horseback riding, drives over the mountains to photograph panoramic views, and collecting sea glass on Sandy Beach. Because of the numerous tourists, this is as good a place as any to try authentic Creole food, as the waiting staff are likely to speak English very well. And if you are there in the month of June, the dozens of lush mango trees that line the south end of Route 115 will be dropping ripe fruit all over the road. Pull over and harvest some; they are free for the taking and delicious.

Mayagüez – looking forward

Known as *La Sultana del Oeste* (The Sultaness of the West), **Mayagüez** ❽ *(see map below)*, a one-time colonial gem, is undergoing a transformation. The third-largest city in Puerto Rico, its port once flourished and its tuna-canning factories provided as many as 8,000 jobs until the mid-1980s. Dolphin-safe tuna-fishing regulations, instituted since the 1990s, reduced the amount of tuna that needed canning, and when Section 936 of the US Tax Code began to reduce the benefits of running a factory in Puerto Rico, StarKist International and Bumble Bee began to pull out. It has been a devastating blow. Today Bumble Bee retains

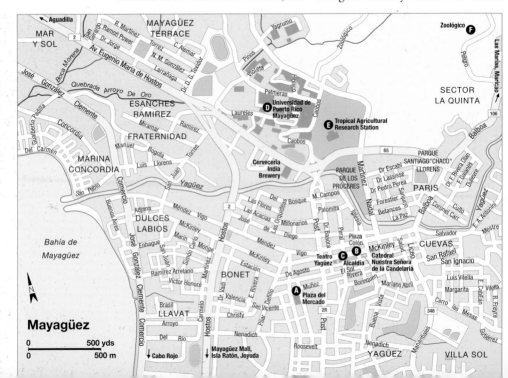

Mayagüez

| 0 | 500 yds |
| 0 | 500 m |

just a small presence, employing around 600 workers, and there is not a whole lot of industry going on to replace the lost jobs.

But Mayagüez has survived devastating blows before. The earthquake of 1918 practically swallowed up the town; a fire took out the imposing Teatro Yagüez in 1919; and then Hurricane San Cipriano almost blew away the city and the surrounding farms in 1932.

Today the town is benefiting from a multimillion-dollar investment program by the central government that will provide much-needed infrastructure in time to host a major sporting event: the Central American-Caribbean Games in 2010. An apartment complex is being constructed to provide housing for athletes during the games, which will be sold off after the competition. It is hoped that the development will strengthen the city as a tourism hub and complement the role of Mayagüez's port, home to **Ferries del Caribe**, a passenger ferry that links Puerto Rico to the Dominican Republic.

Juxtaposed among Mayagüez's modern structures are architectural treasures that happily coexist. Wooden homes with gingerbread trim dating back to the 1800s, which somehow survived the disasters, and colonial mansions are part of the mixed-up cityscape.

The **Plaza del Mercado** Ⓐ (Market Square) is one of the most active and traditional around, despite modernization. Once an open-air covered market filled with the sounds of chickens and roosters, it is now positively deluxe, with air conditioning and no more livestock. Although many of the exotic fruits and vegetables come from the Dominican Republic and Costa Rica, you can still buy *productos del país* (local products) such as bananas, plantains and the prized, small, round, yellow Mayagüez mangoes. Mayagüez is also famous for its *brazo gitanos*, a jellyroll-style cake, and the family-made Sangría de Fido.

Ladies of Barcelona

Mayagüez continues to battle decay valiantly, slowly but surely. The central **Plaza Colón** Ⓑ has been restored. Under the enormous shade of its trees a large statue commemorates Christopher

BELOW: sprawling modern Mayagüez.

Making Waves and Watching Whales

In winter weather, northwestern Puerto Rico becomes heaven on earth for the Hang Ten set and whale-watchers

The cold fronts blowing southeast from Canada may drop unwelcome snow and ice on New England, but those same weather systems push wind toward the Caribbean. That wind ruffles the Atlantic into waves – big waves – that hit the northwest corner of Puerto Rico and produce the Caribbean's best surf.

The first place on the island to become a surf mecca was the town of Rincón, a pointy peninsula at the western tip of the island which held its first World Amateur Surfing Competition in 1968. This tropical corner was rapidly colonized by serious surfers, who began opening campsites and bunk-bed accommodations especially for fellow big-wave seekers.

Rincón has continued evolving into a guesthouse and resort town where surfers are still the main – but not the only – avid repeat guests. Several high-end resorts, including the Horned Dorset Primavera

(see page 252), Puerto Rico's only Relais & Châteaux property, pamper the wealthy, while beach bungalows cater to the bargain hunters among us.

Tourists from the north are not the only ones escaping winter in Rincón. Humpback whales are regular visitors from January through March, calving and frolicking in the warm waters. While there is at least one tour operator taking whale-watchers out on boats to get close to the magnificent mammals, most locals prefer not to disturb the animals and limit themselves to lookout towers along Road 115, afternoon observations with binoculars at the Punta Higüero lighthouse and random sightings along Sandy Beach.

Around the first half of November each year, thousands of humpback whales (ballenas corcovadas) make their way from the North Pole to Atlantic waters north of the Dominican Republic to practice their mating rituals. At times they also cross into the Caribbean Sea through Canal de la Mona (La Mona Channel), the deep trench that separates the Dominican Republic from Puerto Rico.

North of Rincón, the towns of Aguadilla and Isabela are following the surf town's lead. They also have superior surf locations and now more enterprising surfers and hoteliers are opening up businesses to service the growing interest in watersports.

Among the best northwestern surf spots are Tres Palmas (the heaviest spot in the Caribbean), Domes (next to a closed nuclear facility and the lighthouse), and Sandy Beach (beginners) in Rincón; Hawaiian-style Table Rock in Aguada; Gas Chambers, Wilderness, and Pressure Point in Aguadilla; and world-famous Jobos (heavily territorial), left-breaking Golondrines and Sálsipuedes (which means get out if you can) and not-so-Secret Spot in Isabela. Lock your car and leave nothing attractive inside; these are often isolated places and break-ins do happen.

And all of the towns are playing up their year-round aquatic attributes: windsurfing and kiteboarding are world-class and attract adventurous Europeans who don't mind simple amenities. Reefs just offshore create tranquil pools for swimming, snorkeling, and diving, perfect for beginners – manatees are frequently spotted – while the more expert divers can scuba in the underwater karst caves.

Although there are ever more upscale hotels and restaurants popping up, Puerto Rico's northwest remains a more rugged destination, with rough winding roads and deserted beaches with few, if any, amenities. ❏

LEFT: humpback whales are seasonal visitors.

Columbus. He is surrounded by a court of 16 aristocratic bronze ladies brought from Barcelona. He is also often surrounded by transvestites; Mayagüez is well known for its coterie of exclusive cross-dressers who have made Plaza Colón their weekend evening catwalk for the past 50 years.

Around the plaza, the restored Corinthian **Alcaldía** (Town Hall) **C** is an experience in filigree. Just opposite, the long-suffering cathedral of **Nuestra Señora de la Candelaria** underwent a multimillion-dollar restoration, completed in 2003, which was paid for by generous parishioners who raised funds through extra collections; even the two towers that fell in the 1918 earthquake were finally replaced.

Around the corner from the plaza, the historic **Teatro Yagüez** (tel: 787-832 5882; Mon–Fri 8am–4.30pm) has also been totally restored, as part of a project that was completed in 2004; its colorful dome is a beloved Mayagüez landmark. And the surrounding small businesses – the mom-and-pop shops of downtown Mayagüez continue to bustle, even with intense shopping-mall competi-

tion – are taking their cue from the restoration, and painting and smartening up their own historic buildings.

Natural sciences

The **Universidad de Puerto Rico Mayagüez** **D** campus on Route 108 is an engineering and agricultural powerhouse that draws students from neighboring islands and Latin American countries. The campus is hilly and green and has some notable buildings, as well as a noisy flock of emerald-green parrots. The adjoining **Tropical Agricultural Research Station** **E** (Mon–Fri 7am–4pm; free), run by the US Department of Agriculture, offers wonderful grounds for strolling and learning about the many tropical trees and plants brought here from around the world.

Across the street, **Parque de los Próceres** (Patriots Park) is a riverside park with walkways and fountains and new gazebos popular with families and early-morning walkers. And on the northeastern outskirts of the city is the **Zoológico** **F** (tel: 787-834 8110; Wed–Sun and holidays 8.30am–5pm; entrance and parking charge), the island's premier

BELOW: off to work.

The Basilica of Our Lady of Montserrat in Hormigueros is a major pilgrimage site for Puerto Ricans.

collection of animals, which roam freely in an environment as close to their natural habitat as possible.

The Taíno Indians had numerous settlements in the Mayagüez area. It is no wonder. With the many streams and rivers criss-crossing their way toward the sea, it is a fertile plain. While the years of tuna-canning have left Mayagüez bay in need of a clean-up, nearby **Joyuda**, a strip of seaside restaurants a few miles south of Mayagüez, does have some shoreline suitable for swimming. However, most visitors prefer to limit themselves to a rustic, slap-up seafood meal overlooking tiny **Isla Ratón** (Rat Island).

Head for the hills

Just 5 miles (8km) south of Mayagüez, inland off Route 2, is the tiny *municipio* of **Hormigueros** ❾. This is a city with the slow pace of the northwest and the layout of a Cordillera town, with narrow winding streets and one of the finests cathedrals on the island. The **Basílica Santuario Nuestra Señora de la Montserrate** (Our Lady of Montserrat) is at once breathtaking and unas-

suming. Bone-white towers of varying dimensions rise to silver domes, topped with austere white crucifixes of wood. Its hilltop position gives the impression that it is soaring into the sky, and it makes a useful landmark for finding your way around. The red-brick stairs up to the cathedral are a workout, but the view from the top is worth it.

The region of what is now Hormigueros belonged to the Guaynia region, on the southernwest portion of Puerto Rico. Archeological finds have established there were tribes already settled here around 820 BC. Spanish colonists moved into the area at the beginning of the 16th century. By 1640 it was known as the Hermitage or Sanctuary of Hormigueros, part of San Germán. It was officially founded on April 1, 1874, separating it from San Germán.

The word *hormiguero* means anthill or ant trail. It has been speculated that the name of the town could derive from the Taíno word *horomico*, for the Horomico River. Some historians also have documented that the Horomico River was one of the main sources of gold during the rush of the era.

Current public works, including brick paving, are making Hormigueros a tiny treasure, worth a stop as you travel between bigger towns along Route 2.

Heading back toward the coast via Cerrillos you'll reach **Laguna Joyuda** ⓾, a mangrove swamp that is a sanctuary for native birds. Mangroves, in addition to being the nursery for all the delicious crustaceans and fish served in the local restaurants, are hotbeds for semi-tropical bird life, and this 300-acre (120-hectare) expanse is one of the most populated. Herons, martins, and pelicans, including the lovely maroon pelican, make their home here, and the lagoon itself is full of fish. On moonless nights, it is reputed to be phosphorescent, due to a concentration of the marine dinoflagellate organism *Pyrodinium bahamense*.

To the point

Washed by coral-studded Caribbean waters, bathed in dry tropical heat year-round and sculpted into an odd network of cliffs, lagoons, promontories, and swamps by fickle surf and tides, the district of **Cabo Rojo** ⓫, to the south, shows Puerto Rico's landscape at its most alluring. Stretching along 18 miles (29km) of coast from Mayagüez, this region is among the most remote on the island; whether approaching from Ponce or Mayagüez, you notice the landscape becoming drier, the population more sparse, and the scenery more beautiful.

But for those to whom the name "Cabo Rojo" has become synonymous with isolated retreats and breathtaking vistas, the town of Cabo Rojo is worth exploring to see the sewing factories that are open onto the street, and the shoe-repair shops and variety stores that are reminiscent of the 1950s.

A battery of beaches

When it comes to picking a favorite beach along the Cabo Rojo coastline, there are plenty to choose from, but mention **Playa Buyé** ⓬ to a Puerto Rican and you are sure to receive a nos-

talgic sigh for an answer. The houses in tiny Buyé, just southwest of Cabo Rojo town on Route 307, come up close to the water's edge, and there is something magical about its half-moon curved beach that inspires love. At the other end is **Puerto Real** ⓭, perhaps the last authentic fishing village in the region. Stroll around for more nameless hidden beaches. The landscape changes with shocking suddenness just south of Buyé, as the cliffs of **Punta Guaniquilla** give way to the swamps and mangroves of tiny **Laguna Guaniquilla**.

The cliffs and lagoon are best reached by making the ¾-mile (1km) walk south out of Buyé or by taking the dirt road that leads out of the tiny settlement of **Boca Prieta**.

And more beaches

Just 7 miles (11km) south of the town of Cabo Rojo on Routes 4 and 101 lies **Boquerón** ⓮, a one-time fishing port turned recreational beach town. It is blessed with a mangrove forest which shelters some of Puerto Rico's loveliest birds – the Laguna Rincón and surrounding forests have been designated

The infamous Puerto Rican buccaneer Roberto Cofresí made Cabo Rojo his base during his 19th-century raids on European merchant ships.

BELOW: contemplation on the beach.

TIP

The cabins around Boquerón's beach are popular among weekenders; to rent one, contact the Department of Recreation and Sports in San Juan at least four months in advance, through the Puerto Rico Tourism Company, tel: 1-800-866 7827 or 721 2400.

BELOW: a jetty spans white sand and turquoise waters at El Combate Beach.

a bird sanctuary as one of three parts of the **Boquerón Nature Reserve**. But what really brings visitors to the town is the 3-mile (5km) long curving bay whose placid coral-flecked waters and sands backed by a palm grove make **Playa Boquerón** ⓯ almost without question the finest beach on the island. In a place like Puerto Rico, where regional rivalries are intense, the fact that even Luquillo residents concede that this beach is the best is significant. However, Boquerón at the weekends is often a frenzied, crowded, and noisy place, and it is impossible to get into the small town at night because of the wild revelries. To enjoy its wooden shacks, fried snacks, and tranquil waters in peace, go on a weekday.

At the end of Route 301, a circuitous 6 miles (10km) south of Boquerón, **El Combate** ⓰ is another remarkable stretch of beach along the Cabo Rojo coastline with few services and a park-in-the-sand atmosphere, which provides a perfect setting for concerts.

The salt flats at the dirt-road end of Route 301 give a view into Puerto Rico's past which continues as you hike over the promontory to reach **El Faro de Cabo Rojo**. One of the island's historic lighthouses, it overlooks another of the island's most beautiful crescent beaches.

Punta Jagüey ⓱, a kidney-shaped rock outcrop, supporting the lighthouse, is connected to the land by a narrow isthmus which is flanked by two lovely bays – **Bahía Salinas** and **Bahía Sucia**, also called **La Playuela**.

If you have never seen how sea salt is harvested, now is your chance. On the east of the isthmus that connects to the lighthouse you can see the grid for the evaporation system as well as piles of harvested salt. The salt flats are considered very important for migratory birds in the Caribbean. Around 40,000 birds visit this place every year.

Herons and eelgrass

Here too is a nature reserve of grand proportions; both the peninsula and the surrounding waters are protected as part of the same Boquerón system that embraces Laguna Rincón. But there is more to Punta Jagüey than herons and eelgrass. The **Faro de Cabo Rojo** is a

breathtaking specimen of Spanish colonial architecture, with a low-lying, pale-sided main building and squat, hexagonal light-tower. It perches atop dun-colored cliffs at the very extremity of the peninsula and commands views of almost 300 degrees of the Caribbean. The *faro* was built in 1881 over limestone cliffs that drop 200ft (61 meters) into the sea and is also known as "Faro de Los Morrillos." This old lighthouse was automated and electrically charged in 1967. The structure is at its most awe-inspiring when given a faint blush of color by either sunrise or sunset. However, it's more likely that you'll see the latter, as many excursions to Cabo Rojo are conceived as day trips and somehow carry on into the evening.

The southwest corner

La Parguera ⓲, on the southern coast, leads a dual life as a quiet coastal town and – on summer nights and weekends – a party town alive with young *sanjuaneros* and thrill-seeking tourists. This is not to say the place is spoiled; it serves a useful function of diverting crowds from the area's more delicate attractions.

Boats ply the waters between the village and the bay with reassuring frequency. For a few dollars, you'll most likely get an hour in the flying Caribbean spindrift and one of the rare opportunities Puerto Rico affords to make use of a warm sweater. Leaving the docks, cruises run through the yachts and fishing boats of Parguera's poorly sheltered harbor and past a tiny chain of islets whose focus is **Isla Magueyes**, home to a colony of lizards.

As cruise boats enter the bay, their wakes turn an eerie pale green. Captains invite the passengers to trail their hands over the gunwales and into the water to produce odd, remarkable patterns. A bucket is generally brought on board for the curious to play with, and in cupped palms the water breaks into shapes resembling splattering mercury. The phosphorescence is produced by billions of micro-organisms which belong to the family of dinoflagellates known as *Pyrodinium bahamense*. Try to see this unique phenomenon on a cloudy night with a light breeze, when no other light sources muddle the brilliance of the waters, and wavelets make

Fisherman and anglers also enjoy the calm waters of Playa Boquerón.

BELOW: San Germán is an architectural gem.

ever-changing patterns on the surface. Unfortunately, in recent years the effect has been reduced owing to pollution.

San Germán

Seeds of colonization in the New World have not always brought culture, but they have generally created overpopulation, and the large cities of the Americas, with their millions of citizens, were generally in place if only as minor outposts more than a couple of centuries ago. **San Germán** ⓳, with a population of 30,000, is a different sort of locale – it is one of those major 16th-century towns which has been blessed by never having been too thoroughly dragged into the squalid rat race of the modern world. Although old, it has never grown into a sprawling urban center.

San Germán – Puerto Rico's second-oldest town – is a diamond in an emerald setting, a pearly-white town tucked into an uncharacteristically lush and verdant section inland from the south and west coastlines, about halfway between Ponce and Mayagüez on pretty Route 119.

RIGHT: José Campeche's *Virgen de la Leche*, inside Porta Coeli Church.

Founded in 1510 by the second wave of Spanish colonists, San Germán was San Juan's only rival for prominence on the island until the 19th century. Forces invading or retreating from San Juan, notably the English, French, and Dutch, often stopped here to arm themselves or lick their wounds. In the 19th century it became one of Puerto Rico's great coffee towns, with magnates building some of the truly unique homes on the island.

Today, San Germán owes its prominence and cultural vibrancy to the Inter-American University, which has 8,000 students and well-tended grounds, and the diligence with which it has preserved some of the earliest European architectural works to survive in the Western hemisphere.

Heaven's gate

The **Museo Porta Coeli** (tel: 787-892 5845; Wed–Sun 8.30am–noon and 1–4.15pm; free) is San Germán's – and arguably Puerto Rico's – greatest architectural inheritance. Founded in 1606, it is the oldest church under the United States flag. It is also one of only a few

The Art of José Campeche

It is no surprise that the work of José Germán's Porta Coeli, one of Puerto Rico's most architecturally important churches. Many of the island's churches – as well as the cathedral in Old San Juan – feature paintings by Campeche, Puerto Rico's first native painter and its first artistic genius. He was born José de Rivafrecha y Jordán in 1751; his father, Tomás Rivafrecha y Campeche, was a black freeman and his mother, María Jordán y Marques, was a Spaniard from the Canary Islands. Campeche, like his brothers, learned about art and painting through Tomás, who was a master gilder and carver, a painter, and an ornamentalist.

But José excelled at more than art: he was also a professional musician, sculptor, surveyor, and decorator, as well as an architect. Well educated and a devout Catholic, he was considered a gentleman. He was fortunate to live after Puerto Rico's towns and cities were established: before that, not much emphasis had been given to the arts.

Through his approximately 400 paintings of religious themes and historical events, and portraits of prominent politicians and local landed gentry, he gained a deserved reputation as "the most gifted of Latin American rococo artists." Campeche died in 1809 and is buried in San Juan Cathedral.

buildings in the New World constructed in the Gothic architectural style. It is one of the great glories of Spanish colonization that the conquest came about early enough to ensure that this neo-medieval style, which peppers all the countries of Europe with some of the greatest monuments to man's artistry, could also flourish in the New World.

Porta coeli means "heaven's gate" and, indeed, the church portals are of great importance to its artistry. A squat little whitewashed building standing at the top of a broad, spreading stairway of scrabbly brick and mortar, its large doors are of beautiful *ausubo*, a once-common Puerto Rican hardwood.

Inside, the pews and altar are all original, with embellishments. The altarpiece was painted by the first great Puerto Rican artist, José Campeche *(see panel opposite)*, in the late 18th century, a fact that would indicate the church was fairly well established as a historical landmark even by then. Today the church is a small religious museum containing some ancient *santos (see page 69)*. Porta Coeli overlooks one of the most beautifully landscaped plazas in Puerto Rico, with terraced benches and beautifully groomed trees.

Name that church

San Germán, like Ponce, is a two-plaza town, and its second, the **Plaza Francisco Mariano Quiñones**, is no less impressive than that overlooked by Porta Coeli, with the same lovely walks, period lamplights, and marvelous topiary. But it also has a church to rival Porta Coeli in appeal, if not in age. The church of **San Germán de Auxerre** commemorates the French saint who is the town's patron. Its steeple does not face the plaza directly, but has its facade on a nearby side street. While less important than much of San Germán in historical terms, it dominates the town, and is particularly impressive when viewed from the surrounding hills on a bright and sunny day.

Ancient homes

San Germán's oldest attractions – the two churches, in particular – have always captured the attention of visitors, but there is much more: 249 noteworthy sites, to be exact. But few have stopped to examine this ancient town with the rigor and delight that tourists have always brought to San Juan and Ponce. The marvelous haciendas of the late 19th-century coffee barons are abundant, and demonstrate a style which, while it can be seen throughout the southwest – in Yauco, for example – is as much San Germán's own as Porta Coeli.

These houses must be entered to be appreciated, as much of their charm lies in the way in which the interior spaces are divided. Beautiful *mediopunto* carvings – delicate lacy half-screens of snaking wood – create conceptual divisions between rooms without actually putting up substantial physical barriers. Some of them are astounding harbingers of Art Nouveau, as are the simple and sinuous stencilings which grace the walls of many of the houses.   ❏

One of the many santos displayed in the Porta Coeli Church, now a museum.

BELOW: the nave in San Germán de Auxerre Church.

PUERTO RICO'S FANTASTIC FLORA

One would expect luxuriant flora on a tropical island, but Puerto Rico's exceeds all expectations, and much of it is protected in forest reserves

Everything seems to grow in Puerto Rico – and in abundance. This lush, green island produces a vast array of flora which ranges from myriad varieties of orchid to a cornucopia of trees, many of them bearing fruit, including coconuts, limes, pineapples, and the exotic starfruit.

Puerto Rico's flora is as colorful as the many other aspects of the country. Visitors will at once notice the exotic splashes of bougainvillea that adorn homes, businesses, and even bridges. Gardenias and jasmine fill the air with their fragrance, while pink oleander and red hibiscus dot the countryside and towns.

The forests of Puerto Rico are home to more than 500 species of trees. Bamboo, mahogany, and *lignum vitae*, the hardest wood in the world, are cultivated for local use as well as international export.

The 200-acre (80-hectare) Botanical Garden in Río Piedras *(see page 132)* is a particularly good place to see much of the island's tropical plant life in one location. Along similar lines, the Tropical Agricultural Research Station in Mayagüez *(see page 187)* has one of the largest collections of tropical and semi-tropical plants in the world.

Although various hurricanes have taken their toll, Puerto Rico also provides ample locales to explore the island's flora in its natural state, including the Caribbean National Forest – better known as El Yunque *(see pages 141–3)*.

There are also well-kept hiking trails in the Guánica Forest Reserve, which is known for its bird life as well as for its endangered plant species. Puerto Rico's wild karst country *(see page 170)* can also be discovered via the trails running through that area's four national forests – Cambalache, Guajataca, Rio Abajo and Vega Alta.

ABOVE: bright-red blossoms of the flaming royal poinciana, known locally as the flamboyant tree, light up the Puerto Rican countryside in June and July.

BELOW: Cassia Polyphylla at the University of Puerto Rico's Botanical Garden at Río Piedras. This tree can be seen throughout the island.

LEFT: carambola or starfruit grow wild in Puerto Rico. The fruit is entirely edible, including the slightly waxy skin.

FRUITS OF A FERTILE LAND

It would probably come as no surprise to a Puerto Rican if a planted toothpick took root, so fertile is the soil on the island. Fruit-bearing trees are a prime example: oranges, lemons, mangoes, papaya, and guava grow wild on the island, although many fruits are also cultivated. Pineapple, *parcha* (passion fruit) and *quenapa* (Spanish lime) are also abundant on the island.

The country's most unusual fruit has to be the weird, head-sized breadfruit *(pictured above)*, from a flowering tree of the mulberry family, which islanders prepare in a number of ways, but most commonly as *tostones* – fried green-breadfruit slices – that accompany many main courses. When cooked, the taste is described as potato-like, or similar to fresh baked bread (hence the name).

More familiar to visitors is the banana, which grows in abundance here, alongside its close relative, the plantain, which cannot be eaten raw. You'll see plantains on menus everywhere, most commonly in the form of appetizer *tostones* or fried up in *mofongo*, a particular island favorite.

The rich and fertile fields of Puerto Rico produce a wide variety of vegetables. A favorite is the *chayote*, a pear-shaped vegetable called christophone throughout most of the English-speaking Caribbean. Its delicately flavored flesh is often compared to that of summer squash.

ABOVE: the University of Puerto Rico's Botanical Gardens at Río Piedras are considered to be one of the best in the Caribbean.

RIGHT: the Caribbean National Forest (El Yunque) is home to 240 species of tropical trees, flowers, and wildlife, including more than 50 kinds of orchid.

RIGHT: the island's beautiful flora isn't limited to reserves – in nearly every garden and around every corner are brilliant tropical blossoms.

THE SOUTH

Salinas is known for seafood restaurants,
Coamo for springs, and Ponce is rich in history.
Guayanilla is a good base point, and
bird watchers and snorkelers head for
the Guánica Forest Reserve

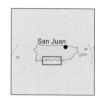

San Juan

When the Las Américas Expressway, or the Autopista Luis A. Ferré, between San Juan and Ponce, was completed in 1975, it cut travel time in half between the traditionally separated north and south of the island. The toll road, which goes through mountains and valleys and is big on scenery, makes the one-hour trip a treat. As you descend from the central mountain range, you discover more arid, sweeping vistas with the clear, blue Caribbean Sea opening out in front of you.

The southern region, christened Porta Caribe by the Tourism Company, is home to 15 municipalities. The city of Ponce is at its epicenter, driving the economy and culture, but there are more waterside towns nestled at the foot of mountain ranges and valleys that offer visitors the chance to explore off-the-beaten-path cultural attractions that stand out in this tropical beach setting.

Porta Caribe offers world-class fishing excursions, fine dining, golf by the sea at spectacular golf courses, and quaint accommodations.

Ponceños, inhabitants of the south coast's largest city, are as proud as ever of their charming, marble-lined streets and rich city center that harks back to the 17th century.

And Ponce's neighbors have equal pride in the landscape. Here you will find the remains of a once-flourishing sugar-cane industry.

Eastern allure

Salinas ❶ is a lip-smacking destination, famed across the island for its seafood restaurants, which can be found tucked behind a beautiful bay edged with mangroves. This small town, criss-crossed by narrow roads, is considered the birthplace of *mojo isleño*, the sautéed onion, pepper, and tomato sauce that all Puerto Ricans love to smear on their fish.

Salinas is also home to the **Albergue Olímpico Germán Rieckehoff** (Olympic Training Center; tel: 1-800-981

Main attractions
SALINAS
SANTA ISABEL
COAMO
PONCE
  PLAZA LAS DELICIAS
  CAJA DE MUERTOS NATURE RESERVE
YAUCO
GUÁNICA

PRECEDING PAGES:
the photogenic
Victorian Fire Station
in Ponce.
LEFT AND BELOW:
picturesque Salinas.

BELOW: enjoying a *piña colada*.

2210; daily 6am–10pm; charge) where so many of Puerto Rico's world-class athletes come to train before international events. Automotive sports are also big in this area, and the **Puerto Rico International Speedway** on Route 3, Km 155.2, is one of the largest (tel: 787-824 0020; www.salinasspeedway-pr.com; Wed 5pm–midnight, Sat 4pm–midnight, sometimes Sun).

Southeast of Salinas is **Aguirre**, the site of a former sugar mill where many of the old buildings still stand. A nine-hole public golf course, built here in 1926, is claimed to be the oldest one on the island (tel: 787-853-4052). Aguirre is framed by the **Jobos Bay Estuarine Reserve**, a research site encompassing mangrove forests, a series of cays, and salt flats, where you can rent a kayak, bird-watch, and hike *(see page 156)*.

Driving around the area, you will come across seafood kiosks such as La Casa del Pastelillo, a waterfront deck with hammocks and seafood-stuffed pastries of every description. If you see an inviting beach, ask around first before stopping for a dip, as some parts along here have dangerous currents.

Hidden gem

Santa Isabel ❷ is a hidden gem that lays south of Coamo, east of Juana Díaz, and west of Salinas. This charming coastal town was founded in 1842 and commemorated in honor of Santa Isabel de Hungría, a 13th-century Hungarian princess who dedicated her life to serving the poor and the sick. It is known as *La Ciudad de los Potros* (Colts City) and *La Tierra Fértil* (The Fertile Earth) because of the fruits cultivated here, in some of the most fertile lands on the planet.

The town center features the typical layout of a square plaza, Plaza de los Fundadores, fronted by the church, Iglesia Santiago Apóstol. It also has a breathtaking view from its *malecón*, or seaside boardwalk, and *villa pesquera*, or fishing village. Neighborhood eateries offer fresh seafood options like crab *empanadillas* (fritters) and other delights.

Locals and visitors alike enjoy the waters at either Jauca Beach or Punta Águila, wading pools gentle enough for the children and lined with palm trees and mangroves.

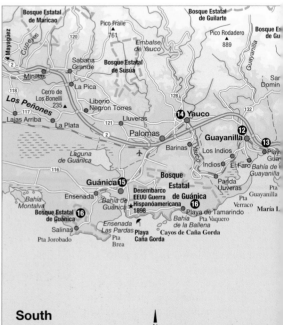

South

0 _____ 5 miles

0 _____ 5 km

Music plays a large part in the life of the town, taking center stage during the patron saint's festival in July. In fact, one of the folk-art specialties of Santa Isabelinos is producing a type of drum used to play *bomba* music.

Santa Isabela's economy is a mix of old and new, ranging from agriculture and manufacturing to biotechnology research. The town's celebration of the arts comes in the form of festivals: the Mango Festival in May, the Crab Carnival in June, its patron saint celebrations in July, and the Cemí Carnival in October.

Bathing beauty

Moving westward across the mountains from Aibonito *(see page 223)* farther inland, Road 14 goes directly to **Coamo ❸**. Its thermal springs – known to the Taíno Indians, who considered them sacred – were discovered by the Spanish in 1571 and the city itself founded in 1579, making it one of the oldest cities in Puerto Rico. Some say that the springs are the Fountain of Youth that Ponce de León was looking so hard for. In the early part of the 20th century, the springs (located at the end of Road 546) grew into a major Caribbean resort and attracted an international clientele. After World War II, however, the resort fell into decay.

Today, a new resort stands on the ruins of the old one and once again visitors join locals in taking to the waters at the pool, staying at the atmospheric Parador Baños de Coamo, whose foundations date from 1848. Top international runners flock to the town in early February to take part in the San Blás Half Marathon. There is an adjacent golf course, Coamo Springs, which could be developed in the future to include a condo-hotel on the site as well.

In the **Museo de Coamo** (tel: 787-825 1150 ext. 206 for times) on José Quinto Street, several rooms are furnished with antiques to recreate a typical 19th-century household.

Continuing west, you reach the town officially called **Juana Díaz ❹**, but also known as *La Ciudad del Río Jacaguas* (City of Jacaguas River), *La Ciudad del Poeta* (City of the Poet – Luis Llorens

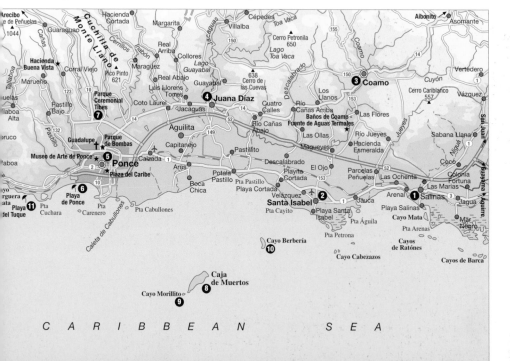

Ponce

0   200 yds
0   200 m

Calle Llanos
Calle Martines
Calle Martines

El Vigía Observation Tower O

EL VIGÍA

Calle Pico Dulce

Castillo Serallés N

Avenida Betances

Calle Intendente Ramires

Calle Húcar

Calle Puerto Rico

12 de Octubre

Calle Las Casas

Calle San Juan

Calle Antocha

Calle León

Calle Mayor

Calle Cantera

Calle Virtud

Calle las Flores

C. Berlin

Calle Guadalupe

Calle Jalome
C. Nueva Atenas
Mendez
Union
Vigo
Arenas

2 de Mayo

Avenida Betances

C. Esmeralda

Calle Tricoche

Calle Guadalupe

ALHAMBRA

Protestante

VIEJO CEMENTERIO

Calle Tricoche

Bertoli

Rosch

Calle Guadalupe

Correo

Estrella

Calle León

14

Plaza Ponce de León

Plaza del Mercado L

Calle A. C. Olivieri

Calle A

Escuela de Bellas Artes de Ponce

Museo Francisco Pancho Coimbre

Calle Frontispicio

C. los Placeres

Calle Victoria

C. Fco. Valls

Calle Union

Plaza del Mercado Isabel II

Vives

Castillo

Salud

Virtud

PARQUE CHARLES H. TERRY

Charles H. Terry Athletic Field

Calle A

Torres

Vives

Calle Sol

14

Calle Sol

Calle León

Calle Sol

Calle Sol

14

Portugués

Puente de los Leones

Casa Wiechers-Villaronga / Museo de Arquitectura de Ponce I

Fox Delicias Hotel

Museo de la Historia de Ponce

Calle St. Isabel G

Museo de la Música Puertorriqueña

M

PARQUE TRICENTENARIO

Calle St. Isabel

Plaza las Delicias A

1

Teatro La Perla F E

1

Calle Trujillo

Cn. Comercio

Calle Molina

Catedral de Nuestra Señora de la Guadalupe B C

Parque de Bombas

Hostos

Calle Cristina

C. Juan Seix

Calle Amor

Mayor

Avenida

Calle Trujillo

Calle Torres

Alcaldia D

Calle Federico P. Duperán

Calle Simon Bolivar

10

Calle Luna

Mendez

Calle

Luna

FRANCISCO

Calle Federico P. Duperán

Calle Aurora

Vigo

Marina

Casa Paoli H

Calle Cruz

Calle Aurora

Calle Wilson

Casa de la Masacrede de Ponce

EL BOSQUE

Calle

Roosevelt

Calle Jobos

10

14

Calle Jobos

Gran

Via

Calle Num 1

Calle Num 2

Calle Num 3

Calle Num 4

Calle Num 5

Calle Num 6

Lucas

Amadeo

Calle Baldorioty

Calle Americo Capo

Aires

Calle

Buenos

Calle

Campos

BELGICA

Martin

Corchado

Calle Sultana

Torres

(Concordia)

Campeche

Calle C

Ferrocarril

Institución Ferrán

Avenida

Hostos

Calle la

Calle Cruz

Calle Num 1

Num 2

Num 3

Calle Num 4

Calle Num 5

Calle Num 6

Campos

Centro Comercial Santa Maria

Molina

Providencia

Calle

SANTA MARIA

Calle A

Calle A

Num 2

Num 3

Num 4

Num 5

Num 6

Museo de Arte de Ponce J

Avenida Las Americas

Avenida Las Americas

Guayanilla

Santa Isabel

Plaza del Caribe K ↓ **Playa de Ponce**

Torres) and Ciudad del Maví (City of Maví, a fermented bark drink). Quiet for most of the year, Juana Díaz comes to life on the Feast of the Epiphany or Three Kings Day on January 6, when an enormous street festival celebrates the African, Taíno, and European roots of modern-day Puerto Rico.

Ponce

The honors for most fabulous city in Puerto Rico is a theme that *sanjuaneros* and *ponceños* have fierce and passionate arguments about. But even the *capitalinos* from the northern coast admit to what *ponceños* proudly claim as the sobriquet of their city. **Ponce ❺** is indeed *La Perla del Sur* or "The Pearl of the South."

Perhaps the most surprising thing is that Ponce, Puerto Rico's second-largest city, actually *is* a pearl of sorts. Though not so distant in the imagination of travelers as Mayagüez, it's still far enough away from the San Juan/Dorado/Palmas del Mar circuit to seem to belong to another place entirely.

However, Ponce is an easy 90-minute drive from San Juan – take Expressway 52 from San Juan all the way there – and so there's very little excuse for not heading south to see what all these southerners are bragging about.

Hot stuff

To begin with, Ponce has the best weather on the island. It's located in what ecologists call a "rain shadow"; the afternoon storms which beleaguer the north coast are stopped dead by the peaks of the Cordillera Central. You can see the rain from Ponce – it's in those purple clouds pulsing above the hills 10 miles (16km) north – but you're not going to feel any of it.

The landscape surrounding the city is a typical southwestern palette of tumbling grasslands, parched to gold by the Caribbean sun, against purple-and-lavender skies.

This is no Atlantic coast – although a place as far south as Ponce can take on that ocean's hostile cobalt aspect – as a look from the hills above the town will demonstrate. Especially from El Vigía, the view across Ponce shows the coral and white of the town's stately houses, the turquoise

> *Ponce is one of the oldest towns on the island… It is located on a big plain covered with trees… 115 houses form an irregular square. The parish church [Guadalupe], which is small and deteriorated, is on one side; 5,038 souls live here.*
> Historian Iñigo Abbad y Lasierra, 1784

LEFT: Ponce policewoman.

Port of the Americas

The development of the Port of the Americas, an ambitious $250-million project to make Ponce Port a Caribbean transshipment hub, is currently in its third of four phases. The first phase, completed in December 2004, included the renovation Ponce Port's existing Piers 4, 5, and 6. The second phase began with a 50ft (15-meter) deep dredging project completed in November 2006. The next part of the second phase, building a new terminal to accommodate some 250,000 containers, known as TEUs, was completed in December 2008. The third phase includes rehabilitating and building the infrastructure to accommodate logistics warehouses and distribution centers. It includes expanding the container terminal to double its capacity, from 250,000 containers to 500,000 containers. It also entails relocating a rain channel of 1 mile (1.6km) on Route 52, which will give the port more space for maritime cargo businesses and enable the municipality of Ponce to develop a housing project in La Playa sector.

The potential of the Port of the Americas hinges on its offering value-added transshipment facilities to be able to integrate into routes from Europe, Asia, and Latin America. While the development of the Port of the Americas is ongoing, it is fully operational and ready to receive Post-Panamax cargo ships, which are large ships that exceed the maximum dimensions of vessels that fit through the Panama Canal.

waters of its Caribbean harbor, and the stripes of green mangrove and travertine coral formations of the archipelago that surrounds the isle of Caja de Muertos.

The inland port

Ponce proper – and if there's a proper city in Puerto Rico, it's Ponce – is perhaps the archetype of a strangely Puerto Rican sort of city: a bustling port with an enviable natural harbor which has nonetheless developed around a city center some distance inland. A left turn off the *autopista* will take you, not to the center of a busy waterfront town, but to the interesting outpost at **Playa de Ponce ❻** – a collection of old brick warehouses and more modern storage areas – and the wharf at **Muelle de Ponce**. On evenings and weekends, **La Guancha Board Walk** is a popular gathering place, where there are plenty of seafood restaurants, shops, an open-air stage, and a massive playground.

To get into the heart of Ponce, continue in a northwesterly direction on Road 133 as it passes over the sluggish

There is a continual raging academic controversy about how Ponce (pronounced Pon-tse) got its name – some say it's from the first governor of the island, Ponce de León; others argue that it was taken from his great-grandson.

RIGHT:
Ponce Cathedral.

Río Portugués and becomes **Calle F.P. Duperán**, the main commercial street, also known as Calle Comercio. If you are coming from San Juan, leave the *autopista* at the Ponce/Road 1 exit and head into the historical district, which has earned Ponce the epithet Museum City *(see page 208)*, where you can take advantage of the trolley system.

Here, you'll see the results of the $450-million "Ponce en Marcha" program, begun in 1986 by former Puerto Rican Governor Rafael Hernández Colón, himself a *ponceño*, and Rafael "Churumba" Cordero, Ponce mayor from 1989 until his death in 2004. The massive beautification effort resulted in the burying of unsightly phone and electric cables, the repaving of streets, and the renovation of nearly every structure in the downtown district.

Hernández Colón is no longer governor, and the program has recently run out of money, but its astounding success was enough to transform Ponce into one of the Caribbean's most beautiful cities. Its image was further boosted in 1993 when Ponce

Fantasy Fire Station

What must be the oddest – and certainly most whimsical – fire station ever built, Ponce's Parque de Bombas was originally erected as an exhibit for the 1882 Trade Fair. It was one of two structures built in Arabic architectural style for the fair; the other, known as the Quiosco Arabe, was destroyed in 1914, although a glassed-in scale model of it can be viewed in the Industry Room at the Museo de la Historia de Ponce. The Parque de Bombas was put into use as a fire station the year after the fair, and it remained the headquarters of the Ponce Fire Corps for over a century, until 1989.

The following year the remarkable red-and-black wooden structure was restored and reopened as a museum featuring fire-department memorabilia. The old fire-fighting equipment on display includes antique fire trucks and hand-pulled tanks, which needed the movement of rushing to the scene of a fire to build up the pressure.

The exhibits in the upstairs museum also detail fire-fighting techniques of the late 19th century and provide interesting information on the Great Fire of 1906. With its playful collection of poles, sideboards, crenellations, and cornices, the Parque de Bombas is a gaudy and riotous building with a playful, truly *ponceño* spirit – and has come to symbolize Ponce itself.

hosted the 17th Central American and Caribbean Games.

A square deal

At the end of Calle Duperán is the cluster of architectural beauties which gives Ponce its reputation as being one of the most Spanish of Puerto Rican cities. Here the magnificent **Plaza las Delicias A**, lush and beautifully landscaped, sits pounded by sunlight amid a pinwheel of centuries-old streets. Huge fig trees stand in lozenge-shaped topiary, and large, shady islands of grass are punctuated by dramatic fountains. Broad paths of rose-colored granite weave through the squares, bordered by slender old lamp-posts which make the plaza both attractive and accessible in the evening.

Plaza las Delicias is dominated by the **Catedral de Nuestra Señora de la Guadalupe** (Our Lady of Guadalupe) **B** (daily with limited hours, so call first, tel: 787-842 0134) named for the patron saint of Ponce. It's a pretty, low, pink structure, reminiscent in its colors and rounded turrets of San Juan Cathedral.

Though not as old as San Juan's, built in the late 17th century, Ponce's cathedral makes ample use of the reflected sunlight from the plaza. Its silvery twin towers – a characteristically Puerto Rican touch in religious architecture – are shaped like little hydrants, and glow oddly at midday. This gives the building a bright and inviting look, against which the eerie stillness of its lofty interior creates a startling contrast.

A museum tour

Our Lady of Guadalupe may hold the religious high ground, but the fancy-looking red-and-black-striped building behind it cuts more ice with the tourist crowd. This is the **Parque de Bombas C** (Wed–Mon 10am–6pm; free), Ponce's unmissable Victorian fire station and perhaps the most photographed building in all of Puerto Rico (*see panel opposite*). The **Alcaldía D**,

diagonally across the plaza from the two buildings, has a pleasant hacienda feel to it and contrasts in a lively way with its two more renowned neighbors. Across from the fire station, King Cream ice-cream shop sells some of the island's best homemade ice cream. Delicious flavors to try are coconut, mango, or almond.

The Pearl Theater

About a block away from the cathedral, at the corner of calles Cristina and Mayor, is the stately **Teatro La Perla E**, where plays are performed by local theater companies. On occasion, productions shown in San Juan go on the road to Ponce. Built in 1864 but partially destroyed in the 1918 earthquake, it is also the home of Ponce's annual Luis Torres Nadal Theater Festival.

Around the corner on Calle Isabel, history comes to life at the **Museo de la Historia de Ponce F** (tel: 787-844 7071; Mon and Wed–Fri 9am–5pm, Sat–Sun 10am–6pm). A fascinating feature outside is a 1,500lb (680kg) marble bathtub, built by Samuel B. Morse, inventor of the telegraph (*see*

Ponce's week-long Carnival in February is the oldest in the country and where the vejigante *masks were first created.*

BELOW: the view across Ponce from El Vigía lookout.

TIP

Free Internet access is widely available thanks to the City of Ponce. This is the latest initiative to bring wireless public-access zones to citizens and visitors. These WiFi zones are: Plaza las Delicias at the heart of the city; La Guancha – Ponce's low-key seaside recreational, cultural, and food zone, and the Julio Enrique Monagas Recreational Park.

BELOW: La Perla del Sur Restaurant on Calle Cristina, Ponce.

page 156). The museum was inaugurated on December 12, 1992 – Ponce's 300th anniversary – and is considered Puerto Rico's best civic museum.

Two hours here and you'll emerge an expert on all aspects of Ponce's history: economic, political, racial, medical, educational, and industrial. This is also the starting point for a walking (or trolley) tour of the historical area.

Close by on the corner of calles Isabel and Salud is the **Museo de la Música Puertorriqueña G** (tel: 787-290 6617; www.icp.gobierno.pr/myp/museos/m15.htm; Tue–Sun 8.30am–4.20pm; charge), where you can see some of the instruments and history of the island's music, which has evolved from African, European, and native traditions, and watch videos of it in action.

Famous homes

On Calle Mayor, at No. 14, **Casa Paoli H** (tel: 787-840 4115; Mon–Fri 10am–noon, 2–5pm) is the home of the renowned tenor Antonio Paoli (1871–1946), heralded as the "King of Tenors" in the early 1900s in competition with Enrico Caruso.

Approximately four blocks westward from the History Museum stands the pink confection of the **Casa Weichers-Villaronga/Museo de Arquitectura de Ponce I** (Tue–Sun 8.30am–4.20pm; free). This beautiful colonial home was built by the architect Alfredo Weichers for himself in 1912 and illustrates life at around that time, when Ponce was enjoying its absolute heyday.

Jewel in the crown

The jewel in the city's crown is the **Museo de Arte de Ponce J** (tel: 787-848 0505; www.museoarteponce.org), farther south in Avenida Las Américas, across from the Catholic University. Mostly dedicated to Western art, with contemporary and classical works, the museum houses more than 3,000 pieces of art, including paintings, sculptures, and works on paper.

Established in 1959 with just 71 paintings, MAP was the brainchild of *ponceño* founder of the pro-statehood New Progressive Party and former governor Luis A. Ferré, who wanted to broaden the understanding of the

arts in Puerto Rico and who, until he died in 2003 at the grand old age of 99, was still one of the island's most vigorous supporters of the arts.

The Italian Baroque School and 19th-century pre-Raphaelite paintings are among its greatest strengths. However, Lord Frederick Leighton's *The Flaming June* (1894) is its most treasured work of art, which has become iconic on the island, inspiring local theater and dance performers.

Designed by world-renown architect Edward Durell Stone, the Museo de Arte de Ponce opened its doors to the public 50 years ago. Temporarily closed for major renovations until early 2010, the museum has moved part of its permanent collection and has a new exhibit space at Plaza Las Américas in Hato Rey (tel: 787-200 7090). Some of its most famous pieces, like *The Flaming June*, are traveling around the world. Check out www. museoarteponce.org for details.

Shopping experiences

Continuing south on the road to Playa de Ponce, shopaholics may wish to experience Ponce's **Plaza del Caribe** **K**, a vast shopping center rivaling San Juan's Plaza Las Américas, where you can purchase anything from a flat-screen TV to a designer gown. The more traditional shopper may prefer the buzz of the finest market in town, in the **Plaza del Mercado** **L**, which spreads across several blocks north of the Plaza las Delicias.

Here, the merchants haggle with the customers over anything that can be worn, ogled or eaten, in an atmosphere as charged with excitement as any world market.

Opposite Plaza las Delicias is the new **Fox Delicias Hotel**, a movie theater from 1931 to 1980 and then a shopping mall in the 1990s.

There are plenty of peaceful perambulations to be made around Plaza las Delicias. **Calle Cristina** and **Calle Mayor** are particularly renowned for the wrought-iron grilles and balcony work which evoke in Ponce, as in San Juan, the spirit of European cities. Even the highly commercialized Calle Duperán has a number of quaint shops and a shady marketplace.

In March every year, the largest artisans' fair on the south coast is held in Ponce. In addition to some wonderful handiwork, this regional craft fair features folklore shows, plentiful Puerto Rican food, and a children's folk-music contest.

LEFT: Puerto Ricans have practiced hammock-weaving for many centuries.
BELOW: Castillo Serrallés.

A Museum City

Ponce is not only filled with museums – the town itself is a museum

While the city center bustles with real people going about their real business, it is also a living museum of unusual architecture that has been well preserved and, these days, celebrated on a national scale.

This town, established in the late 1600s, was first populated by Spanish farmers and ranchers. Spanish policies of encouraging immigration to boost coffee and sugar-cane production in the 1800s brought many adventurers from Spain, particularly Catalonia.

As *ponceños* became more wealthy, they began to visit the countries of Europe, bringing back architectural trends that they applied to their own homes. The result is an almost whimsical blend of neoclassical, Spanish Revival, Creole, and even Moorish styles that change from house to house and block to block.

It is such a wonder that the US National Endowment for the Humanities and Puerto Rican Foundations for the Humanities have designated 45 sites singled out for their architectural beauty and historical importance.

Of course you can just wander around on your own, but with a deposit of $20, you can borrow a guidebook for two days to take you through the historical and architectural importance of the city in English and Spanish. The book is available from the Museo de la Historia de Ponce, the first stop on the museum trail *(see page 205)*.

From there, you can walk or take the free trolleys that leave from Plaza las Delicias. The first stops on the plaza are the Parque de Bombas *(see panel, page 204)* and the Cathedral of Our Lady of Guadalupe.

The neoclassical Museo de la Música Puertorriqueña, which has some magnificent stained-glass panels, is next. You can see Catalan-styled furniture and curious bathroom fixtures at the Residencia Weichers-Villaronga and the precious, Moorish-style "Dog Plaza" (Plaza Ponce de León).

Even the home of the late renowned tenor Antonio Paoli is now a cherished museum. Currently on exhibit are documents and memorabilia that belonged to this well-known singer.

Further away from the center, but no less important to Ponce or to the Caribbean, is the impressive Museo de Arte de Ponce, which has closed for extensive renovations and is set to reopen early in 2010.

Ponce Museums

Casa de la Masacre de Ponce
Calle Aurora, corner of Marina, tel: 787-844 9722

Casa Wiechers-Villaronga (Architecture Museum)
Calle St Isabel, tel: 787-843 3363

Casa Paoli
14 Calle Mayor, tel: 787-840 4115

Museo de la Historia de Ponce
53 Calle St Isabel, corner of Mayor,
tel: 787-844-7071

Museo de la Música Puertorriqueña
Calle St Isabel, corner of Salud,
tel: 787-848 7016

Museo Francisco "Pancho" Coimbre
Calle Lolita Tizol, tel: 787-284 4141 ext. 2508 ❑

LEFT: a bright-red Victorian fire engine takes pride of place in Ponce's Parque de Bombas.

Also well worth a visit is the **Parque Tricentenario**  and the Puente de los Leones, called the Lion Bridge because of its twin lions, at the eastern end of Calle Isabel.

The people and the city

Ponceños have always been a breed apart from other Puerto Ricans. Their insularity is legendary, and some Puerto Ricans claim that even the dialect here differs slightly from that spoken on the rest of the island. They're also racially different: you'll see more people of African descent here than anywhere else on the island save Loíza Aldea, because Ponce's prominence as a port antedates slavery.

As a result, a great deal of African and other regional customs live on in the city. Every February, at the Festival of Our Lady of Guadalupe, *ponceños* parade around the city in colorful and carnivalesque masks made of local gourds. The tradition actually derives from medieval Spain, but it's unquestionable that such a transoceanic transplant required a soil as culturally fertile as Ponce's in which to take root.

A walk on the nice side

There's no better way to take in all the beauty and diversity of this city than to stroll north of Plaza las Delicias for several hundred yards to **El Vigía**. This hilly neighborhood is so beloved of *ponceños* that you'll surely be directed to the place if you show the slightest interest in the city.

From the winding road to the top you can see the mansions of Ponce's great families, the roofs of its 17th- and 18th-century townhouses and the turquoise glint of the Caribbean below, which does more than any questions of demography, government or economics to shape the daily lives of the proud inhabitants.

The most important of these mansions is the magnificent **Castillo Serrallés** (tel: 787-259 1774; www.castillo serralles.org; Tue–Sun 9.30am–5.30pm; charge), located right next to the huge,

100ft (30-meter) high cross-shaped **El Vigía Observation Tower** .

Castillo Serrallés was formerly the home of Don Juan Serrallés, whose family became rich and powerful during the rum- and sugar-boom years of the early 20th century. The castle itself was designed by architect Don Pedro Adolfo de Castro y Besosa in the Spanish Revival style popular throughout the 1930s. The Serrallés family moved in around 1934 and stayed until 1979. In 1986, the City of Ponce bought it from the estate for $500,000 – an unbelievable bargain – and spent the next three years restoring it in painstaking detail.

Among the castle's highlights are a formal dining room with the table set for 12; a vestibule decorated with furniture of the era; an 1865 rum-distilling unit in the central interior patio; and an octagonal fountain with tiles imported from Spain. Even the kitchen is preserved with its original stove and refrigerator made of metal and porcelain. An upstairs terrace offers a spectacular view of Ponce and the Caribbean.

TIP

Island Ventures offers private day trips to Caja de Muertos (by appointment only). For more information, tel: 787-842 8546.

BELOW: El Vigía Observation Tower, or Cruz del Vigía (Virgin's Cross), is a 100ft (30-meter) structure with lateral arms measuring 70ft (21 meters) long.

Just outside Ponce are two other interesting sites. The **Parque Ceremonial Tibes** (Tibes Indian Ceremonial Park) (tel: 787-840 2255; Tue–Sun 9am–4pm; charge) is the first. It is a 10-minute drive north of the city and one of the most important archeological discoveries made in the Antilles. The discovery provides an insight as to how the indigenous tribes of the Igneri and Taínos lived and played during and before the arrival of Christopher Columbus in the New World. An archeological treasure, it features rectangular ball-courts and ceremonial plazas dating from AD 300 to AD 700. Note that you can only visit the site with a guide (free of charge).

The second is **Hacienda Buena Vista** (tel: 787-722 5882; Fri–Sun, by reservation; charge), about 7 miles (11km) north of Ponce on Road 10. This is a restored coffee-and-corn plantation from the late 19th century, complete with working original machinery, that details every step in the coffee-harvesting process. Reservations are required.

Southern isles

It's almost true that it never rains in Ponce, but at times the weather on Puerto Rico's sun-bombarded south coast can get so hot and steamy that you may wish that some of those hanging clouds would make it over the Cordillera Central.

Fortunately, however, the environs of Ponce offer strategies for cooling off as diverse as they are effective. Nautical enthusiasts head their boats into the breezy waters for a trip to the fascinating rock archipelago that is located 8 miles (13km) south. You can charter a boat at the Ponce Yacht and Fishing Club (see page 265) or take a ferry (Island Venture Water Tours; tel: 787-842 8546).

This string of Caribbean islets centers around **Caja de Muertos** (Dead Men's Coffin) . Largest of the islets at 2 miles (3km) long and 1 mile (1.6km) wide, Caja de Muertos is as popular with bird watchers and botanists as it is with sailors.

This being one of Puerto Rico's driest regions, the majority of Caja de Muertos' flora resembles that of the

BELOW: Route 52, the toll road which links Ponce with San Juan.

Guánica Forest Reserve *(see page 213)*. Some of the more prevalent plant species include certain herbs, some dwarf forests of white mangrove, and great quantities of bindweed.

Four of the plant species on Caja de Muertos are extinct on the Puerto Rican mainland and classified as endangered. This is also a haven for endangered reptiles: iguanas and wall-lizards abound, and two species of Culebra lizard live here.

In different cays

Caja de Muertos is only one of the three islets that make up the **Caja de Muertos Nature Reserve**. The others, though far smaller, are no less enticing. **Cayo Morillito** ❾, just a few hundred yards across flat sea, is the smallest, with only a few acres of territory, but is home to more endangered birds than the other two combined. Among these is a variety of gulls, pelicans, and sea eagles.

Cayo Berbería ❿, which is the closest of the cays to the mainland at 3 miles (5km), is blessed with a fauna no less extensive and no less idiosyn-cratic. Most of the fish – many of them endangered species – for which the southern isles are famous, populate the waters around its shores, and consequently some of them put in an appearance on the menus of the south coast's seafood restaurants.

Though the charms of the rippling, brown-green, semi-arid landscapes of Puerto Rico's southwest are well known to those who love the island, few travelers get this far. Its towns are small, but surrounded by natural preserves that Unesco has recognized as World Heritage sites.

Road 2 moves westward out of Ponce and hugs the shore for about 2 miles (3km). It meets the coast of popular **Playa del Tuque** ⓫, which houses a hotel (Quality Inn El Tuque; tel: 787-290 2000), the Speed & Splash water park operating in the summer, and an auto racetrack complex just 3 miles (5km) outside the city.

Continue westward and you will find **Balneario Las Cucharas**, a tiny bathing beach more notable for the excellent seafood restaurants that overlook the bay.

Poster advertising the Carnival Masked Ball in Ponce.

BELOW: lottery tickets for sale.

Some beautiful architectural touches grace the homes of the inhabitants of Yauco.

Guayanilla and Guánica

Another 6 miles (9km) on is the **Guayanilla** ⑫ exit. This pretty town was founded in 1833, but its history goes back to one of the Taínos' most important *caciques*, Agüeybaná. A mile away, at the mouth of the Río Guayanilla, is the desolate and hushed fishing port at **Playa de Guayanilla** ⑬. And this is where the fun starts. With hundreds of species of wild birds and small creatures, mangrove forest, and a beautiful bay formed by Punta Gotay and Punta Verraco, you can spend hours here just enjoying the natural beauty of the region.

The town of Yauco

The attractive town of **Yauco** ⑭ lies 3 miles (5km) west of Guayanilla on roads 2 and 127. The latter is probably the more pleasant drive, except when it rains, which on this arid coast is about once every millennium.

Anyone with even the most cursory experience of driving in the southwest region knows that those little oily bushes huddled on the brown hillsides are coffee trees, but few know the pre-eminence that the Yauco area holds as a coffee capital.

By the late 19th century, Puerto Rico had developed the most advanced coffee industry in the world. In the coffee houses of late-colonial Europe – in Vienna, London, Paris, and Madrid – Puerto Rican coffee was considered the very best that one could drink. "Yauco" was that coffee's name.

Whatever can be said about its other effects, the 20th-century presence of Americans on the island removed Yauco from this position of pre-eminence, as emphasis on manufacturing and cane production sapped the industry's resources. Fortunately, vestiges of that halcyon era remain – the stately homes of Yauco's coffee barons.

Owing to the variety of sub-climates in the southwest, coffee was a mobile industry, and its gentry and their residences were no less itinerant than their crops. As a result, Yauco shares with San Germán and Mayagüez an architecture that is distinctively Puerto Rican and among the best Spanish-influenced work of its day.

Some of these old residences are open to the public; for information on the southwestern style and how to see it, the best source is the **Colegio de Arquitectos**, located in the Casa Rosa in Old San Juan (*see page 118*).

Even more fortunate is the fact that Yauco has regained some of its old prominence as a coffee producer and exporter. One of Puerto Rico's most successful brands, Yauco Selecto, is now sold in Japanese gourmet coffee shops for over $20 a pound.

Warships by woodlands

On to **Guánica** ⑮, 5½ miles (9km) past Yauco on Road 116. About the same size as Guayanilla, but with an understandably more oceanic ambience, Guánica might be worth visiting even without the historical significance which draws so many travelers and historians. In the midsummer of 1898, at the height of the Spanish-American War, General Nelson Miles, having had

BELOW: the main square in Yauco.

no success in a month-long attempt to break the Spanish defenses around San Juan, landed in Guánica with some troops before traveling on to Ponce. He had come, he said, "to bring you protection, not only to yourselves but to your property, to promote your prosperity, and to bestow upon you the immunities and blessings of the liberal institutions of our government."

Out of this promise came American Puerto Rico, and the degree to which the promise has been kept or breached has defined almost all political arguments on the island for the past century. The commemorative stone placed at the edge of Guánica harbor by the local chapter of the Daughters of the American Revolution is encased in a wrought-iron cage guarded by lock and key – presumably to protect the marker against political vandalism.

The birds of Guánica

Guánica is the ornithological capital of Puerto Rico. Covering 1,570 acres (635 hectares) of subtropical dry forest, the **Guánica Forest Reserve** ⓰ is home to half of Puerto Rico's bird species. Most treasured among these is the highly endangered Puerto Rican whippoorwill (found here in the 1950s, some 80 years after it was thought to be extinct).

This low-lying area also has 48 endangered plant species, 16 of which are endemic to the forest. Well-kept hiking trails and a pleasant beach make the reserve a good respite in a hectic sightseeing schedule. Unesco has designated the area a World Biosphere Reserve, and it is also part of the US National Forest network.

Some of the best bathing, snorkeling, and diving can be found here. **Caña Gorda** is the public beach which acts as a springboard for the popular **Cayos de Caña Gorda** – a string of mangrove cays dotting a large and shallow bay protected by an extensive reef – and Ballena Beach at the easternmost point of the cays. Small launches leave from a tiny dock on the beach several times a day, costing about $4, or you can rent a kayak and paddle your own way there. The bay area gets extremely crowded and noisy at weekends, so try to visit there during the week. ❏

Among the flora found in the Guánica Forest Reserve is the knotted guayacan tree, or lignum vitae *– a wood so hard it was once used to replace metal propeller shafts and ball-bearings.*

LEFT: subtropical Guánica Forest Reserve.
BELOW: pastel-colored houses vie for space on this Yauco hillside.

CORDILLERA CENTRAL

This remote heart of the island features characterful villages, forest-covered mountains, and some spectacular scenic views

San Juan

The Cordillera Central or "central spine" towers over the middle of the island, its peaks and valleys stretching 60 miles (96km) from east to west. It is a region of superlatives and extremes – the highest, the deepest, the roughest, the coldest. And also the remotest: most visitors to the island choose to ignore its allure, staying on the beaches or in San Juan.

This is perhaps due to lack of publicity. It is true that the charm of the Cordillera has little to do with the shops of Old San Juan or the sun-drenched beachfronts of Dorado and Humacao. Rather, it offers cool mountain lakes and streams, isolated green spots, and remote country inns. The temperature in the mountains drops one degree for every 500ft (150-meter) increase in elevation. This means that when San Juan is broiling, you just might need a sweater on Cerro de Punta. The contrast between Puerto Rico's urban industrial character and its countryside is both delightful and thought-provoking.

The best way to see the Cordillera is by car. Allow at least two full days, and find a good road map of the island. Getting around in the mountains is half the fun.

Two-lane blacktop is the rule for mountain roads; some two-lane roads are major ones, others minor, and others again turn into dirt tracks halfway up deserted hillsides. Be prepared for some arduous driving on hairpin and switchback curves. The roads connecting most mountain towns run from plaza to plaza, making navigation easy. Here, you are never more than a few minutes away from the next *colmado* – a roadside store selling cold drinks, essential groceries, and perhaps a sandwich or two.

Land of mountain peasants

The Cordillera was the last retreat of the once-ubiquitous *jíbaro*, the hardy Puerto Rican mountain peasant, whose exploits had been the stuff of legend

Main attractions

CAGUAS
CIDRA
CAYEY
AIBONITO
SAN CRISTÓBAL CANYON
VILLALBA
JAYUYA
GUILARTE FOREST RESERVE

PRECEDING PAGES: flower nursery in Aibonito. **LEFT:** Toro Negro Forest. **BELOW:** the aptly named Aibonito.

The pink-hued Centro de Bellas Artes in Caguas was inaugurated in 1993.

and literature from the chronicles of the early settlers to the stories of Emilio Belaval. The virtually extinct *jíbaros* were to Puerto Rican consciousness what cowboys are to the Americans, or bushrangers to the Australians. The *jíbaro*, frequently the butt of jokes by more sophisticated city slickers, was nevertheless shaped by an exacting landscape and possessed of pride, resourcefulness, and a wry pessimism.

Along Highway 52, just after the Cayey turn-off on the way to Ponce, stands the Monumento al Jíbaro Puertorriqueño – a huge white statue dedicated to these machete-swinging philosophers who today live on in songs, paintings, and the memories of their descendants.

Eastern Cordillera

Two roads connect San Juan with **Caguas ❶**, 20 miles (32km) to the south: Route 52, the fast modern tollway that runs all the way to Ponce, and the older and slower Route 1, with no toll collectors. Caguas, whose 133,000 people make it the largest city in the island's interior, lies in the broad and fertile **Turabo Valley**. Three different mountain ranges form the valley's walls, accounting for its

unusual expanse. To the north and east rises the **Sierra de Luquillo**, which runs almost to the coast. To the south, the **Sierra de Cayey** climbs rapidly, blotting out the horizon. And to the west, the Cordillera Central stretches up and across the island.

Caguas is named after the Taíno *cacique* Caguax, who ruled the people of the Turabo Valley area at the time of the Spanish Conquest. Caguax was one of the two *caciques* who made peace during the Indian uprisings of 1511. The Indians, fearing reprisal after drowning a Spanish boy, revolted. Several *caciques* led guerrilla bands on raids in the following weeks, but Ponce de León, with the help of peaceful *caciques*, soon restored order. A large allegorical painting, depicting Caguax's conversion to Christianity, exists.

In many ways Caguas is typical of a moderate-sized Latin American city. **Plaza Palmer**, one of the most appealing plazas in Puerto Rico, is the center of civic and spiritual life. Almost as large as the one at Ponce, it is dominated by two ancient rubber trees with benches built into their huge trunks. Pigeons inhabit the plaza, some in an aviary and others flocking freely. In the middle, a solemn statue of the 19th-

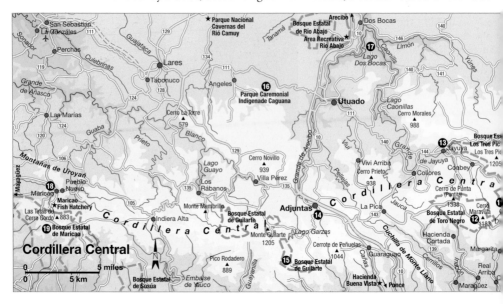

century poet José Gautier Benítez, Caguas's most famous son, stands on a pedestal. Goldfish sun themselves in a mossy pond, and, on weekends, musicians bring salsa rhythms to a small bandstand. There is also the Daliesque **Reloj Florido**, a giant clock face planted with flowers.

The imposing cathedral of the **Dulce Nombre de Jesús** (Sweet Name of Jesus) faces one side of the plaza, directly across from the **Alcaldía**, which boasts an 1856 facade. The church has been rebuilt and enlarged several times as hurricanes destroyed the original building. The first Puerto Rican to be beatified, namely Charlie Rodríguez, is buried here.

On any afternoon the plaza attracts a good number of people: couples sit quietly holding hands; old men move from bench to bench, following the shade; and kids plan mayhem while their mothers shop. Every city or town in Puerto Rico has its plaza, but few as lively or picturesque as this.

A walk down Calle Ruiz Belviz reveals a tiny 19th-century **Baptist church**. Farther along, on a side street, the historic **Piedra de Polanco** can be found. This large rock was once used to mount and dismount from horses. Today it is part of a jewelry store. You can also look into the small tobacco museum, **Museo del Tabaco Herminio Torres Grillo** (tel: 787-744 2960 ext. 2908 or 2959; Wed–Sun 9am–4pm) on Calle Betances, the corner of Luis Padial.

Botanical Gardens

The **Jardín Botánico y Cultural de Caguas** (tel: 787-653 8990; http://portalesp.caguas.gov.pr/jardin_botanico/index.html; Thur–Sun 10am–4pm) opened its doors to the public in 2007. The 58-acre (23-hectare) gardens in the Cañabón region cover what was once Hacienda San José, a vital agricultural center and sugar plantation of the 19th and early 20th centuries, and grounds inhabited by pre-Columbian Taínos.

As a means to educate the public, the gardens illustrate Puerto Rican culture and its relationship with Mother Nature. Among the attractions are the Taíno arboretum – with over 50 species of indigenous trees, an artistic re-creation of a Taíno ceremonial *batey*, and authentic Taíno petroglyphs lining the river.

The African arboretum houses a 14ft (4-meter) bronze statue of Osaín, the Yoruba nature god, by Puerto

Economic activity in Caguas includes diamond-cutting, tobacco processing, and manufacturing. Caguas is also the island headquarters for US retail giant Wal-Mart and Sam's Club, which is Puerto Rico's largest private employer.

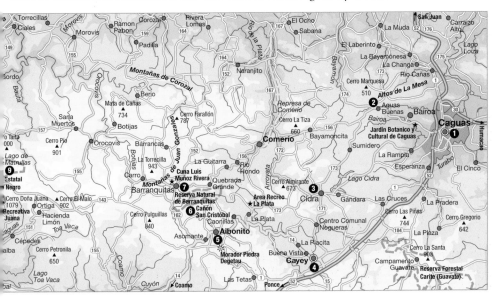

Rican artist Samuel Lind, 40 species of trees, and plants from different regions of Africa.

Visitors are invited to reflect on the importance of conserving and protecting at the endangered species grove. The gardens also feature a butterfly house, a flowering tree arboretum, and a *manigua* (Taíno word for marsh), used as an education and research center and home for various species of birds. One trail over a bridge leads to a typical 19th-century farmhouse with a working vegetable-and-herb garden.

The facilities include a greenhouse, a cafeteria, an artisans' shop, an amphitheater, and a lakeside recreational spot. Tours of the ruins and the gardens are available in English or Spanish.

The southern tip of **Lago Loíza** may be reached by taking Route 796 northeast out of town. The road skirts the lake's banks, with several likely picnic or fishing spots, before circling back to join Route 1 north of Caguas.

Rising mountains

The 6 miles (10km) between Caguas and **Aguas Buenas** ❷ to the west

mark a profound change in the landscape. Route 156 begins to climb as soon as it leaves the city behind. Aguas Buenas is perched on a hill that is part of the far northeastern extension of the Cordillera Central.

Mountain palms and bamboo start to line the roadside. The lush green miniature valleys glimpsed through the breaks in these trees are a rugged preview of the contours of the Cordillera, and the hills and curves of Route 156 serve as a beginner's course in Cordillera driving.

Is it the change in temperature? The sweet, cool air? The first sight of a little boy leading a skinny black-and-white island cow? Whatever it is, the city seems much farther than a few miles away, and the intangible yet universal mountain mindset of isolation and wonder begins to take hold.

Aguas Buenas is dashed across the hillside as if with one hurried stroke of a paintbrush. A modern church and a school struggle for space on the small plaza, which often fills with children.

The town was once known for the nearby **Aguas Buenas Caves**. The

SHOP

Look for the roadside fruit stands along Route 172 between Caguas and Cidra, where you can pick up some delicious local fruits and vegetables (some varieties of which are never seen in San Juan), or a bunch of fresh flowers for your hotel room.

BELOW: food kiosk in Caguas.

Department of Natural Resources used to run tours at weekends, but the caves have been closed for some time. It is, however, possible to enter them off Route 794, but only experienced spelunkers should attempt serious exploration. The road, at any rate, has some interesting views as it leads down out of the town and then up to rougher country.

Dammed Cidra

Nine miles (14km) southwest of Aguas Buenas is **Cidra ❸**, which can also be reached from Caguas on Route 172. This road offers excellent panoramic views of the entire **Turabo Valley**, including Caguas. With more than 30,000 residents, Cidra is a larger town than it seems. There is always a line of young people waiting to play video games at Café la Estrella, one block off the plaza.

In Cidra, in three closely guarded factories that stand only a few miles apart from one another, Coca-Cola Inc. and Pepsico Inc. produce the top-secret flavoring concentrates that are eventually shipped out to Coke, Pepsi, and Seven-Up bottling plants all around the world.

Lago Cidra, 5 miles (8km) long, supplies water to San Juan, Cataño, and other cities. The lake, an artificial one, was dammed in the 1940s. While there is no boating, residents claim that the fishing is well worth a try. The houses around the lakeshore, with their serene views, give quiet testimony to the gracious lifestyle of their lucky inhabitants. A restaurant on the shore with outdoor tables shares the view.

An interesting local legend of buried treasure dates from the early 20th century. One night during an epidemic of smallpox, a wealthy peasant fearful of losing his fortune rode his horse into the forest and buried a quantity of gold. Upon returning home the man fell sick and soon died without disclosing the location of his treasure. To this day the old peasant appears as a skeleton atop a black horse, unable to rest because his sons inherited nothing.

Between Cidra and Las Cruces on Route 787, **Rancho Pepón** provides a pleasant family *pasadía* (picnic ground). Rancho Pepón looks like the country

The Sierra de Cayey is home to the 6,000-acre (2,400-hectare) Carite (Guavate) Forest Reserve, which harbors some 50 species of bird, plus waterfalls and a small pool with water of an incredible blue color.

BELOW: mountains in the mist.

Puerto Ricans are fiercely proud of their multi-faceted island.

ranch that it is. Its facilities include a large covered patio, a swimming pool, and a restaurant that is open on weekends. The Caraballo family runs the facility, which can accommodate groups of up to 300.

Cayey

Whether you follow either the tollway or the lesser Route 1 south of Caguas, the next major town is **Cayey ❹**, 12 miles (19km) away. The first view of Cayey is of a modern strip-cum-shopping center at the highway exit. Founded in 1773, Cayey is a city of nearly 50,000 people, with a university and bustling industry. The city sits on the northern slope of the Sierra de Cayey; from the *autopista* you can see the huge AT&T earth stations that carry most of Puerto Rico's long-distance telephone calls.

Southeastern Puerto Rico is a tobacco-growing region, and Consolidated Cigars has a large plant in Cayey. Here popular brands like Muriel and Dutch Masters are manufactured.

Cayey's **plaza** features a large church, built in 1813, with an extremely long

BELOW: going for a stroll in Cayey.

nave, a single square tower, and a dome overlooking the transept. The museum at the university displays works by major Puerto Rican artists.

South of the *autopista* in the town of Guavate on Route 184, open-air restaurants prepare roast suckling pig to the sounds of live music at weekends.

Road with a view

The Ruta Panorámica avoids Cayey, passing several miles to the south, but that doesn't mean the city's vistas are second-rate. It does mean, though, that Cayey is a good place to pick up the Ruta Panorámica from San Juan, little more than 30 minutes' drive from Condado. Route 1 becomes the Panorámica about 2 miles (3km) past the town. Care should be taken, for the Panorámica shifts to Route 772 after another 3 miles (5km).

The Ruta Panorámica, as its name suggests, is rich with vistas. Remember, though: Cordillera driving is no picnic. Don't forget the essential map for winding road navigation, and pack some motion-sickness pills – you never know.

Valley jewel

Set in a narrow valley, **Aibonito** ❺ is a pretty jewel of a place. The Ruta Panoramica narrowly misses the town, which can be reached from Cayey via Route 14, a road rivaling the Panorámica both for valley viewing and for its great number of curves. Aibonito, at 2,400ft (730 meters), has the highest altitude of any town in Puerto Rico, and the lowest average temperature. In 1911, the recorded temperature reached 40°F (8°C).

One story of how Aibonito was named features a wandering half-starved 17th-century bandit who stumbled on the valley and then exclaimed *"Ai, que bonito!"* (How pretty!) Another – possibly more plausible – explanation is that it is derived from the Indian name for the town, *Jatibonuco*, which means "river of the night." In 1887 Aibonito was the provisional capital of the island for seven months. In that year, known as *El Año Terrible*, an independence movement was bloodily suppressed by a military governor, the hated General Palacios González.

Aibonito is famous for its flower and nursery industry. **The Flower Festival**, which takes place in late June and early July, is one of the most popular events on the island. To appreciate fully the view from the town, visit the **Mirador Piedra Degetau** observation tower on Route 7718. On a clear day you can even see San Juan. Restaurant La Piedra offers homegrown organic vegetables and delicious Creole food.

A slit in the hills

Near Aibonito is the **Cañón San Cristóbal** ❻, the deepest gorge on the island. Formed by the Río Usabon, this canyon, with walls up to 700ft (210 meters) high, is so deep and narrow that from the air it looks like a slit in the hills. From the ground, the only way to see it is to stand on the very rim. The view is indeed impressive.

To approach the canyon, follow Route 725 to the north. In this area, businesses tend to call themselves El Cañón – Tienda el Cañón, Ferrenta el Cañón, and so on. One of the most *simpático* of these establishments is the **Bar el Cañón**, at Km 4 on Route 725. Among its attributes

LEFT: the annual Aibonito Flower Festival is a popular summer event in this area.

A Man Who Made a Difference

Luis Muñoz Rivera, one of the most famous men in the political history of Puerto Rico, devoted his life to the struggle for his country's autonomy. Born in Barranquitas on July 17, 1859, he attended a local private school and later worked in his father's store. Muñoz Rivera was one of the founders of the Autonomist Party and its newspaper "voice," *La Democracia*. In 1897, he was appointed Secretary of State and Chief of the Cabinet of the newly independent Government of Puerto Rico. After the Americans arrived on the scene in 1898, he again turned to journalism, founding the newspaper *El Territorio* and later, while living in New York, the *Puerto Rican Herald*.

After returning to Puerto Rico in 1904, Muñoz Rivera became one of the founders of the Unionist Party and served in the House of Delegates until 1910, when he was elected Resident Commissioner to the US House of Representatives. Here, he pushed to amend the Foraker Act. His work led to the passing of the Jones Act, which, among other things, gave Puerto Rico more autonomy and granted United States citizenship to Puerto Ricans. He did not live to see the bill signed into law by President Wilson in 1917; Muñoz Rivera returned to Puerto Rico in September 1916, ill with cancer, and died on November 15 of that year.

TIP

If you're interested in Puerto Rican political history, you may want to visit the small museum in the Barranquitas house where Luis Muñoz Rivera was born.

are a jukebox and canned beer at country prices. The canyon can be reached from here, but it is a rough hike, so it's better to go on to Km 5.5, where a narrow unmarked side road comes a little closer to the edge. From there it is a short hike down to the canyon and a 100ft (30-meter) waterfall. For guided tours of the area in English, call Restaurant La Piedra (tel: 787-735 1034).

Hills and heroes

Four miles (6km) north as the crow flies, but double that by car, the town of **Barranquitas** ❼ overlooks the other side of San Cristóbal Canyon. The best place to view the canyon is on Route 156 east of the town. At Km 17.7 the Lions Club has a view which gives the traveler a much better perspective.

Barranquitas is known as the birthplace of Luis Muñoz Rivera, the autonomy-minded statesman (see panel, page 223). Muñoz Rivera and his son Luis Muñoz Marín, governor of the island from 1948 to 1964, are both buried near the plaza in a small complex that includes a museum full of Muñoz Rivera memorabilia.

In Spanish, *una barranca* means a cliff or gorge, but it can also mean great difficulty or an impassable obstacle. This "Birthplace of Patriots" has a beautiful church in the plaza with an impressive wooden ceiling and glowing stained glass all around. The only collection of Greco-Roman art in the Caribbean can be found at the Museo de Arte y Antropología.

Another attraction in Barranquitas is the annual Artisans' Fair in July, when some 130 Puerto Rican artisans sell their work at reasonable prices – the perfect time to buy a painting, a flute, or jewelry made from local stones. Traditional music and food are also a major part of the fair, which began in 1964.

There is a more direct route from San Juan to Aibonito and Barranquitas, a pleasant drive through hilly country. Take Route 2 from San Juan to Bayamón, and from there take Route 167 south until it intersects Route 156, which goes to Barranquitas. This route looks less taxing on the odometer; in reality, it involves nearly 30 miles (48km) of demanding two-

BELOW: big trucks are a common sight in this part of the island.

lane roads. If you plan any mountain driving beyond Aibonito or Barranquitas, it is probably better to take the *autopista* to Cayey.

Route 167, though, is worth a trip in itself, especially on a Sunday afternoon. Immediately south of Bayamón, the road begins playing a game of peek-a-boo with the **Río de la Plata**, named after the mighty South American river, and its subsidiary streams. The streams jump back and forth across the road until at last, near **El Ocho**, a panorama of the broad river unfolds.

Look out for the green-and-white colors of the PIP (Puerto Rican Independence Party) splashed on walls, houses, and trees with great regularity from just outside Bayamón. Whether this attests to a rural base of support for the *independentistas* is a matter of conjecture; perhaps graffiti is more noticeable in the country.

Route 167 passes through or near settlements with rustic names: Pájaro Puertorriqueño, Sabana, Naranjito (Puerto Rican Bird, Savannah, Little Orange). On Sunday afternoons in nearly every one of these little towns,

musicians will be tuning up in bandstands and *colmados*. They will start to play as the sun's rays stretch out, singing to audiences of 20, 30, or 50. If there are no musicians around, a group of men in a bar will begin to sing and keep singing until long after sunset. Thus the country people – and the city visitors – squeeze every moment out of the weekend.

Toro Negro

In the southwest of the Cordillera, the town of **Villalba** ❽ is surrounded by some of the most incredible scenery on the island, including Puerto Rico's highest peak. From Coamo, Route 150 reaches Villalba in 14 tortuous mountain miles (22km).

Villalba itself is not as interesting as the nearby peaks and forest reserves, although it was the first town on the island to get electricity and telephones. North of town, Route 149 begins to climb in earnest. And you thought you were in the mountains! A stop at the *colmado* **La Collaloma**, within sight of the intersection with Route 514, feels like a reward for

The superb Art Deco bandstand stands on Plaza Bicentenaria Monseñor Miguel A. Mendoza in Barranquitas.

BELOW: welcome to Toro Negro Forest.

BELOW: snapshot along Route 149.
RIGHT: practicing the Puerto Rican art of relaxation.

leaving civilization behind. Here you can catch your breath sipping a relaxing *bebida* (drink) and sitting on a handmade bamboo bench. From this vantage point, Villalba and **Lago Toa Vaca** spread out far below, and in the distance the blue Caribbean waters shimmer in the sunlight. High above, terraced gardens line the slopes, and farther up still, the peaks disappear into the mist.

Route 149 continues to climb until it intersects Route 143 inside the **Toro Negro Forest Reserve** ❾. Route 143 is an east–west road that follows the backbone of the Cordillera Central from Adjuntas to a point near Barranquitas. This 30-mile (48km) section of road is the longest continuous stretch of the Ruta Panorámica; views along this section pan north and south to both coastlines.

To the east of the intersection is the **Doña Juana Recreational Area** ❿, a *pasadía* viewpoint that features a large freshwater swimming pool and several trails through dense forests of large mountain palms. There is a campground, and a ranger station. A

trail leads from the pool to a deserted lookout tower about 2 miles (3km) away; the first quarter of the trail is paved with uneven, mossy stones, and moss turns very slippery with the smallest amount of water, so make sure you take care on wet days. The **Doña Juana Falls**, a 200ft (60-meter) waterfall, is nearby.

Climbing the peaks

West of the intersection, the road climbs into the silent peaks. **Lago Guineo** ⓫ (Banana Lake), the highest lake on the entire island, hides at the end of a gravel road marked only by a wooden sign reading *Prohibido Tirar Basura* (Do not Drop Litter).

A dam across the Toro Negro River keeps the lake full. It's difficult to find, walled about by steep red clay banks choked with bamboo. Only the high-pitched chatter of the *coquí* disturbs the perfect isolation of this little round lake. The clay banks demand caution; clay is another surface that gets very slippery when wet.

Farther west (and higher up), the road passes **Cerro Maravilla** ⓬, a lofty

peak that bristles with antennae and relay towers. This mountain, at 3,970ft (1,183 meters) one of the island's highest, occupies a tragic place in 20th-century history: on July 25, 1978, two young independence supporters planning to blow up the WRIK-TV transmitter atop the mountain were killed by policemen who had been tipped off. The deaths triggered an investigation and an ongoing political controversy.

Oddly, no sign directs visitors to the spot where it all happened, and the gravel road leading to Cerro Maravilla – Route 577 – doesn't appear on the official highway map. If you make a left turn at 577 and ascend the hill for half a mile, however, you'll see two stone crosses marking the graves of the two revolutionaries murdered there – Arnaldo Darío Rosado and Carlos Soto Arriví.

The men's graves are surrounded by flowers and Puerto Rican flags. Don't be surprised to find several people at the site. Since the events of 1978, it has become a shrine for those who support the cause of Puerto Rican independence.

The highest point

Across the road from the peak, a grassy picnic area overlooks the entire south coast. A gravel parking lot on the north side of the road at Km 16.5 marks the base of **Cerro de Punta**, at 4,390ft (1,338 meters) the island's highest peak. The summit can be reached on foot or by car up a treacherously steep paved road considerably less than one lane wide.

On top, the solitude is shared by more antennae and a shed. On a clear day you can see for 50 or 60 miles (80 to 100km). The view includes San Juan, unless of course a stray cloud happens to get in the way. To be on Cerro de Punta when the mists roll in is a powerful experience.

A few miles directly north of the mountain, **Jayuya** ⑬ nestles in its valley; unfortunately for the driver, no road connects the two points. Take Route 144 to the town from either the east or the west.

The hidden treasure of Jayuya, a Taíno stronghold, is *La Piedra Escrita* (The Written Rock). A large boulder that forms a natural pool in Río

Even the smallest buildings in the Cordillera – like this barber shop – are splashed with color.

BELOW:
Lago Toa Vaca.

TIP

A good time to visit Jayuya is in November during the Jayuya Indian Festival, which focuses on the Taínos' culture and traditions, including their music, food, and games.

Saliente, it features petroglyphs from prehistoric inhabitants and is located off Route 144 at Km 2.3.

In Jayuya, a short stay in the stately **Hacienda Gripiñas**, a *parador* situated on an old coffee plantation, might be tempting. A wide porch on the restored 200-year-old house overlooks a cool valley. As the sun sets so many *coquí* begin singing that their performance is even featured in the hotel brochure. A trail connects the *parador* with Cerro de Punta just a short distance away.

The Western Cordillera

West of Toro Negro, the mountains start to change character once again. The stately peaks give way to rougher, lusher country. The valleys are smaller, shallower, and more numerous. The tall mountain palms yield to bamboo, ferns, and hardwood trees like teak. Flowering bushes intermittently line the roadsides.

The town of **Adjuntas** ⑭ marks this area of transition. It is a rugged town filled with no-nonsense hardware stores and lumberyards; local produce includes coffee, bananas, oranges, and other fruits. Adjuntas also has the **Monte Río Hotel**, a clean establishment near the plaza. New attractions include the **Mariposario** (Butterfly Garden), and there's now easier access via Route 10 from Ponce.

Guilarte – land of the *jíbaros*

The **Guilarte Forest Reserve** ⑮ west of Adjuntas is another good place to get back to nature. A hillside *pasadía* is set near a eucalyptus grove whose fragrant, blade-shaped leaves litter the ground. A few hundred feet up the road, a well-marked trail leads to the top of 3,900ft (1,205-meter) **Monte Guilarte**. Watch out for any slippery clay on the trail.

Between Adjuntas and Monte Guilarte are many small farms, tended by the last of the *jíbaros* (mountain smallholders). This area is one of the few places on the island with such a concentrated population of these legendary people. The Ruta Panorámica passes right through their farmland, and they enjoy the opportunity to

BELOW: coffee at Hacienda Buena Vista, a restored plantation south of Adjuntas.

talk to travelers in a Spanish that is nasal, twangy, and high-pitched.

North of Adjuntas toward **Utuado**, the Cordillera begins its descent to the coastal plain. But that does not mean the land gets flat. The haystack karstic hills north of Utuado march all the way to the Atlantic.

Land of the Indians

West of Utuado on Route 111, the **Parque Ceremonial Indigenade Caguana** 🔟 (tel: 787-894 7325; www. icp.gobierno.pr/myp/museos/m19.htm; daily 8.30am–4.20pm; free) should not be missed. Built by the Taínos nearly a millennium ago, the ballpark includes 10 *bateyes* (ball courts) on which the early Indians played a lacrosse- or *pelota*-like game in a blend of sport and religious ceremony.

Overlooking the courts, a small rocky peak has been guarding the park for centuries, and looks as though it will continue to do so for centuries to come. Strange sounds echo back and forth over the landscaped grounds. An owl hoots. A dry leaf rasps across one of the *bateyes*. The Taíno gods Yukiyu and Juracán continue to make their presence felt here.

North of Utuado on Route 10, **Lago Dos Bocas** 🔟 (Two-Mouthed Lake) curves into a U-shape around steep hills. At Km 68, Route 10 skirts the lake-shore. From there, a launch service carries passengers back and forth across the lake at the weekends, while restaurants situated by the lake also pick up passengers in their private boats to take them across for lunch.

Land of the baby fish

On the far western edge of the Cordillera, not far from Mayagüez, is **Maricao** 🔟, one of the smallest *municipios* in Puerto Rico. Route 120 approaches the town from the south through the **Maricao Forest Reserve** 🔟, or you can take Route 105 out of downtown Mayagüez. By the roadside in the middle of the forest is a castle-like stone tower, four stories tall,

which overlooks the entire western half of the island from 2,600ft (800 meters). There is also a campground.

Maricao's tiny plaza features a rustic cream-and-brick-colored church. Just outside the town is the **Maricao Fish Hatchery**, where many species of freshwater fish are hatched and raised, then dumped in 26 lakes around the island to replenish their indigenous stocks. On the road to the fish hatchery is a mountainside shrine, a haven of serenity and dignity.

The **Hacienda Juanita** in Maricao is yet another coffee plantation converted into a *parador*, surrounded by groves of oranges, bananas, and avocados. Guests are invited to pick their own breakfasts. For the lazy ones, bowls of fragrant fruits are always within reach, and bunches of bananas hang from 150-year-old beams.

Some of these beams are hewn from the precious *ausubo*, a type of ironwood native to Puerto Rico. This wood, prized for its resistance to rot and termites, was once plentiful, but today it is among the rarest of the world's hardwoods. ❑

The Los Chorros restaurant at Lago Dos Bocas takes its name from a nearby cave, which can be reached on foot.

BELOW: one of the Cordillera's many lovely *paradores*, the Hacienda Juanita in Maricao.

BIO BAY
TOURS
SNORKEL
TOURS
KAYAK
RENTALS
SNORKEL
GEAR
RENTALS
GIFT SHOP

OUTER ISLANDS

**Off the east coast of Puerto Rico, Culebra and
Vieques beckon with their pristine beaches and
wild horses, while untouched Mona, far off the
west coast, has unique charms of its own**

S ix miles (10km) off the east coast
of Puerto Rico lies **Vieques**, with
twice the acreage of Manhattan
and twice the charm of some islands
many times its size. Like Culebra,
Vieques belongs geologically to the Virgin Islands, but this is not all that separates it from mainland Puerto Rico.
The island has grown in popularity
among expatriates, although traditional
ways live on. Islanders still refer to
crossing the sound as "going to Puerto
Rico," and the more formal *usted* form
of second-person address, which is
extinct on the mainland, is still heard in
everyday conversation here.

Vieques's varied terrain

Much of Vieques looks like Califor-
nian cattle country: dry, rolling hills,
scattered lazy herds and flocks of
white egrets. But the island also enjoys
scores of beaches, a small rainforest,
exotic wild flowers, and a healthy
population of tree frogs, mongoose
and horses. A hundred or so beautiful
paso fino (fine-gaited) horses,
descended from 16th-century Spanish
steeds, roam wild over the island.

The Taíno Indians who first settled
the island called it *Bieques*, or "small
island"; Columbus named it *Graciosa*
(gracious). English pirates called it
"Crab Island" for the still-common
land crabs they depended on for a
tasty dinner. And the Spanish (who
built the lighthouse and an unfin-
ished fort) called Vieques and Cule-

bra *las islas inútiles* – the "useless
islands" – because neither had gold.
The island took a direct hit in September 1989, when Hurricane Hugo
passed directly overhead, its 200mph
(320kph) winds destroying many
houses and businesses before moving
on to "mainland" Puerto Rico.

For years, the island was beset by protesters demanding the exit of the US
Navy, which had a base on the island for
more than 50 years. They moved out in
2003, and since then property values in
Vieques have more than doubled as the

Main attractions
VIEQUES
  ISABEL SEGUNDA
  ESPERANZA
  SUN BAY
CULEBRA
  DEWEY
  FLAMENCO BEACH
ISLA MONA

PRECEDING PAGES:
Punta Mulas
lighthouse, Vieques.
LEFT: trips for sale.
BELOW: slice of life
in Isabel Segunda.

Exotic Caribbean flora on the island of Vieques.

affluent clamor for a piece of what may be the last affordable, unspoiled paradise in the Caribbean.

Tucked into various spots on the island are some first-rate inns and hotels, such as the eco-friendly Hix Island House, built on 13 acres (5.25 hectares) mid-island, and the Inn on the Blue Horizon perched on a bluff overlooking the Caribbean Sea.

Isabel Segunda

Vieques is accessible by air from San Juan or by sea from Fajardo (a twice-a-day, 18-mile/29km journey). Unless you have a tight timetable, the latter is the preferable route, offering an exhilarating excursion through brisk, choppy waters; a distant view of stormy El Yunque; and – with luck – a full double rainbow stretching for miles across blue waters. During high season (Dec–Apr) you can also reach Vieques and Culebra via the **Island Hi-Speed Ferry** (tel: 877-899 3993; www.islandhispeedferry.com; Thur–Sun), which leaves from Pier 2, the public ferry dock in Old San Juan in the morning. The 40mph (65kmph) cata-

maran skims the coastline from San Juan to Fajardo, providing great views, although the sea can be rough coming out of San Juan Bay. The return trip to San Juan is usually smoother.

Near the ferry landing, **Isabel Segunda ①**, Vieques's only town, has the staples of any modest Puerto Rican municipality. Many of the island's 9,000 residents live here or nearby. Some work in factories, but unemployment remains relatively high. Agriculture, which has been in decline for many years, may yet become an important source of income. In spite of its problems the town is dotted with trendy restaurants, upscale bakeries, and real-estate offices, and the sound of construction is in the air as mansions and small developments are built.

The town has the distinction of having the last fort built by the Spaniards in the New World, **El Fortín Conde de Mirasol**. Although it was never completed, what was there has been well restored and has an excellent historical museum (tel: 787-741 1717; Wed–Sun 10am–4pm, other days by appointment; free). There's also an

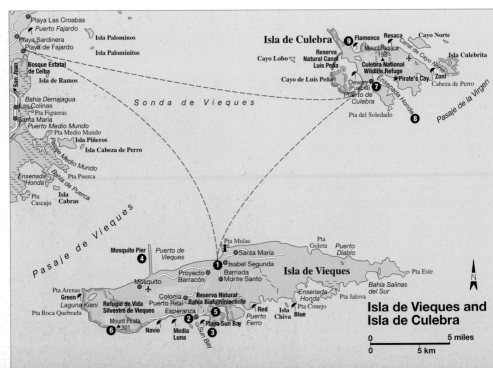

Isla de Vieques and Isla de Culebra

0   5 miles
0   5 km

interesting exhibit (and great views) at the **Punta Mulas Lighthouse** (tel: 787-741 0060; daily 8am–4.30pm; free) to the north of town.

The place to be

A 10-minute drive across the 25- by 4-mile (40 by 6km) island is **Esperanza** ❷, a small fishing village consisting of little more than a strip of guesthouses and restaurants overlooking the water. Do not be fooled: this is *the* place to eat well, sleep well, sunbathe, and explore. A lovesick French army general turned sugar-plantation owner bought the **Casa del Francés** here in 1910 for his pretty young bride. Word has it that the spoiled girl was impressed with neither the island, the house, nor even the husband, and promptly fled back to Paris. Today it is a rather dilapidated guesthouse, but still a landmark. Once the only place to stay on the island, Casa del Francés has been eclipsed by a half-dozen ultra-chic or ultra-charming boutique hotels and the Martineau Bay resort. Visit the **Esperanza Archeological Museum** (tel: 787-741 8850; daily 11am–3pm; free) for a historical look at pirate and Indian life around these parts. If it's nightlife you're after, try Banana's, Tradewinds and (Saturdays) Cerromar. Saturday nights are especially lively, when pretty much the entire town turns out along the seafront to promenade in their finest, talk, and flirt. During the *Fiesta Patronal* (Patron Saint's Festival), which takes place in the last two weeks of July, things really hop.

Just outside Esperanza, **Sun Bay** ❸ (Sombé to locals) glistens with a popular crescent-shaped beach. Camping is permitted here, as long as campers have the free permit. Beyond Sun Bay, and more secluded, lie **Media Luna** and **Navio** beaches. Final scenes from Peter Brook's classic 1963 movie *Lord of the Flies* were shot at Navio, a favorite spot for locals. The other good beaches to visit are not far away, within former **US Navy land**. In 1941 the Navy acquired over 70 percent of Vieques to use for land and sea exercises. As an impediment to development, the Navy was partly responsible for the island's charm. Though the inhabitants protested at the military presence, the Navy

Vieques has some 40 palm-lined white-sand beaches on its 60-mile (96km) coastline. It is hoped that the entire stretch of beach will be open to the public now that the US Navy has returned the property to the control of the Puerto Rican government.

BELOW: ponies abound on Vieques.

built roads, let cattle owners use Navy land, and left reserves open for public access to beaches.

Colorful beaches

With characteristic imagination, the Navy named three of the island's beaches Red, Blue, and Green. Merely getting to these places is a small adventure; rocky approach roads wind through thick seagrape overbrush. **Red** and **Blue** beaches are ideal for swimming, snorkeling, and scuba-diving. Just 75yds/meters off Blue Beach lies a cay to swim to and explore for helmet shells and coral. The way to **Green Beach** is long, bumpy, and tortuous. If you make the trek, stop to see **Mosquito Pier ❹**, a mile-long dock built earlier in the last century when sugar production still flourished.

Vieques has many minor expeditions on which to embark. Ask a local fisherman to take you out at night in a boat to the **Reserva Natural Bahía Bioluminiscente** (Phosphorescent Bay) **❺**, considered to have the best phosphorescent display in the world. Billions of luminescent microscopic creatures emit a green fluorescence when the water stirs. The best time to come here is on a moonless night, when swimming becomes quite a scintillating experience.

Or climb to the cave atop **Mount Pirata ❻**, where the ancient *cacique* Bieque allegedly hid his tribe's treasure once he realized the conquistadors' murderous intentions. Islanders say the sound of the cave's ceaseless roar attests that the great chief's ghost still rages. And while on the subject of superstitions, on Vieques's north coast near **Roca Cucaracha** (Cockroach Rock) is **Puerto Diablo** (Port Devil), said to be the third point of the notorious Bermuda Triangle.

Pirate's Cay

From Isla Grande Airport, the short flight to isolated **Culebra** to the north of Vieques overlooks dramatic coastline, dozens of varied cays, and a turquoise-green Caribbean Sea. Columbus reportedly discovered this island on his second voyage in 1493. The first known inhabitants, the Taíno Indians, sought refuge on Culebra after the Spanish started colonizing the

A gallon of water from Mosquito Bay may contain almost three-quarters of a million tiny (¹⁄₅₀₀-inch) bioluminescent swimming creatures, which are a type of dinoflagellate called Pyrodinium bahamense.

BELOW: sunbathing on Blue Beach.

Puerto Rican mainland. Before long, pirates and privateers began to use Culebra's Pirate's Cay as a hiding place and supply base before sailing off to raid ships in the Virgin Islands. Infamous corsairs, including the Welshman Sir Henry Morgan, may have buried their treasure on and around Culebra; according to local legend, a road near Punta del Soledado, a bend on Los Vacos Beach, a clump of large trees near Resaca Beach, and a rocky mound at the end of Flamenco Beach might be good spots to start looking for the 17th- and 18th-century fortunes.

By 1880, settlers from Puerto Rico and Vieques were braving severe droughts and swarms of mosquitoes to build a colony which grew tamarind, mango, cashew, and coconut trees. Then, a few years after the Spanish-American War of 1898, the US Navy opened facilities on Culebra, making Ensenada Honda its principal Caribbean anchorage. About this time, the island's town moved from what is now Campamento to Dewey. In 1909, one of President Theodore Roosevelt's last executive orders established parts of Culebra as a National Wildlife Refuge, one of the oldest in the US.

By the end of World War II, the US Navy had begun to use Culebra for gunnery and bombing practice. Sea vessels and fighter planes from the United States and its allies pummeled target areas; islanders recall days and nights of constant bomb bursts.

The Culebrans protested bitterly for many years. In 1971, Navy personnel and Culebrans exchanged tear gas and Molotov cocktails, for which some islanders were imprisoned. Finally, President Nixon decided that all weapons training on Culebra should be terminated. President Ford's National Security Council reaffirmed the decision, and Culebra was left alone in 1975.

Probably the most important feature of Culebra is its arid climate; with only 35 inches (89cm) of rain a year, there's always some sunshine here. Its 24 islands comprise 7,700 acres (3,100 hectares) of irregular topography and intricate coastline. Most of the terrain is good only for pasture, forest, or wildlife. Much of the land is administered by the US Fish and Wildlife Service,

Grazing livestock and fishing are the two principal activities of Culebra's inhabitants.

LEFT:
the San Juan ferry sailing on the azure waters to Vieques.

Sea Legs for the San Juan Ferry

Vieques and Culebra are accessible by air from San Juan or by sea from Fajardo. The latter is the scenic route, but people who suffer from motion sickness need to come prepared. Some people become ill on the ferry ride. In fact, an attendant distributes barf bags and collects them during the short trip.

Be prepared. Get an over-the-counter preventative drug such as Dramamine or a wristband device. Eat before you travel so that if you do vomit, you'll expel something besides stomach bile. Once motion sickness strikes, try looking at the horizon; focus on a distant point. Go to the top deck as fresh air helps.

You should also carry or have access to lots of liquids – club soda is a great stomach settler. Some people actually plug the nose in case they throw up – this keeps any vomit from clogging and paining your nostrils. And it keeps the smell of vomit out of your nose.

If you vomit severely, you will need to drink plenty of water and electrolytes so as not to become dehydrated. Drink at least 8 oz (0.2 liters) of liquid every time you throw up. Take precautions so you can actually enjoy your time once on the ground.

The fare to Vieques is $2 per person, while the fare to Culebra is $2.25 per person, and both trips take about an hour and a half.

TIP

To see giant leatherback turtles laying their eggs between April and July is a truly worthwhile experience. The best beaches are Resaca and Brava; you may wish to go with a guide.

which aims to maintain the diverse fauna and flora of the islands. Culebra's cays provide flourishing nesting colonies for a dozen marine bird species, including brown boobies, laughing gulls, sooty terns, and Bahama ducks. The brown pelican, an endangered species, can often be spotted in mangrove areas. Rare leatherback turtles nest on many of Culebra's beaches from April through July. Turtle-watchers on Resaca and Brava beaches frequently stay up from 6pm to 6am in order to catch sight of the large, lumbering reptiles delivering and protecting their eggs. Call 1-877-772 6725 to make reservations with a qualified guide.

Because the island has no freshwater streams, sedimentation is low, and Culebra enjoys one of the healthiest coral ecosystems in the Caribbean. Remarkable reefs make for an abundance of fish species and clear water.

More than 2,000 people now live on Culebra, many in pastel-colored houses amid scrubby hills. Roads and front yards abound with jeeps and chickens. Time passes slowly; the atmosphere is one of tranquillity and bonhomie.

BELOW: postcard-perfect beach.

Main town

The town of **Dewey** ❼ (which locals defiantly call **Puebla**), a 10-minute walk from the airport, covers only several blocks. (Be sure to remember Culebran law – no walking around town without a shirt!) At one end of town is the Fajardo ferry dock, known as the waterfront. Nearby you will find a dive shop, guesthouses, gift shops, a deli, and the highly recommended **Mamacita's Restaurant**. Down the road are two markets, the bank, the post office, and, across the bridge, you'll find Dinghy Dock Restaurant & BBQ for a lively bar crowd and American and Creole seafood dishes.

Just beyond town is one of the few drawbridges in the Caribbean. Nearby is **Ensenada Honda** ❽ ("Deep Bay"), surrounded by mangrove forests and one of the most secure hurricane harbors in the area, not to mention a nice spot for windsurfing. Smack in the middle of the bay is **Pirate's Cay**.

Much to the dismay of locals, who prefer to keep tourism to a minimum in Culebra, several boutique hotels have opened here, among them Club Sea-

borne and Bahía Marina. The central government began work in 2006 on the installation of a modern sewage system for Culebra, which it is hoped will help keep Culebra's waters pristine.

Perfect beach

While on Culebra, make a point of seeing **Flamenco Beach** ❾. A *público* (bus) can take you there, or you can make the long walk from Dewey. This is the sort of beach you have always heard about – soft white sand, clear blue water, and no one to kick sand in your face. A few hundred yards down the beach rest two archaic US Marine Corps tanks. Hikers occasionally find unexploded shells in the vicinity. Another fine beach is **Zoni Beach**, on the island's northeastern edge, some 7 miles (11km) from Dewey.

Half a mile uphill and east of Flamenco Beach stands **Mount Resaca**, the highest summit on Culebra, with a formidable 360-degree view of cays and some of the Virgin Islands. Resaca hosts a dry subtropical "rock forest" where exotic Caribbean flora thrives amid thousands of large boulders. Last officially sighted in 1932, the Culebra giant anole, an extremely rare lizard, is still believed to survive in the forested areas of the mountain.

The best way to see Culebra is by packing a picnic and hiring a boat for the day. Do some snorkeling or scuba-diving from the boat as you travel to otherwise inaccessible beaches, lagoons, forests, and rocky bluffs on **Cayo de Luis Peña** and the mile-long **Culebrita**. Here you will find the most exuberant wildlife on the island. On Culebrita, you can also see tidal pools and more spectacular, virtually deserted snow-white beaches.

Untouched island

Throughout the Caribbean it is hard not to feel that, however breathtakingly beautiful the landscape may be, it must *really* have been heart-stopping before the European settlers arrived. There are still a few places that the reckless hand of civilization has not reached, though, and one of them, the tiny **Isla Mona**, belongs to Puerto Rico. Stuck 45 miles (72km) out to sea, in the Mona Passage halfway to the Dominican Republic to

BELOW: poster advertising Conga music at Mamacita's Restaurant, Culebra.

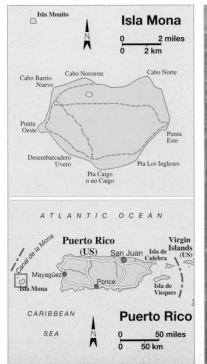

Map on page 239

the west, this rugged island of 25 sq miles (65 sq km) is a haven for some of the oddest and most interesting wildlife in the Antilles.

Mona is protected by the Department of Natural Resources, which also supervises the use of Cabo Rojo and other spots of great scenic beauty on the mainland's west coast. Nobody lives there now, but Mona has had a long history of habitation. Christopher Columbus found Taíno Indians there when he landed on the island, and Spanish settlers visited for many years in hopes of finding habitable and pleasant spots to settle. For centuries it was the stronghold for some of the most notorious of European and Puerto Rican pirates. Only a few naturalists and hermits visit the place now.

The landscape these solitary types have found is reported to be astounding. Except for an isolated lighthouse on a remote promontory, Mona is much as the Taínos left it. Cliffs 200ft (61 meters) high ring the tiny island, and are laced with a cave network which some say rivals that of the Camuy. Much of the island's ground is covered by small cacti that resemble a miniature version of Arizona's organ-pipe cactus, and tiny barrel cacti are common here as well.

Booby "trap"

Some of the vegetation on the island is known nowhere else in the world, while the fauna is even more astounding. Here are found the biggest lizards in Puerto Rico, as well as three species of endangered sea turtle. Besides an extensive variety of gull, there lives on Mona a red-footed bird beloved by visitors and known disrespectfully as the "booby."

There are those who would claim that anyone who wished to visit Mona could be called a booby as well. Those hardy souls who are not dissuaded would be best advised to charter a boat or private plane in Mayagüez. Planes can be chartered from San Juan's Isla Grande Airport as well. Official information on hiking trails and on the island's topography is hard to come by, but try contacting the Department of Natural and Environmental Resources at www.drna.gobierno.pr or by calling 787-999 2200. ❏

TIP

If you decide to make the long journey to Mona, make sure to take everything you need (including water); there are no facilities.

BELOW:
trailing for shellfish.
RIGHT: a wonderful gradation of blues on Culebra.

243

TRANSPORTATION

ACCOMMODATIONS

EATING OUT

ACTIVITIES

A – Z

LANGUAGE

☆ INSIGHT GUIDES TRAVEL TIPS
PUERTO RICO

TRANSPORTATION

GETTING THERE AND GETTING AROUND

GETTING THERE

By Air

Luis Muñoz Marín International Airport (tel: 787-791 4670/3840), just to the west of San Juan in Isla Verde, is one of the largest and busiest airports in the Caribbean. It serves not only as Puerto Rico's main port of entry but also as a stopping point for most American and European flights to the Caribbean. The main international carriers serving San Juan include the following:

Air Canada
www.aircanada.com
In Canada and the US, tel: 1-888-247 2262 (toll-free); 514-393 3333 (regular toll charges apply)
In Australia, tel: 1300-655 767 (toll-free within Australia)
In Ireland, tel: +1-800-709 900
In New Zealand, tel: 0508-747 767
In South Africa, tel: +27-21-422 3232
In the UK, tel: 0871-220 1111
American Airlines
www.aa.com
In North America, tel: 1-800-433 7300 (toll-free)
British Airways
www.britishairways.com
In Australia, tel: 1300-767 177 (toll-free)
In New Zealand, tel: 09-966 9777
In North America, tel: 1-800-247 9297 (toll-free)
In South Africa, tel: 11-441 8400
In the UK, tel: 0844-493 0787
Continental
www.continental.com
In North America, tel: 800-523 3273; 800-231 0856 (toll-free)

Delta
www.delta.com
In the US, tel: 800-221 1212 (toll-free); 404-765 5000
International, tel: 800-241 4141 (toll-free in the US)
Iberia
www.iberia.com
In Canada and the US, tel: 800-772 4642 (toll-free)
In Ireland tel: 0818-462 000 (Spanish and English)
In the UK, tel: 0870-609 0500 (Spanish and English)
Jet Blue
www.jetblue.com
In Canada and the US, tel: 800-538 2583 (toll-free)
International, tel: 1-801-365 2525
Lufthansa
www.lufthansa.com
In Australia, tel: 1300-655 727 (toll-free)
In Canada, tel: 1-800-563 5954
In Ireland, tel: 0184-45544
In New Zealand, tel: 0800-945 220
In South Africa, tel: 0861-842 538
In the UK, tel: 0871-945 9747
In the US, tel: 800-399 5838/800-645 3880 (toll-free)
Northwest
www.nwa.com
In Australia, tel: 02-9767 4333; 1300-767 310 (toll-free)
In the UK, tel: 0870-507 4074
In the US, tel: 800-225 2525 (toll-free)
Spirit
www.spiritair.com
In the US, tel: 800-772 7117 (toll-free)
United
www.ual.com
In the US, tel: 800-864 8331 (toll-free)
In the UK, tel: 0845-844 4777

US Airways
www.usairways.com
In Ireland, tel: 1890-925 065
In the UK, tel: 0845-600 3300
In the US, tel: 800-428 4322 (US and Canada); 800-622 1015 (international destinations) (toll-free)
Virgin Atlantic
www.virgin-atlantic.com
In Australia, tel: 1300-727-340 (toll-free); 0830-1730
In South Africa, tel: 011-340 3400
In the UK, tel: 08705 747 747
In the US, tel: 800-821 5438 (toll-free)
A free shuttle bus service operates between the airport itself and each car rental agency located in or close to the airport.

The Metropolitan Bus Authority runs to various parts of the city, 9 miles (14km) away, for a small charge, and you can only take carry-on luggage on the buses.

Taxis from the airport operate on a fixed-rate zone system for tourist areas; meter charges apply to places outside tourist locations.

By Sea

San Juan is the most popular cruise port in the Caribbean, receiving over 1 million visitors annually. Several modern "tourism piers" have been constructed at the harborside in Old San Juan, with the result that most cruise companies plying the South Atlantic make at least an afternoon stop in San Juan.

Specialist Tours

Following is a list of tour companies operating trips to Puerto Rico:
Acampa Nature Adventure Tours
Tel: 787-706 0695
www.acampapr.com

This company specializes in customized trips with tour guides to waterfalls, caves, rainforests, or mountains. Also available are hiking, camping, rappelling and/or rock climbing in Toro Negro, the Tanamá River in Utuado, El Yunque in Río Grande, the San Cristóbal Canyon, Mona Island and the Monagas Park in the San Juan metropolitan area. Adventure gear and gadgets are available to buy.

Aventuras Tierra Adentro
Tel: 787-766 0470
www.aventuraspr.com
One-day adventures are provided, including rappelling, rock climbing, zipping down tyroleans, free jumping, rock climbing, body rafting, and exploring caves and canyons. Tours depart from San Juan metropolitan area to El Yunque and Río Camuy Cave Park. A little pricey but thoroughly exciting.

Captain Duck Tours
Tel: 787-725 0077
www.captainduck.com
A 90-minute land and sea tour on an amphibious bus through Old San Juan and the San Juan Bay.

Encantos Ecotours
Tel: 787-272 0005; 808 0005
Outdoor activities, historical, cultural, and nature tours throughout Puerto Rico. Activities include kayaking, snorkeling, biking, hiking, and sailing lessons with gear rental available. Serves the San Juan metropolitan area and the southwest of the island.

Rico Suntours
Tel: 787-722 2080
www.ricosuntours.com
This established company provides tours and transfers, and specializes in team-building groups. Serves San Juan metropolitan area, northwest, northeast, and southwest of the island. Accommodates travelers with wheelchairs.

United Tour Guides
Tel: 787-723 5578/725 7605
www.unitedtourguides.com
Experienced tour operators for main cruise lines and groups. Tours in San Juan, Coamo, the northwest, and the northeast of the island.

Wheelchair Transportation
Tel: 800-868 8028; 787-883 0131
Transportation and customized tours are provided for disabled travelers, mostly in the San Juan metropolitan area, but also to more locations around the island.

Cruise Companies

The following cruise lines include San Juan as a regular port of call.

Carnival Cruises
Tel: 1-888-CARNIVAL (2276 4825; US); 020-7940 4466 (UK)
www.carnival.com

Celebrity Cruises
Tel: 1-800-647 2251 (US); 0800-018 2525 (UK)
www.celebrity.com

Costa Cruises
Tel: 1-877-882 6782 (US); 0845-351 0552 (UK)
www.costacruises.co.uk

Cunard Line
Tel: 1-800-728 6273 (US); 0845-071 0300 (UK)
www.cunardline.com

Holland America Line
Tel: 1-877-932 4259 (US); 0845-351 0557 (UK)
www.hollandamerica.com

Norwegian Cruise Line
tel: 866-234 7350 (US); 0845-658 8010 (UK)
www.ncl.com; www.uk.ncl.com

Princess Cruises
Tel: 1-800-774 6237 (US); 0845-075 0031 (UK)
www.princesscruises.com

Radisson Seven Seas
Tel: 1-877-505 5370 (US)
www.rssc.com

Royal Caribbean International
Tel: 866-562 7625 (US); 0845-165 8414 (UK)
www.royalcaribbean.com; www.royalcaribbean.co.uk

Seabourn Cruise Line
Tel: 1-800-929 9391 (US)
www.seabourn.com

Silver Sea Cruise Line
Tel: 1-800-722 9955 (US)
www.silversea.com

Windstar Cruises
Tel: 1-800-258 7245 (US); 020-7292 2387 (UK)
www.windstarcruises.com

GETTING AROUND

On Arrival

Be sure to keep the ticket for your checked-in luggage because airport officials in the baggage-claim area at the Luis Muñoz Marín International Airport will require this to verify ownership of your bags before allowing you to exit.

Porters or *maleteros* from the Operativa de Servicio de Equipaje are available in all baggage-claim areas, they will help carry bags for a fee of $1 per bag, regardless of size. The *maleteros* can be identified by their light-blue shirts and dark-blue pants and an ID tag with *Operativa de Servicio de Equipaje*.

If you arrive between 9am and 7pm, stop by the Tourism Company Information Center (tel: 787-791 1014) in concourse C at street level. Pick up a copy of *¡Qué Pasa!*, *Bienvenidos*, or *Places To Go* magazines.

Airport/City Transportation

Taxis
The best way to get from the airport to your destination, if it's in the San Juan tourist areas, such as Condado, Isla Verde, and Ocean Park, is by taxi.

Taxis are regulated by Transportación Turística. To take a cab, you must stand in line and obtain a transportation voucher from the Ground Transportation stand (orange with the Tourism Company's logo), located at street level and on the second (first) floor of all terminal exits. The voucher indicates the price and address of your destination.

BELOW: San Juan is the most popular cruise port in the Caribbean.

Travel Times

Estimated travel times by car from Luis Muñoz Marín International Airport when traffic is not heavy:

Airport to Dorado   30 mins
Airport to Río Grande 45 mins
Airport to Fajardo   1hr
Airport to Humacao   1hr 20 mins
Airport to Isabela   2hrs 30 mins
Airport to Aguadilla 3hrs
Airport to Mayagüez   3hrs
Airport to Ponce   1hr 15 mins
Airport to Rincón   2hrs 30 mins

Taxis are plentiful, especially in tourist areas. Some metropolitan-area taxi companies include:

Capetillo Taxi, tel: 787-758 7000
Major Taxi Cabs, tel: 787-723 2460
Metro Taxi, tel: 787-725 2870, email: metrotaxipr@hotmail.com
Rochdale Radio Taxi, tel: 787-721 1900

Fixed taxi rates apply under the Taxis Turísticos program, sponsored by the Puerto Rico Tourism Company. Participating taxis are white with the Taxis Turísticos logo on the door. Keep in mind that rush hour brings traffic jams and heavy rain also slows things down.

Note that all tolls must be paid by the passenger. The Teodoro Moscoso Bridge toll is $2. A surcharge of $2 each applies to the sixth and seventh passenger in a vehicle, while $0.50 is charged for each of the first three pieces of luggage and $1 each for the fourth piece of luggage and thereafter. Tips are not included in the set fare.

Metered taxi rates apply outside of the set San Juan tourism zones. The initial charge is $1.75, with $0.10 charged for every nineteenth of a mile or every 25 seconds of waiting time. The same luggage charges as in the transportation zones are applicable, as are the fees for the sixth and seventh passenger. There is a $1 call charge, and the minimum charge for a trip is $3. Hourly rent charge is $36, and the night rate (from 10pm to 6am) is $1 over the meter charge.

If visitors wish to visit parts of the island outside the metropolitan area, ask for a metered journey or negotiate a flat price with the driver before setting off. However, such trips are expensive, so it is best to take a tour or rent a car for sightseeing trips around the island.

By Air

Most international and many domestic flights (including those from the United States) to San Juan land at Luis Muñoz Marín International Airport in Isla Verde, while others use San Juan's second airport, Isla Grande, just across the estuary south of Puerta de Tierra. Ponce and Mayagüez have modern, small airports which provide access to the capital in 20 minutes.

Ponce's airport accommodates flights from Atlanta, Newark, and New York in the US. Aguadilla Airport, which was created from part of Ramey Air Force Base, also accepts flights from the US and Canada.

Vieques has a good airport, and the Vieques Air Link (tel: 787-741 8331), which leaves Isla Grande daily is a pleasant way of getting to and from that lovely island.

Small planes can be chartered at Isla Grande Airport.

Airports

Aguadilla
Rafael Hernández Airport
Tel: 787-890 6075
Arecibo
Antonio (Nery) Juarbe Municipal Airport
Tel: 787-881 2072
For private planes.
Ceiba
Aeropuerto José Aponte de la Torre
Tel: 787-534 4101
Culebra
Benjamín Rivera Noriega
Tel: 787-742 0022
Humacao
Humacao Airport
Tel: 787-852 8188
For private and skydiving planes.
Isla Grande
Isla Grande Airport
Tel: 787-729 8790
Isla Verde
Luis Muñoz Marín International Airport
Tel: 787-791 3840
Mayagüez
Eugenio María de Hostos Airport
Tel: 787-833 0148
Patillas
Patillas Airport
Tel: 787-852-8188
For private planes.
Ponce
Mercedita Airport
Tel: 787-842 6292
Vieques
Antonio Rivera Rodríguez Airport
Tel: 787-741 0515

By Bus

There is a wide-ranging public transport system. Most towns have private bus services. The only public bus service is in the San Juan metropolitan area. The Metropolitan Bus Authority has routes through Bayamón, Guaynabo, Río Piedras, San Juan, Carolina, and part of Trujillo Alto. Adults pay $0.75 per trip. Buses run daily from 4.30am–10pm; they are air-conditioned but can get crowded and don't operate on a set schedule. Buses can be hailed where you see signs: *Parada de Guaguas*. For information about bus routes and terminals:
Tel: 787-250 6064; 787-294 0500, ext. 524 or 514; 800-981 3021
www.ati.gobierno.pr

By Public Car

Puerto Rico's major cities are linked by *públicos*, independently owned small vans which can be found at stands all over San Juan and other smaller cities. *Públicos* are good value and comfortable, and probably the best alternative to having one's own car. To arrange a pick-up call one of the following companies:
Blue Line
Tel: 787-765 7733
Río Piedras, Aguadilla, Aguada, Moca, Isabela, and others.
Choferes Unidos de Ponce
Tel: 787-764 0540
Ponce and others.
Línea Caborrojeña
Tel: 787-723 9155
Cabo Rojo, San Germán, and others.
Línea Sultana
Tel: 787-765 9377
Mayagüez and others.
Terminal de Transportación Pública
Tel: 787-250 0717
Fajardo and others.

By Urban Train

Puerto Rico's commuter rail system has 16 modern stations, it connects downtown Bayamón with eastern Santurce near Sagrado Corazón University, passing through the Torrimar neighborhood, the Centro Médico (the island's main medical center), the University of Puerto Rico at Río Piedras, and the financial district of Hato Rey. Route expansions are planned to Old San Juan, Carolina, and Caguas. The fare is $1.50 per ride on air-conditioned cars, which includes a bus connection. For information, contact: Tren Urbano, tel: 866-900 1284, or visit www.ati.gobierno.pr.

By Water

Ferries

The country lacks the extensive water transportation networks of other islands in the Caribbean. But the ferry that operates from the tourist piers of San Juan to Cataño, a mile across San Juan Bay, is a time-saver (less than 10 mins) and a bargain at $0.50 per ride. The ferry runs from 6am–10pm. Call 787-788 0940 for schedules.

Ferries also run from Fajardo to Vieques and Culebra and vice versa. They leave the docks at Fajardo for Vieques at 9.30am, 1pm, 4.30pm, and 8pm weekdays; 9am, 3pm, and 6pm weekends and holidays. Ferries leave Vieques for Fajardo at 6.30am, 11am, 3pm, and 6pm on weekdays; 6.30am, 1pm, and 4.30pm on weekends and holidays. Ferries from Fajardo to Culebra leave at 9am, 3pm, and 7pm daily. Ferries from Culebra to Fajardo depart at 6.30, 1pm, and 5pm daily. A one-way journey takes approximately 1hour 15 minutes and costs $2.25 per adult from Fajardo to Culebra or $2 per person to Vieques. Children and seniors pay $1 to either island. Seats can be reserved, but it's best to arrive an hour early. Ferries don't always stick to the schedule, so leave extra time if making connections.

For information and reservations:
Fajardo Port, tel: 800-981 2005
Vieques, tel: 787-741 4761
Culebra, tel: 787-742 3161

A high-speed ferry also links Old San Juan with Culebra and Vieques, though it's pricey – $68 for a round trip to Culebra, $78 for a round trip to Vieques, $33 between Culebra and Vieques (excluding port fees). One-way fares are available. Service is seasonal, so check availability. For reservations call 877-899 3993 or visit www.islandhispeed ferry.com/puertorico.

Boat Trips

Charter a boat in Mayagüez for the arduous but fascinating 45-mile (72km) trip to the Isle of Mona. Companies that operate tours include:
Adventours or Excursiones Guariquén, tel: 787-530 8311, www.adventourspr.com
Copladet, tel: 787-765 8595, www.copladet.com

By Car

Car Rental

Puerto Rico has one of the highest per-capita rates of car ownership in the Americas, and an automobile is a necessity for anyone who wants to see the island. The drive from east to west across the island is little more than a 3-hour trip. Puerto Rico therefore has many car rental companies. Avis, Budget, Hertz, and

ABOVE: on the bus to El Morro, San Juan.

National have offices in the baggage-claim area of terminal E at the Luis Muñoz Marín International Airport, while others are a short shuttle-bus trip away. Most have unlimited mileage. Smaller companies often have excellent automobiles and are less expensive. Even though insurance usually costs extra you would be advised to purchase it. And always carefully check the terms and conditions of the rental agreement detailing insurance coverage.

To rent a car visitors must be fully qualified drivers of at least 25. Some allow drivers under 25, requiring an extra insurance fee. Agencies will usually require a deposit using a major credit card to secure the vehicle. However, some will accept a large cash deposit in lieu of the credit card. Foreign drivers must also produce either an international driver's license or a license from their home country. US licenses and international licenses are valid for use in Puerto Rico for up to 3 months.

Rules of the Road

Driving is on the right-hand side of the road. Speed limits are listed in miles, paradoxically – distance signs are in kilometers. The speed limit on the San Juan–Ponce highway and other expressways is 65mph (104kph), although in some places the limit is 55mph (100kph). Limits elsewhere are lower, especially in urban areas, where speed-bumps (lomos) provide a natural barrier to excess.

Puerto Rico's older coastal highways are efficient routes but can be slow going, due to never-ending traffic lights. Roads in the interior are narrow, tortuous, poorly-paved, and dangerous. Often, they run along dizzying cliffsides.

Hurricanes, too, take their toll on the roads, and traffic signals are regularly out of order, so drivers go at their own pace, which usually means too fast, weaving in and out of traffic. Also be aware that road signage is poor, and many of the smaller roads do not appear on any map. Be careful too with the many potholes you may encounter along the road.

By law, you must wear seat belts in Puerto Rico. As in some parts of the US, turning right on a red light when traffic allows is permitted – except at a few intersections, where a sign advising you not to do so is indicated. Be advised that hitchhiking and picking up hitchhikers can be extremely dangerous.

In general, most Puerto Rican drivers tend to follow the rules of the road, but a formidable group do not, which can make driving hazardous. The best advice is to be aware of where you are at all times, drive defensively, and don't take anything for granted. Traffic signs and lights may not be heeded by other road users.

Be sure to carry change for the numerous tolls throughout the road network. There is a speed pass system, so check with the car rental company for availability.

If your car breaks down and you do not have roadside assistance, try the following 24-hour towing companies:
Central Towing and Transport, tel: 800-981 0087
Grúas Pachi, tel: 787-728 8140 (non-English)
Metropolitan Tow Service, tel: 787-518 6244

Road Safety

Slow down if you see a sign indicating any of the following:

Desprendimiento	**Landslide**
Desvío	**Detour**
Carretera Cerrada	**Road Closed**

A CCOMMODATIONS

HOTELS, YOUTH HOSTELS, BED AND BREAKFAST

Choosing a Hotel

Puerto Rico has a wide range of accommodations available, but big resorts set the tone. Still, guesthouses, beach houses, grand hotels, and camping grounds, as well as a host of less conventional settings, round out a growing and expensive lodging situation.

The island's large and splashy beach resorts come in two main varieties. The first comprises pricey beachfront resorts with casinos, plenty of bars, and fine restaurants, as well as beautiful golf courses. Each is characterized by excellent sports facilities such as large swimming pools, well-maintained tennis courts, a gym, spa, and long stretches of beach.

The second type is less lavish and tends to be only half as expensive. These include the white high-rises of San Juan's Condado and Isla Verde areas, which cater to a mix of holiday-makers and businesspeople.

Guesthouses tend to be less costly and more intimate than the big resorts, with around a dozen rooms. Many have beachfront locations, about half have bars, and almost all have swimming pools.

If you prefer to be independent, renting an apartment or condominium is a good self-catering option.

San Juan Vacations (tel: 787-727 1591; www.sanjuanvacations.com) has a comprehensive listing of condominiums available in Isla Verde and Condado.

Avoid shady hotels, and play it safe by sticking to the list endorsed by the Puerto Rico Tourism Company

(www.gotopuertorico.com/puerto-rico-accommodations.php).

The *parador* presents a unique lodging option in Puerto Rico.

A *parador* is a small, privately owned hotel participating in a special government program that assures a certain level of quality.

These family-run country inns, often old coffee or sugar haciendas, offer the authentic ambience of Puerto Rican rural life. Beautiful old furniture and elegant dining facilities make them worth trying. Many are located in particularly scenic areas. Rates are mostly reasonable, often around $70–90 per night for a double room, and the food is usually much better than what you may find at nearby restaurants.

Be warned, however, some *paradores* have a distinctly utilitarian flavor with dormitory-style rooms. It pays to do a little research. Try to obtain photos of the establishment before making a reservation.

From the US mainland, *parador* reservations can be made through a central toll-free number: 800-866 7827. In Puerto Rico, call 800-981 7575 (toll-free). For more information visit www.gotoparadores.com.

The Puerto Rico Tourism Company currently certifies 18 *paradores*, which are listed in the box.

Paradores

Bahía Salinas, Cabo Rojo, tel: 787-254 1213; www.bahiasalinas.com **$$**
Boquemar, Boquerón, tel: 787-851 2158; www.boquemar.com **$**
Caribbean Paradise, Patillas, tel: 787-839 5885; www. caribbeanparadisepr.com **$**
El Buen Café, Hatillo, tel: 787-898 1000; www.elbuencafe.com **$**
El Faro, Aguadilla, tel: 888-300 8002; www.farohotels.net **$**
Hacienda Juanita, Maricao, tel: 787-838 2550; www.haciendajuanita. com **$**
J.B. Hidden Village, Aguada, tel: 787-868 8686; www.jbhiddenhotel. com **$**
Joyuda Beach Hotel, Boquerón, tel: 787-851 5650; www.joyudabeach. com **$**

Palmas de Lucía, Yabucoa, tel: 787-893 4423; www.palmasdelucia. com **$**
Perichi's, Joyuda, tel: 787-851 3131; www.hotelperichi.com **$**
Villa Antonio, Rincón, tel: 787-823 2645; www.villa-antonio.com **$**
Villa del Mar, La Parguera, tel: 787-899 4265; www.pinacolada.com/ villadelmar **$**
Villa Parguera, La Parguera, tel: 787-899 7777; www.villaparguera.net **$**
Villas del Mar Hau, Isabela, tel: 787-872 2045; www.hauhotelvillas. com **$**
Villas Sotomayor, Adjuntas, tel: 787-829 1717; www.paradorvillas sotomayor.com **$**
Vistamar, Quebradillas, tel: 787-895 2065; www.paradorvistamar.com **$**

ACCOMMODATIONS LISTINGS

OLD SAN JUAN

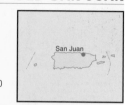

Chateau Cervantes
329 Recinto Sur Street
Tel: 787-724 7722
www.cervantespr.com
Boutique hotel in the heart of San Juan with six deluxe rooms and six suites, all simply yet elegantly

decorated. There is also a good restaurant on the property. **$$$**
The Gallery Inn
204 Norzagaray Street
Tel: 866-572 2783; 787-722 1808
www.thegalleryinn.com

Art gallery and 22-room guesthouse in a 16th-century mansion. Eclectic funky elegance. **$$**
Hotel El Convento
100 Cristo Street
Tel: 800-468 2779; 787-723 9020
www.elconvento.com
Convent dating to the 16th century, now a 71-room, gay-friendly hotel. **$$$**
Howard Johnson Plaza de Armas
22 San José Street
Tel: 787-722 9191
Convenient location near restaurants, bars, stores. With 51 rooms, rate includes continental breakfast. **$$$**

Sheraton Old San Juan
100 Brumbaugh Street
Tel: 866-653 7577; 787-721 5100
www.sheratonoldsanjuan.com
This is a hotel with 240 rooms, built as part of the waterfront expansion. It also has a restaurant, lounge, rooftop pool, and a large casino. **$$**

BELOW: the yellow facade of Hotel El Convento.

METROPOLITAN SAN JUAN

Puerta de Tierra

Caribe Hilton
Los Rosales Street
San Gerónimo Grounds
Tel: 800-468 8585; 787-721 0303
www.hiltoncaribbean.com/sanjuan
The 646-room Caribe Hilton is the only hotel in Puerto Rico with a private beach. Several restaurants, spa, and fitness center. **$$$**
Normandie Hotel
499 West Muñoz Rivera Avenue
Tel: 877-987 2929; 787-729 2929
www.normandiepr.com
Art Deco hotel, most of its 173 rooms include a parlor with a working and sitting area and sun room. Gay-friendly. **$$**

Condado

Atlantic Beach Hotel
1 Vendig Street
Tel: 787-721 6900
www.atlanticbeachhotel.com
Beach hotel with 36 rooms. Rate includes continental breakfast, beach chairs, and towels. Gay-friendly. **$$**
At Wind Chimes Inn
1750 Ashford Avenue
Tel: 800-946 3244; 787-727 4153
www.atwindchimesinn.com

Lovely 22-room guesthouse on the tourist zone's main avenue. **$**
Casa del Caribe
57 Caribe Street
Tel: 877-722 7139; 787-722 7139
www.casadelcaribe.com
The hotel has 13 intimate rooms decorated with Puerto Rican original art. Complimentary breakfast can be taken on the wrap-around veranda. **$**
Comfort Inn San Juan
6 Clemenceau Street
Tel: 787-721 0170
www.choicehotels.com
Next to the Condado Lagoon, this watersports center has 56 rooms. **$**
Condado Plaza Hotel and Casino
999 Ashford Avenue
Tel: 866-317 8934; 787-721 1000
www.condadoplaza.com
With 570 units, top-notch restaurants, casino, pool, and business center. **$$$**
Diamond Palace Hotel and Casino
55 Condado Avenue
Tel: 800-468 2014; 787-721 0810
www.diamondpalacehotel.net
A good choice for budget travelers who want to be close to where it's

happening. With 133 rooms and a small casino. Near popular restaurants. **$**
Doubletree by Hilton
105 De Diego Avenue
Tel: 800-528 1234; 787-721 1200
www.doubletree.com
Traditional hostelry that caters to families and business clientele. Its 184 units are well proportioned and equipped with air con and cable TV. **$$**
El Canario by the Lagoon
4 Clemenceau Street
Tel: 800-533 2649; 787-722 5058
www.canariohotels.com
With 44 rooms, this comfortable bed and breakfast hotel is located on the Condado Lagoon. **$**
El Canario by the Sea
4 Condado Avenue
Tel: 800-533 2649; 787-722 8640
www.canariohotels.com
Small, 25-room guesthouse near the beach. All rooms are air-conditioned with private bath. Complimentary breakfast provided. **$**
El Canario Inn
1317 Ashford Avenue
Tel: 800-533 2649; 787-722 3861
www.canariohotels.com
Lovely 25-room small hotel/bed and breakfast inn with

lots of character. **$**
Holiday Inn Express
1 Mariano Ramírez Street
Tel: 888-826 2621; 787-724 4160
www.hiexpress.com
Simple chain hotel near Condado Lagoon and beaches. The hotel has 115 rooms, a pool, and price includes continental breakfast. **$$**
Iberia Hotel
1464 Wilson Avenue
Tel: 787-722 5380
www.hoteliberia.net
This 30-room hotel in a residential neighborhood includes air conditioning, phone, and bath; decorated in cozy Spanish style. **$**

PRICE CATEGORIES

Price categories are for a double room in high season:
$ = under $150
$$ = $150–250
$$$ = more than $250

ABOVE: beautiful beach setting.

La Concha A Renaissance Resort
1077 Ashford Avenue
Tel: 877-524 7778; 787-721 7500
www.laconcharesort.com
A retro-urban showcase and architectural landmark, it was originally built in 1958 and reopened in 2007 with 248 state-of-the-art rooms. Casino, pool, restaurants, bars, and lounges. **$$$**

Le Consulat
1149 Magdalena Ave Condado
Tel: 787-289 9191
www.choicehotels.com
Elegant European-style bed and breakfast. 28 rooms. **$**

Quality Inn El Portal
76 Condado Avenue
Tel: 787-721 9010
www.qualityinn.com
Traditional small hotel with 47 well-equipped rooms. **$**

Radisson Ambassador Plaza
1369 Ashford Avenue
Tel: 888-201 1718; 787-721 7300
www.radisson.com/ambassador
This 233-unit hotel has a pleasant piano bar adjacent to the casino, a restaurant and sports bar, and two lounges with live music. Features lavish concierge floor with two-room suites. **$$**

San Juan Beach Hotel
1045 Ashford Avenue
Tel: 800-468 2040; 723 8000
www.sanjuanbeachhotel.com
Located on the beach, this colorful 95-room hotel with a pool caters to tourists and businesspeople. **$$**

San Juan Marriott Resort and Casino
1309 Ashford Avenue
Tel: 888-817 2033; 722 7000
www.marriott.com/sjupr
Grand 525-room hotel that is popular with Puerto Ricans. Large casino and several fine restaurants on site. **$$$**

Ocean Park

Hostería del Mar
1 Tapia Street
Tel: 877-727 3302; 787-727 3302
www.hosteriadelmarpr.com
Delightful 24-room hostelry on the beach; breakfast included. Thrilling view of the Atlantic. Restaurant. Gay-friendly. **$**

Numero Uno Guesthouse
1 Santa Ana Street
Tel: 866-726 5010; 787-726 5010
www.numero1guesthouse.com
Intimate beachfront inn with 14 tastefully decorated rooms, and restaurant. Gay-friendly. **$$**

Miramar

Courtyard by Marriott Miramar
801 Ponce de León Avenue
Tel: 800-593 8620; 787-721 7400
www.courtyardsj.com
Business hotel with 140 rooms with easy access to Old San Juan and Puerto Rico Convention Center. Popular restaurant. **$$**

Hotel Miramar
606 Ponce de León Avenue
Tel: 877-647 2627; 787-977 1000
www.miramarhotelpr.com
Comfortable hotel accommodation and has a capacity of 50 rooms. **$**

Hotel Olimpo Court
603 Miramar Avenue
Tel: 787-724 0600
Email: hotelolimpocourt@hotmail.com
In a residential area, the 45-room hotel has guest rooms and studio apartments with fully equipped kitchenettes. **$**

Isla Verde

Best Western San Juan Airport Hotel
Luis Muñoz Marín International Airport
Terminal D, Second Floor
Tel: 800-981 1701; 787-791 1700
www.bestwestern.com/pr/sanjuanairporthotel
Lodging with 125 sound-proofed rooms. Flat-screen TV; breakfast included. **$$**

Borinquen Beach Inn
5451 Isla Verde Avenue
Tel: 866-728 8400; 787-728 8400
www.borinquenbeachinn.com
On tourist strip near beach; 12 rooms and free parking. **$**

Casa Mathiesen
36 Calle Mar Mediterráneo, Villamar
Tel: 800-677 8860; 787-726 8662
www.coqui-inn.com
Lovely 30-room hotel located just off the beach. Two restaurants. **$**

Coral by the Sea
2 Rosa Street
Tel: 787-791 6868
www.coralbythesea.com
This low-priced 68-room hotel is best known for its restaurant. Basic rooms have satellite TV; cocktail lounge and live entertainment. **$**

El San Juan Hotel and Casino
6063 Isla Verde Avenue
Tel: 866-317 8935; 787-791 1000
www.elsanjuanhotel.com
Lavish resort with 382 rooms and casino. The resort has some of San Juan's best restaurants. **$$$**

Embassy Suites Hotel and Casino
8000 Tartak Street
Tel: 800-362 2779; 787-791 0505
www.embassysuitesanjuan.com
Spacious 300-room luxury resort with one-bedroom suites that include a living/working area. Large casino and huge banquet hall. **$$$**

ESJ Towers
6165 Isla Verde Avenue
Tel: 800-468 2026; 787-791 5151
www.esjtowers.com
On the beach, this 450-room complex features air-conditioned studios and apartments with kitchens and private balconies. **$$$**

Green Isle Inn
36 Calle Mar Mediterráneo, Villamar
Tel: 800-677 8860; 787-726 4330
www.coqui-inn.com
Comfy 26-room hotel. One of the best deals in town. **$**

Hampton Inn and Suites
6530 Isla Verde Avenue
Tel: 800-426 7866; 787-791 8777
www.hamptoninn.com
This 200-room resort has two-room suites with lounge, bar, meeting rooms, and fitness center. **$$**

Hotel Villa del Sol
4 Rosa Street
Tel: 787-791 2600
www.villadelsolpr.com
Spanish villa-style hotel with 24 rooms, one block from the beach; free parking. **$**

Howard Johnson Hotel
4820 Isla Verde Avenue
Tel: 800-446 4656; 787-728 1300
www.hojo.com
This 115-room hotel has deluxe rooms on executive floor complete with jacuzzi; cable TV; restaurant. **$**

InterContinental San Juan Resort and Casino
5961 Isla Verde Avenue

Tel: 877-721 0185; 787-791 6100
www.ichotelsgroup.com
Beautiful, modern hotel with
402 rooms. Las Vegas-style
entertainment at night. Five
restaurants. **$$$**

**San Juan Water and
Beach Club Hotel**
2 Tartak Street
Tel: 888-265 6699; 787-728 3666
www.waterbeachclubhotel.com
Boutique hotel with vibrant

lounge bars and restaurant.
Located on Isla Verde Beach.
Gay- and pet-friendly. **$$$**
**The Ritz-Carlton San Juan
Hotel, Spa, and Casino**
6961 Los Gobernadores Ave.

Tel: 800-542 8680; 787-253 1700
www.ritzcarlton.com/hotels/san_juan
Luxurious 416-room resort
with casino, spa and fitness
center, private dining room,
and chic boutiques. **$$$**

THE NORTHEAST

**El Conquistador Resort
and Golden Door Spa**
1000 El Conquistador Avenue,
Fajardo
Tel: 888-543 1282; 787-863 1000
www.elconresort.com
This 972-room luxury resort,
recently branded as a
Waldorf Astoria Collection
resort, has a private island
and 18-hole championship
golf course. A funicular
transports guests to La
Marina Village, which
overlooks the sea and is
home to the exclusive Coquí
Water Park and private
marina. **$$$**
The Fajardo Inn
52 Parcelas Beltrán
Puerto Real Area, Fajardo
Tel: 888-860 6006; 787-860 6000

www.fajardoinn.com
This 97-room hotel offers a
panoramic view of the
Atlantic and is located on 5
lush acres (2 hectares). **$$**
Gran Meliá Puerto Rico
Route 3, Intersection with PR-955,
200 Coco Beach, Río Grande
Tel: 866-436 3542; 787-809 1770
www.gran-melia-puerto-rico.com
All-suite, all-inclusive beach
resort with 486 rooms.
Facilities include a spa, golf
course, live entertainment
and casino, six restaurants,
and bars and lounges. **$$$**
Passion Fruit
Route 987, Int. 9987
Bo. Las Cabeza, Fajardo
Tel: 800-670 3196; 787-801 0106
www.passionfruitbb.com
Comfortable bed and

breakfast with friendly staff
and simple rooms. Enjoy a
drink in the rooftop bar and
breakfast served by the
swimming pool. **$**
**Río Mar Beach Resort and
Spa, a Wyndham Grand
Resort**
Route 968, Km 1.4
6000 Río Mar Boulevard, Río
Grande
Tel: 877-636 0636; 787-888 6000
www.wyndhamriomar.com
Lovely setting, on the
beach and among the hills,
this resort with 600 rooms
is ideal for a secluded
getaway. Views of El
Yunque from the two
championship golf courses.
Tennis courts, a fitness
center and a casino, and a

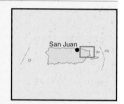

choice of eight restaurants.
$$$
Scenic Inn
52 Parcelas Beltrán
Puerto Real Area, Fajardo
Tel: 787-863 5195
www.fajardoinn.com
Small guesthouse with 10
rooms, ideal for travelers
looking for simple but
inexpensive lodging.
Restaurant and swimming
pool on the property. **$**

THE SOUTHEAST

**Caribe Playa Beach
Resort**
Route 3, Km 112.1, Patillas
Tel: 787-839 6339
www.caribeplaya.com
Simple beachfront studios
with their own kitchens
make self-catering a
breeze in this 30-room

resort. There is also a
seaview terrace restaurant,
barbecue, hammocks to
relax in, and a pool to
keep the children
occupied. **$**
**Four Points by Sheraton at
Palmas del Mar**
170 Candelero Drive, Humacao

Tel: 800-368 7764; 787-850 6000
www.fourpoints.com
This 107-unit suite resort
includes two 18-hole golf
courses, 16 tennis courts,
horseback-riding facilities,
scuba-diving, and several
good restaurants.
$$$

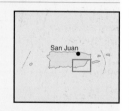

BELOW: the exclusive Palmas del Mar marina is filled with luxury yachts.

THE NORTH AND THE WEST

Dorado

Embassy Suites Dorado del Mar Beach and Golf Resort
201 Dorado del Mar Boulevard
Tel: 800-362 2779;
787-796 6125
www.embassysuitesdorado.com
A great place for a getaway just a few blocks from Isla Verde Beach. With 210 rooms in a modern block, an 18-hole championship golf course designed by local golf legend, Juan "Chi-Chi" Rodríguez, and a beautiful lagoon-style pool with a fine ocean view. There are also tennis courts and two restaurants. **$$$**

Hyatt Hacienda del Mar
301 Highway 693
Tel: 800-926 4447;
787-796 3000
www.hyatthaciendadelmar.hyatt.com
Large, luxury beachfront resort, which has been converted into a pricey timeshare complex. Fully equipped condominiums in modern tower blocks right on Dorado Beach. There is a large swimming pool, a spa and fitness center; residents can also enjoy a plethora of watersports such as sailing and snorkeling. **$$$**

Isabela

Costa Dorada Beach Resort
Route 466, Km 0.1
Tel: 877-975 0101; 787-872 7255
www.costadoradabeach.com
All 52 rooms have a view of the northern coast and offer standard amenities. **$**

Aguadilla

Cielo Mar Hotel
84 Montemar Avenue
Tel: 787-882 5959
www.cielomar.com
The hotel has ocean views; 72 rooms with amenities. **$**

Courtyard Marriott Aguadilla
West Parade/Belt Road, Ramey Base, Aguadilla
Tel: 800-321 2211;
787-658 8000
www.marriott.com/hotels/travel/bqncy-courtyard-aguadilla
Family resort-like setting with 141 rooms, pools, aquatic playground, fitness center, restaurant, bars. **$$**

Hotel El Pedregal
Route 111, Km 0.1,
Cuesta Nueva Street
Tel: 787-891 6068;
787-882 2865
www.hotelelpedregal.com
Landscaped property with ocean views. Pool area, restaurant and snack bar. **$**

Rincón

Casa Islena
Route 413 Interior, Km 4.8
Punta Higuero, Barrio Puntas
Tel: 888-289 7750; 787-823 1525
www.casa-islena.com
Guesthouse with nine rooms. Lovely romantic atmosphere and a friendly restaurant. **$**

Horned Dorset Primavera
Route 429, Km 3.0
Tel: 800-633 1857; 787-823 4030
www.horneddorset.com
With a reputation for privacy, elegance and fine service and 22 secluded suites. Restaurant. **$$$**

Lazy Parrot Inn
Route 413, Km 4.1, Barrio Puntas
Tel: 800-294 1752; 823 0224
www.lazyparrot.com
Funky 11-room guesthouse with pool and shop. **$**

Rincón of the Seas Grand Caribbean Hotel
Route 115, Km 12.2
Tel: 866-274 6266; 787-823 7500
www.rinconoftheseas.com
Comfortable hotel with stylish Art Deco interior and 112 rooms. Restaurant. Ideal for families. **$$**

Villa Cofresí Hotel
Road 115, Km 12.3
Tel: 787-823 2450
www.villacofresi.com
On the beachfront on the south side of the point. A laid-back, family-oriented

place with 68 rooms; continental breakfast included in the price. **$**

Mayagüez

Holiday Inn Mayagüez and Tropical Casino
2701 Hostos Avenue
Tel: 866-621 0183; 787-833 1100
www.holiday-inn.com/mayaguezpr
Centrally located hotel; 141 rooms with air conditioning, cable TV and lounge. **$**

Howard Johnson Downtown Mayagüez
70 East Méndez Vigo Street
Tel: 800-446 4656; 787-832 9191
www.hojo.com
Comfortable hotel with 39 rooms. Centrally located. **$**

Mayagüez Resort and Casino
Route 104, Km 0.3
Algarrobo Sector
Tel: 888-689 3030; 787-832 3030
www.mayaguezresort.com
Family hotel with 140 rooms set in 20 acres (8 hectares) of landscaped gardens. Restaurant. **$$**

BELOW: the Holiday Inn in Mayagüez is centrally located.

THE SOUTH

Copamarina Beach Resort
Route 333, Km 6.5, Guánica
Tel: 800-468 4553; 787-821 0505
www.copamarina.com
Luxury resort with 106 rooms, set in mangroves and forest. Ideal for families. **$$$**

Hilton Ponce Golf and Casino Resort
1150 Caribe Avenue, Ponce
Tel: 800-981 3232; 787-259 7676
www.hiltoncaribbean.com/ponce
Luxurious hotel with 253 rooms and suites. Casino and 27-hole championship golf course nearby. **$$**

Holiday Inn and Tropical Casino Ponce
3315 Ponce Bypass, Ponce
Tel: 866-621 0183; 787-844 1200
www.holiday-inn.com/ponce

Part of the international hotel chain. Some rooms overlook the Caribbean Sea. **$$**

Hotel Bélgica
122 Villa Street, Ponce
Tel: 787-844 3255
www.hotelbelgica.com
A simple 60-room hotel in the heart of town. **$**

Hotel Meliá
75 Cristina Street
Degetau Plaza, Ponce
Tel: 800-448 8355; 787-842 0260
www.hotelmeliapr.com
Lovely hotel with 73 rooms. Friendly staff and complimentary breakfast. Restaurant. **$**

Howard Johnson Ponce
103 Turpo Industrial Park
Mercedita Area, Ponce
Tel: 800-446 4656; 787-841 1000

www.hojo.com
Family accommodations with 120 rooms near the airport, with restaurant and swimming pool. Includes continental breakfast. **$**

Fox Delicias Hotel
6963 Calle Isabel, Ponce
Tel: 787-290 5050
Located in downtown Ponce Historic district, this boutique hotel offers 30 rooms and suites. All rooms have air conditioning, Internet access and cable television. Facilities include two restuarants. **$**

Quality Inn El Tuque
3330 Ponce Bypass, Road #2, Km 220.1, Ponce
Tel: 787-290 2000

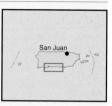

www.qualityinn.com/hotel-ponce-puerto_rico-PR013
The charming Quality Inn El Tuque is ideally located, close to many local points of interest and historic landmarks. Inside the infield of the Ponce International Speedway Park and next to the Speed & Splash Waterpark. The University of Puerto Rico at Ponce is just minutes away. **$**

CORDILLERA CENTRAL AND THE OUTER ISLANDS

Central

Casa Grande Mountain Retreat
Route 612, Km 0.3, Utuado
Tel: 888-343 2272; 787-894 3939
www.hotelcasagrande.com
This small mountain inn is located on a former coffee plantation. Twenty rustic rooms surrounded by lush forest and landscaped gardens. Swimming pool and yoga center on the property. No air conditioning or telephone in rooms. Restaurant. **$**

Monte Río Hotel
18 César González Street, Adjuntas
Tel: 787-829 3705
Hotel with 24 rooms, pool, and meeting facilities. Great views of the countryside. **$**

The Outer Islands

Culebra

Bahía Marina
Punta Soldado Road, Km 2.4
Tel: 787-742 0535
www.bahiamarina.net
Laid-back apartment-hotel complex comprising 16 simple condos with kitchenette and sea views. Near to the beach and a

nature reserve. Facilities include pool and watersports. Restaurant. **$$**

Club Seabourne
Fulladoza Bay
Tel: 800-981 4435; 787-742 3169
www.clubseabourne.com
An intimate boutique hotel with 14 stylish and comfortable villas and rooms set in tropical garden. Facilities include swimming pool. Restaurant; eat inside or out on the deck. Great views of the bay. **$$**

A Happy Vacation
Tel: 787-742 3000
All-inclusive packages for parties of two people and more. **$$**

Vieques

Amapola Inn and Bili Restaurant
144 Flamboyán Street
Esperanza sector
Tel: 787-741 1382
Simple beachfront guesthouse with eight small yet efficient rooms and studios. **$**

The Crow's Nest
Route 201, Km 1.5
Tel: 877-276 9763; 787-741 0033
www.crowsnestvieques.com

The small inn provides basic accommodation with views of the countryside near Isabel Segunda and a short drive to a good beach. Rooms have a kitchenette, and there is also a pool on the premises. **$$**

Hacienda Tamarindo
Route 996, Km 4.5
Puerto Real sector
Tel: 787-741 0420
www.haciendatamarindo.com
Lovely boutique hotel with 16 stylish and rustic rooms. The inn sits on a hilltop, so guests can enjoy some great views. **$$**

Hix Island House
Route 995, Km 1.5
Esperanza sector
Tel: 787-741 2302
www.hixislandhouse.com
Simple but stylishly designed boutique hotel. Concrete buildings surrounded by lovely gardens contain 13 airy rooms with partially open showers for nature lovers. The hotel has an eco-friendly philosophy. **$$**

Inn on the Blue Horizon
La Casa del Francés
Road 996, Km 4.3
Tel: 877-741 2583; 787-741 3318
www.innonthebluehorizon.com
Tastefully decorated

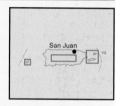

10-room guesthouse with a breathtaking view. Ideal for a relaxing getaway. Swimming pool and other facilities available. **$$$**

W Retreat and Spa – Vieques Island
Route 200, Km 3.2
Tel: 888-625 4988; 787-741 4100
www.whotels.com
(Opening Oct 1, 2009) Part of a hotel group, this health spa has 157 rooms and villa suites. Pretty beachfront and comfortable air-conditioned rooms. Fitness center and a spa offering a wide variety of treatments, some services available in-room. Watersports, tennis. Restaurant. **$$$**

PRICE CATEGORIES

Price categories are for a double room in high season:
$ = under $150
$$ = $150–250
$$$ = more than $250

E ATING OUT

RECOMMENDED RESTAURANTS, CAFÉS, AND BARS

What to Eat

Aside from having a delectable and historic native cuisine, Puerto Rico benefits from its American and Caribbean connections in having just as many of the world's cuisines as you'd find in the largest cities of the United States. Spanish, US, Mexican, Chinese, French, Italian, Swiss, Brazilian, Japanese, and other food is plentiful, especially in San Juan.

Puerto Rican cuisine differs from that of its Spanish neighbors in the Caribbean almost as much as it differs from that of the mainland US. Relying heavily on rice, beans, and whatever Puerto Ricans haul out of the sea, it is a mild, savory, well-balanced style of cuisine. See the feature on page 61 for more details.

Where to Eat

Puerto Rican food can be found in all manner of spots: in the modest urban *fondas*, where a rich *asopao de camarones* will cost you under seven dollars; in the rural *colmados* where delicious roast chicken is the order of the day; and in the posh restaurants of Old San Juan and Condado, such as La Mallorquina *(see opposite)*, the Caribbean's oldest continuously operating restaurant.

The restaurants of San Juan tend to be concentrated in certain areas. While *fondas* are all over town, international cuisine tends to be concentrated in the trendier parts of Old San Juan and in the more expensive areas of Condado and Santurce, such as Ashford Avenue. There is also a high concentration of American fast-food and restaurant chains in tourist areas.

These are found mainly in Isla Verde and Condado, and in the metropolitan area shopping malls, whether it's the food court or in the vicinity of the mall.

Healthy Options

There is a great movement toward health foods in Puerto Rico. Dozens of stores have cropped up dispensing vitamins, herbs, and organically grown foods. Also check out local supermarket chains (Pueblo, Grande, SuperMax) as they expand their gourmet and organic food selections.

Recommended: Mother Earth, Plaza Las Américas, third level, tel: 787-754 1995; Freshmart, an organic food supermarket with stores located on Route 887, Carolina, tel: 787-762 7890, and also on Plaza Montemar, 201 Indo Costa Street, corner with Calaf Tres Monjitas, Hato Rey, tel: 787-282 9108.

Specialty Foods

For those who crave French breads, Japanese green tea, or curry paste, San Juan is home to Asian food markets and other international specialty stores. Recommended: Asia Market, near Stop 18 on Fernández Juncos Avenue in Santurce; Eastern Market in Condado. Both specialize in Chinese and other Asian staples. Some of the more popular items in the stores are Chinese and Japanese medicines and teas.

For French goodies, stop in at La Boulangerie, 174 Taft Street, Santurce, tel: 787-721 6272. This bakery and bistro offers an assortment of French pastries, soups, and sandwiches, as well as pastas and poultry dishes. For classic Spanish fare, such as *paella*, *jamón serrano*, wines, and more, visit La Ceiba, 1239 Roosevelt Avenue in San Juan, tel: 787-782 0419, or Kasalta, 1966 McCleary Street in Condado, tel: 787-727 7340.

BELOW: alfresco lunch in San Juan.

RESTAURANT LISTINGS

OLD SAN JUAN

311 Trois Cent Onze
311 Fortaleza Street
Tel: 787-725 7959
www.311restaurantpr.com
Provence was the inspiration for this formal French restaurant set in a landmark building and decorated with tradition and style. Meals are sophisticated yet simple. Two outdoor patios add to its charm. Reservations recommended. Lunch and dinner Mon–Fri, dinner only Sat, closed Sun. **$$$**

Aguaviva
364 Fortaleza Street
Tel: 787-722 0665
www.oofrestaurants.com
Seaside Latino restaurant with chic and trendy decor. Mouthwatering seafood. Calling ahead to sign up on the waiting list is highly recommended. Lunch and dinner daily. **$$$**

Amadeus Café
106 San Sebastián Street
Tel: 787-722 8635
Caribbean casual and fusion cuisine is a favorite for the neighborhood regulars. Popular dishes include Asian-glazed pork ribs and penne arrabiata. Lunch and dinner Thur–Sun noon–11pm, dinner only Mon 6–10.30pm. **$$**

Barú
150 San Sebastián Street
Tel: 787-977 7107
www.barupr.com
Caribbean- and Mediterranean-influenced tapas and a sexy lounge atmosphere. Reservations recommended. Dinner daily, last order at 12.45am Thur–Sat. **$$$**

Café Berlin
407 San Francisco Street
Tel: 787-722 5205
"Gourmet vegetarian" eatery offering fresh pastas, organic foods, and a delicious salad bar. Daily 10am–10pm. **$$**

Café Manolín
201 San Justo Street
Tel: 787-723 9743

ABOVE: bread baskets at the ready.

www.cafemanolinoldsanjuan.com
Puerto Rican restaurant with excellent authentic cuisine at reasonable prices. Breakfast and lunch daily 6am–4.30pm. **$**

Carli Café Concierto
206 Recinto Sur Street (Banco Popular Building)
Tel: 787-725 4927
www.carlisworld.com
For more than 10 years, a place where locals and international patrons gather to enjoy live music and fine dining in a relaxed atmosphere. Savor exotic assortments of gourmet tapas and exquisite local and international entrees. Dinner Mon–Sat 3.30–11.30pm. **$$$**

Dragonfly
364 Fortaleza Street
Tel: 787-977 3886
www.oofrestaurants.com
Sexy Asian-Latino fare in an intimate space. Small dishes to share. Calling ahead for reservations recommended. Dinner daily 5.30pm until late. **$$$**

El Jibarito
280 Sol Street
Tel: 787-725 8395
www.eljibaritopr.com
Traditional *criollo* fare run for almost 30 years by the same family. Breakfast, lunch, and dinner daily 9am–10pm. **$$**

El Patio de Sam
102 San Sebastián Street
Tel: 787-723 1149
Caribbean cuisine served in a casual setting. Sam's hamburgers are legendary. Reservations are recommended. Lunch and dinner daily until 11.30pm. **$$$**

Il Perugino
105 Cristo Street
Tel: 787-722 5481
www.ilperugino.com
Italian restaurant where chef-owner Franco Seccarelli prepares specialties such as *pasta con vongole*, carpaccio of Angus beef and marinated salmon. Fine wine. Reservations required. Lunch Sat noon–3pm, dinner daily 6.30–11pm. **$$$**

La Bombonera
259 San Francisco Street
Tel: 787-722 0658
Traditional cafeteria-style bakery. The best place for an inexpensive, satisfying *arroz con pollo* and coffee with pastries, especially mallorcas. Breakfast, lunch, and dinner daily. **$$**

La Mallorquina
207 San Justo Street
Tel: 787-722 3261
Puerto Rican cuisine in the oldest restaurant on the island, dating from 1848.

House specialties: *asopao de marisco* and *arroz con pollo*. Worth a visit if only for the interior courtyard. Reservations required. Lunch and dinner Mon–Sat, closed Sept. **$$$**

Marmalade
317 Fortaleza Street
Tel: 787-724 3963
www.marmaladepr.com
Ultra-modern decor, vanguard cuisine. A place to be seen. Reservations are recommended. Dinner Mon–Thur 5–11pm, Sat–Sun until midnight. **$$$**

Nuyorican Café
312 San Francisco Street
Tel: 787-977 1276
This music lounge features salsa, Spanish rock, and reggae. Excellent tapas, pizza, and seafood salads. Dinner daily 7pm–2am. **$**

Old Harbor Brewery
202 Tizol Street, corner of Recinto Sur
Tel: 787-721 2100
www.oldharborbrewery.com
The only microbrewery on the island, it boasts seasonal handcrafted

PRICE CATEGORIES

Price categories are per person for three courses, with a half-bottle of wine:
$ = under $20
$$ = $20–40
$$$ = more than $40

ABOVE: colorful Parrot Club in Old San Juan.

beers in a family-friendly environment where old-world charms meet industrial chic. Top-quality steaks and local lobster. Lunch and dinner 11.30am–1am. **$$$**

Panza
329 Recinto Sur Street, Chateau Cervantes
Tel: 787-289 8900
www.cervantespr.com
Fine dining, with creative international cuisine. Reservations are required. Breakfast, lunch, and dinner daily 8am–midnight. **$$**

The Parrot Club
363 Fortaleza Street
Tel: 787-725 7370
www.oofrestaurants.com
A contemporary Latin bistro and bar featuring live music. Call in advance to put your party on the waiting list. Lunch and dinner daily, breakfast Sat and Sun. **$$$**

Raíces
315 Recinto Sur Street
Tel: 787-289 2121
www.restauranteraices.com
1940s rustic decor, spin-off of original in Caguas, this is a favorite for traditional local cuisine, garb, and all. Reservations are required. Lunch and dinner Mon–Sat 11am–11pm, Sun noon–10pm. **$$**

Sofia
355 San Francisco Street
Tel: 787-721 0396
Italian restaurant with pizzas, *linguine con vongole*

with pancetta, *churrasco*, veal chops, poached halibut, and braised lamb shank. The setting is casual, in a restored colonial house. Call ahead to join the waiting list. Lunch and dinner daily until 11.30, Sun until 10pm. **$$$**

Tantra
356 Fortaleza Street
Tel: 787-977 8141
www.tantrapr.com
Hindu-influenced food with modern flashes. Lunch and dinner daily noon–midnight, after hours midnight–3am excluding Sun. **$$$**

Puerta de Tierra

El Hamburger
402 Muñoz Rivera Avenue
Tel: 787-721 4269
Before fast-food restaurants started to take over the island, El Hamburger was the place to go, and it still draws the crowds. Build your own burger and pick your favorite jukebox song. Lunch and dinner daily, Sun–Thur until 12.15am, Fri–Sat until 4am. **$**

Lemongrass
Los Rosales, Caribe Hilton Hotel Gardens
Tel: 787-724 5888
A fusion of Indian, Thai, and Japanese flavors come together in this casual dining restaurant. Dinner daily. **$$$**

Marisquería Atlántica
7 Lugo Viñas Street
Tel: 787-722 0890
This Spanish seafood eatery prides itself on being the "friendliest fresh food and fish restaurant in town." Try daily specials. Lunch and dinner Tue–Sun. **$$$**

Normandie Restaurant
499 Muñoz Rivera Avenue, Normandie Hotel
Tel: 787-729 2929
www.normandiepr.com
Fine dining steakhouse in a beautiful Art Deco setting. Dinner daily. **$$$**

Condado

Ajili Mójili
1006 Ashford Avenue, Condado
Tel: 787-725 9195
www.hdmdesigns.com/ajili
Authentic local cuisine with a gourmet twist. Dishes include: *mofongo relleño*, *arroz con pollo, fricasé de cabrito, piononos, piñón* and *serenata de bacalao*. These local dishes cost far less in other places. Reservation policy is 72 hours in advance. Lunch and dinner daily. **$$$**

Antonio's Restaurant
1406 Magdalena Avenue
Tel: 787-723 7567
Spanish gourmet cuisine in an elegant atmosphere. Table settings are majestic, service impeccable. Steaks, chicken, and seafood complemented by Spanish wine. Reservations. Lunch

and dinner Mon–Fri, dinner only Sat. **$$**

Budatai
1056 Ashford Avenue
Tel: 787-725 6919
www.budatai.com
Restaurant, bar, terrace. Chef Roberto Treviño serves a blend of Asian-inspired foods with subtle hints of Latin and Caribbean spices and flavors in a posh environment. Lunch and dinner daily. **$$**

Cherry Blossom
1309 Ashford Avenue, San Juan Marriott Resort and Casino
Tel: 787-723 7300
Japanese steakhouse and sushi bar featuring teppanyaki preparation. Guests can order dinner from the bar on the second level. The service is fast and careful. Reservations. Lunch and dinner Mon–Fri, dinner only Sat, lunch only Sun. **$$$**

Cielito Lindo
1108 Magdalena Avenue, Condado
Tel: 787-723 5597
Authentic Mexican cantina with casual decor and dining. The festive atmosphere appeals to both tourists and locals. Less formal than most Condado restaurants. Lunch and dinner Mon–Sat. **$$**

Compostela
106 Condado Avenue
Tel: 787-724 6088
Spanish restaurant highly rated by *San Juan City Magazine*. The Galician

chef-owner, José Rey, prepares the freshest seafood with a deft hand and a creative contemporary spirit. Reservations required. Lunch and dinner Mon–Fri, dinner only Sat. **$$**

Green House
Ashford Avenue, Diamond Palace Hotel, Condado
Tel: 787-725 4036
Short orders and full dinners at this popular place. Stop in after a hard night clubbing. Breakfast, lunch, and dinner daily, Sun–Thur until 2am, Fri–Sat until 5am. **$$**

José José
1110 Magdalena Avenue, Condado
Tel: 787-725 8496
Named after its two owners, this restaurant serves international cuisine with a Creole touch, such as ostrich with chocolate foam and port reduction. Reservations. Lunch and dinner daily. **$$$**

Mandalay
999 Ashford Avenue, Condado Plaza Hotel
Tel: 787-721 9140
Oriental cuisine. The New York Times hails this as one of the best restaurants in Puerto Rico. The menu features Szechuan, Hunan, Mandarin, and Cantonese cuisine, as well as dim sum. Reservations. Lunch and dinner daily. **$$$**

Miró
76 Condado Avenue
Tel: 787-723 9593
Catalan/Spanish fresh fish and shellfish cooked Mediterranean-style. Plates of squid, octopus, oysters, clams, and langoustines abound. Reservations. Lunch and dinner Sun–Fri, dinner only Sat. **$$$**

Portobello
55 Condado Avenue, Diamond Palace Hotel
Tel: 787-722 5256
www.portobellopr.com
Fine northern Italian and international dishes. Ravioli, gnocchi, seafood, and the best pasta sauce on the island. Also paella and asopao. Reservations. Dinner daily. **$$**

Ramiro's
1106 Magdalena Avenue
Tel: 787-721 9049
Among Puerto Rico's finest restaurants featuring imaginative international specialties with a Spanish flair. Chefs/owners Óscar and Jesús Ramiro prepare memorable dishes. Excellent desserts and wine list. Try the white sangria. Reservations. Lunch and dinner Sun–Fri. **$$$**

Ristorante Tuscany
1309 Ashford Avenue, San Juan Marriott Resort
Tel: 787-722 7000 ext. 6219
www.sanjuanrestaurant.com
Italian cuisine, fine dining with an excellent wine list. Reservations recommended. Dinner daily 6–10pm. **$$** (early-bird dinner) **$$$** (à la carte).

Strip House
999 Ashford Avenue, Condado Plaza Hotel
Tel: 787-722 0150
www.condadoplaza.com/hotel_activities/strip_house.cfm
An instant classic, the luscious, all-red interior is adorned with rich, luxurious materials. Start with the lobster bisque and enjoy a perfect strip steak. Signature items include: shellfish plateau, rib-eye, sesame-crusted tuna, Maine lobster linguine. Dinner daily 5.30–11pm. **$$$**

Tony Roma's
999 Ashford Avenue, Condado Plaza Hotel
Tel: 787-722 0322
Baby back ribs with barbecued beans and coleslaw are a pleasing lunch or dinner. The Cajun spiced ribs are great. Lunch and dinner daily. **$$$**

Varita
999 Ashford Avenue, Condado Plaza Hotel
Tel: 787-919 7818
www.wilobenet.com
Puerto Rican favorites like lechón a la varita, rustic baked pastas and the best of good all-American classics are reinvented by Chef Wilo Benet here at his new restaurant. It is the perfect location for those looking for an excellent meal in a comfortable and casual setting. Lunch and dinner daily. **$$$**

Via Appia
1350 Ashford Avenue, Condado
Tel: 787-725 8711
Always busy Italian sidewalk café with pizza and pasta dishes. Lunch and dinner daily. **$$**

Zabó Creative
14 Candina Street
Tel: 787-725 9494
Restaurant in an old beach house in the heart of Condado. Choose from a variety of appetizers or a selection of entrées. Reservations recommended. Dinner Tue–Sat. **$$$**

Miramar

Augusto's Restaurant
801 Ponce de León Avenue, Courtyard by Marriott
Tel: 787-725 7700
Continental restaurant considered to be one of the best on the island. Winner of the prestigious Golden Fork Award. Reservations. Lunch and dinner Tue–Fri, dinner only Sat. **$$$**

Bistro de Paris
801 Ponce de León Avenue, Courtyard by Marriott
Tel: 787-721 8925
Menu favorites such as French onion soup, crushed pepper tenderloin flambé with cognac, cream, and potatoes au gratin, apple tart. Reservations. Breakfast, lunch, and dinner daily, Breakfast only Sun. **$$**

Chayote
603 Miramar Avenue, Olimpo Court Hotel
Tel: 787-722 9385
Contemporary Caribbean cuisine in elegant but casual surroundings. Lunch and dinner Tue–Fri, dinner only Sat. **$$$**

Delirio
762 Ponce de León Avenue
Tel: 787-722 0444
Contemporary local cuisine set in a sophisticated and chic environment. This trendy restaurant opened in 2006 in the former home of the late Raúl Juliá's family. Lunch and dinner Tue–Thur and Sat noon–2.30pm, 6–10.30pm, dinner only Fri from 6–11.30pm. **$$$**

BELOW: drinking in a café on Plaza del Mercado, Old San Juan.

PRICE CATEGORIES

Price categories are per person for three courses, with a half-bottle of wine:
$ = under $20
$$ = $20–40
$$$ = more than $40

HATO REY, RÍO PIEDRAS, AND PUERTO NUEVO

El Zipperle
352 F.D. Roosevelt Avenue, Hato Rey
Tel: 787-751 4335
www.elzipperle.com
German/Spanish cuisine
in an old-time eating
and meeting place.
Reservations. Lunch
and dinner daily.
$$$

Frida's Mexican Restaurant
128 Domenech Avenue, Hato Rey
Tel: 787-763 4827
www.fridasmexicanrestaurant.com
Mexican cuisine, casual
ambience and fine dining. A
local favorite. Reservations.
Lunch and dinner Mon–Sat.
$$$

Jinya's Restaurant
1009 Piñeiro Avenue, Puerto Nuevo
Tel: 787-783 2330
Delicious traditional sushi
rolls and sashimi, as well as

"Japanrican" rolls with
chicharrón and *bacalao*.
This casual-elegant
restaurant also has steak
and chicken teriyaki,
tempura, and soft-shell
crab. Daily specials.
Reservations recommended
on weekends. Lunch and
dinner Tue–Sat, Sun
3–9pm. **$$$**

Los Chavales Restaurant
253 F.D. Roosevelt Avenue, Hato
Rey
Tel: 787-767 5017
www.banqueteloschavales.com
Old-time popular gathering
place with international
Spanish cuisine and fresh
seafood in an elegant
setting. Reservations
recommended. Lunch and
dinner Mon–Sat. **$$$**

Mangère
311 De Diego Avenue, Puerto Nuevo

Tel: 787-728 5901
www.mangerepr.com
Italian cuisine with daily
specials. Reservations.
Lunch and dinner daily.
$$$

Margarita's
1013 F.D. Roosevelt Avenue, Puerto
Nuevo
Tel: 787-781 8452
Mexican, well known for its
margaritas, enchiladas,
and *fajitas*. Mariachi band
on the weekend. Lunch
and dinner daily.
$$

Metropol 3
124 F.D. Roosevelt Avenue,
Hato Rey
Tel: 787-751 4022
www.metropolpr.com
Cuban cuisine that's a
long-time local favorite.
Daily specials include
meat, chicken, and fish

dishes with rice and beans
and fried plantain. Try
natilla and Cuban coffee
for dessert. One of three
Metropols in Puerto Rico.
Lunch and dinner daily.
$$

Puerto Nuevo

Café Valencia
1000 Muñoz Rivera Avenue,
Hato Rey
Tel: 787-764 4786
Traditional Spanish
cuisine. Famous for its
paella. Reservations
recommended. Lunch and
dinner Sun–Fri, dinner only
Sat. **$$$**

Tierra Santa
284 F.D. Roosevelt Avenue,
Hato Rey
Tel: 787-763 5775
Hummus, tabuleh and
shish kebab are favorites
here. Entrées include
kustaleta (lamb chops)
and *gambary* (shrimps
Arab-style). Belly-dancing
Fri–Sat. Reservations
recommended. Lunch and
dinner daily. **$$$**

Yuan Restaurant
255 Ponce de León Avenue, MCS
Plaza, Hato Rey
Tel: 787-766 0666
Set in attractive, dimly lit
decor with roses on each
table. Delicately prepared
Chinese cuisine.
Reservations recommended.
Lunch and dinner daily.
$$$

BELOW: busy in the kitchen.

SANTURCE/OCEAN PARK

Bebo's Café
1600 Loíza Street
Tel: 787-726 1008
Cheap and tasty local
dishes offered like
*pastelones, salmorejo de
jueyes* and roasted *pernil*.
Casual ambience. Breakfast,
lunch, and dinner daily,
kitchen closes 12.30am.
$$

Che's
35 Caoba Street, Punta Las Marías
Tel: 787-726 7202
Argentinian restaurant
specializing in *parrilladas*,

churrasco and *chimichurri*
as well as grilled steaks
and pasta. Reservations.
Lunch and dinner daily.
$$$$

Pamela's Restaurant
1 Santa Ana Street, Ocean Park
Tel: 787-726 5010
www.numerounoguesthouse.com
This quaint little restaurant
is nestled inside a guest-
house right on the beach.
Casual fine dining at its
best, the service is
impeccable and the
Caribbean dishes are

prepared with the freshest
ingredients. Lunch and
dinner daily. **$$$**

Pikayo
299 De Diego Avenue, Museo de
Arte de Puerto Rico
Tel: 787-721 6194
www.wilobenet.com
Celebrity chef Wilo Benet's
first of three restaurants,
Pikayo's creative cuisine
combines gourmet recipes
with local produce and
fresh seafood. Considered
to be one of the best
restaurants in San Juan.

Reservations recommen-
ded. Lunch and dinner
Tue–Fri, dinner only Mon
and Sat. **$$$**

Uvva
1 Tapia Street at Hostería del Mar,
Ocean Park
Tel: 787-727 3302
www.hosteriadelmarpr.com
Caribbean flavors mix with
Mediterranean delights in
this very romantic hotspot
by the beach. Alfresco
dining available. Breakfast,
lunch, and dinner daily.
$$$

partying is generally taken with more reckless abandon. The whole city is crowded with bars and dancing establishments of every description.

In Old San Juan, **Nuyorican Café**, **Los Hijos de Borínquen**, and **El Patio de Sam** provide good spots for drinking and chatting.

What's On

Free publications such as *¡Qué Pasa!* and *Bienvenidos*, usually found at hotels and tourist offices, provide up-to-date information on local nightlife. Websites such as universia (www.universia.pr/home/index.jsp) provide a full calendar of events for the university crowd and beyond. Also check out the local newspaper sites (www.endi.com, www.vocero.com) for the latest happenings.

Gay and lesbian travelers can pick up a copy of *Puerto Rico Breeze*, which can be found at the gay-friendly Atlantic Beach Hotel in Condado.

Nightclubs and Discos

Old San Juan

Café Bohemio
100 Cristo Street,
El Convento Hotel
Tel: 787-723 9300
Open: daily
Professional and gay-friendly crowd, popular on Tuesday.
Carli Café Concierto
Corner of Recinto Sur and San Justo streets, Plazoleta Rafael Carrión
Tel: 787-725 4927
Open: Monday–Saturday
Dining club with live jazz by former Beach Boys pianist Carli Muñoz.
Club Lazer
251 Calle Cruz
Tel: 787-721 4479
www.clublazer.com
Open: Friday–Sunday
Loud youthful disco with hip-hop, R&B, and reggaeton. Open late.
El Batey
Cristo Street
Open: 24 hours
Small, loud dive. Great classic rock jukebox.
Hard Rock Café
253 Recinto Sur
Tel: 787-724 7625
www.hardrock.com
Open: daily
Delicious food accompanied by loud music, with rock 'n' roll memorabilia. Performances by up-and-coming and established acts.
Kudetá
314 Fortaleza Street
Tel: 787-721 3548

Open: Thursday–Saturday, until late Friday–Saturday
Two-floor club with dance floor on the second level and a VIP lounge on the third. Music includes hip-hop, house, techno, and progressive. Dress fashionably; attracts a youngish crowd, age range 18–30.
Nuyorican Café
312 San Francisco Street, entrance through the alleyway
Tel: 787-977 1276; 787-366 5074
www.nuyoricancafepr.com
Open: daily until late
House band plays classic salsa on Wednesday/Friday. Other nights feature Latin jazz, rock, or Latin fusion. Poetry and theater as well. A casual, popular bar and restaurant popular with a diverse crowd.
Rumba
152 San Sebastián Street
Tel: 787-725 4407
Open: Thursday–Saturday
Dance to live salsa on Friday and Saturday with an over-25 crowd. Music varies on Thursdays and the crowd is younger. Popular with locals and tourists alike. Casual attire.

Puerta de Tierra

Kali
1407 Ashford Avenue
Tel: 787-721 5104
Open: Tuesday–Sunday
Dress to impress for this cool restaurant and bar where folks chill to lounge, hip-hop, and electronic music. The place attracts a diverse crowd from 25–50 years old. Open late.
The Lobby Bar at San Juan Marriott
1309 Ashford Avenue
Tel: 800-464 5005; 787-722 7000
www.marriott.com/sjupr
Open: Wednesday–Sunday
Dance the night away to live salsa and

merengue. Attracts a diverse crowd from 25–60. Dress up.
Moorings
1214 Ashford Avenue
Tel: 787-725 2192
Open: Wednesday–Sunday, until late on weekends
Bar and grill with 1980s rock, salsa, merengue and reggaeton, plus karaoke on Wednesday. The crowd ranges from 22–28 years old.
N-Lounge
Normandie Hotel,
499 West Muñoz Rivera Avenue
Tel: 787-729 2929
www.normandiepr.com
Open: Tuesday–Sunday
Electronic lounge music, casual ambience; lounge and terrace. The age of the crowd is 23 and over.

Hato Rey

Club Boccacio
1–2 El Centro Building
Tel: 787-299–1745
Open: Friday–Saturday until late
A casual club that plays merengue, salsa, and dance music. The place to be on Friday for gays and lesbians; the crowd is 21–45 years old.

Santurce

Krash Klub
1257 Ponce de León Avenue
Tel: 787-722 1131
www.krashpr.com
Open: Wednesday–Saturday
Formerly known as Eros, this club plays hip-hop, house, reggaeton, and is popular with gay men aged 18–60.
La Placita
Open: Thursday–Saturday
Historic open-air plaza, during the day a farmers' market; at night the square is filled with young professionals, *fondas*, restaurants, and live music.

BELOW: buzzing nightlife.

Tia Maria's Liquor Store
326 José de Diego, Stop 22
Tel: 787-724 4011
Open: daily, until late on weekends
Casual pub with billiards. During
business hours there is a mixed
heterosexual crowd; after 7pm it
attracts a gay crowd.

Isla Verde

Brava
El San Juan Hotel and Casino
Tel: 787-791 1000
www.bravapr.com
Open: Thursday–Saturday
Elegant yet fun, an old-style disco for
night owls aged 23 and over.
**The Lobby at El San Juan Hotel &
Casino**
6360 Isla Verde Avenue
Tel: 787-791 1000
It feels as if all of San Juan heads for
the lobby on Saturday night for salsa
and merengue at **El Chico Bar** and
drinks and music at the **Oval Bar**.
Dress to impress.
Lupi's
Route 187, Km 1.3
Tel: 787-253 2198
Mexican bar and sports cantina.
Delicious *margaritas*, fabulous *fajitas*,
and live music.
San Juan Water & Beach Club Hotel
2 Tartak Street
Tel: 787-728 3666
www.waterbeachclubhotel.com
Open: Tuesday–Saturday
House, R&B, and techno music is
played in the lobby bar and lounge
called **Liquid**, which is open until very
late. The rooftop bar and lounge,
called **Wet**, features a sushi bar, a
spectacular view, and is open daily.

Shots
677 Isla Verde Avenue, Isla Verde Mall
Tel: 787-253 1443
Open: Wednesday–Sunday until late
Sports bar and restaurant featuring
salsa on Thursday, Friday, and
Saturday with a variety of live bands.
The crowd is aged 18–35. Dress is
casual attire.

Casinos

Gambling is legal in Puerto Rico.
Casinos have blackjack, roulette,
poker, slots, and games of chance.
Casinos are permitted only in hotels
and usually tend to open from noon
until the early hours.

FESTIVALS

Annual Events

Almost every holiday is the occasion
for a festival in Puerto Rico, many of
them legislated, others informal.
Every town has its patron saint, and
every saint a festival. These, known
as *fiestas patronales*, are the biggest
events of the year in their respective
towns. The most famous is probably
Loíza's **Fiesta de Santiago Apóstol**
in July. The largest is certainly San
Juan's **Noche de San Juan Bautista**
in late June, and a very popular one
with islanders is the **San Sebastián
Street Festival** in Old San Juan in
mid-January.
  The **Le Lo Lai Festival** is a year-
round program established by the
Puerto Rican Tourism Company. It

involves evening shows of Puerto
Rican music and dance staged in
hotels and in Old San Juan. For
details contact the Tourism Company
(tel: 787-721 2400, ext. 2715, or
800-866 7827).

SPORTS

Outdoor Activities
Freshwater Fishing

There are 12 private clubs devoted
to freshwater fishing, in the island's
man-made lakes and reservoirs.
  Bass, both large-mouth and
peacock, are local favorites, though
at least four other species like sunfish,
tilapia and catfish are sought after as
well. Plastic worms are the most
popular choice of bait among bass
fishermen. The reservoirs are stocked
with more than 2,000 fish from the
Maricao Fish Hatchery (Los Viveros).
  Only four reservoirs are open to
the public and are managed by the
Department of Natural and
Environmental Resources (DNER).
Facilities include boat ramps,
information centers and restrooms.
For reservoir fishing regulations or
for directions to the facilities, call
the DNER's Reserves and Refuges
Division, tel: 787-999 2200, ext.
2713; www.drna.gobierno.pr.
  The four reservoirs open to the
public are:
Cerrillos Lake
Ponce
Tel: 787-259 9979
Fairly deep and large. Facilities

BELOW: young dancers in the *Parada del Descubrimiento* in Aguada, which commemorates the discovery of Puerto Rico.

include a barbecue. The lake is accessible using Route 139.

Guajataca Lake
Quebradillas
Tel: 787-896 7640
One of the largest reservoirs in Puerto Rico, receives 27,000 visitors per year. Off Route 119 in San Sebastián.

La Plata Lake
Toa Alta
Tel: 787-983 7215
Measuring 26 sq miles (67 sq km), this is Puerto Rico's second-largest lake. It is located between Toa Alta, Bayamón, and Naranjito, and is accessible by Route 167.

Lucchetti Lake
Yauco
Tel: 787-856 4887
Fed by the Yauco River and located 4 miles (6km) outside the town of Yauco. It has a camping area, barbecue, and bathrooms with showers. Accessible through Route 128, Km 12.3.

Saltwater Fishing

Saltwater fishing, particular deep-sea fishing, is also popular, with several bill fish tournaments held off the coast. Shallow-water fishing is also practiced on the island, and there's excellent tarpon fishing. For shallow-water fishing, take a skiff to the coastal mangroves.

For deep-sea fishing, boats can be chartered in San Juan, Fajardo, and Arecibo, which are close to the Atlantic's Puerto Rico Trench, dubbed Blue Marlin Alley. Today, most caught marlin are tagged and released. To fish wahoo, head to deep waters off Humacao. For tuna, head to the Mona Passage on boats departing from Rincón, Mayagüez, Cabjo Rojo, and La Parguera. The best months to catch blue marlin are August and September, while yellow and blackfin tuna, wahoo, and bonito have their own seasons.

Deep-sea and shallow-water fishing charters are available from:

Adventures Tourmarine
Cabo Rojo
Tel: 787-375 2625

Caribbean Outfitters
Carolina
Tel: 787-396 8346

Castillo Tours and Watersports
San Juan
Tel: 787-791 6195

Light Tackle Adventure Fishing
Cabo Rojo
Tel: 787-849 1430

Parguera Fishing Charters
La Parguera
Tel: 787-382 4698

Tropical Fishing Charters
Fajardo
Tel: 787-379 4461

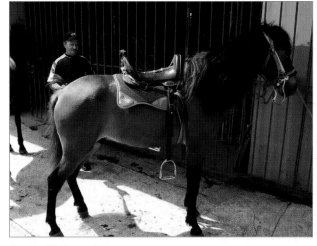

ABOVE: saddled up ready to go.

Hiking

There are several hiking trails in Puerto Rico and a great number afford spectacular vistas. There are particularly good hikes in the Caribbean National Forest at El Yunque, as well as in the Guánica State Forest and on Mona Island. Río Camuy Cave Park and Las Cabezas de San Juan Nature Reserve have what are considered walks rather than hikes, but are still enjoyable. The Puerto Rico Department of Natural Resources in San Juan (tel: 787-999 2200, ext. 5156; www.drna.gobierno.pr) can provide more information on many of the country's trails.

Horseback Riding

Hacienda Carabalí
Luquillo
Tel: 787-889 5820
With *paso fino* horses and an excellent reputation.

Rancho Buena Vista
Palmas del Mar Resort, Humacao
Tel: 787-479 7479
Upscale.

Tropical Trail Rides
Isabela
Tel: 787-872 9256
Horseback riding through forest and on beaches.

Golf and Tennis

Golf courses and tennis courts are scattered throughout the island, though most of the better ones are in the large, more expensive resorts. A variety of hotels sometimes allow access to non-guests for a reasonable fee.

Resorts with 18-hole championship golf courses include:

Embassy Suites Dorado del Mar
Dorado
Tel: 787-796 3070

Palmas del Mar
Humacao
Tel: 787-285 2256

Westin Río Mar
Río Grande
Tel: 787-888 6000

Kayaking

Kayaks are an ecologically friendly way of exploring the island's mangroves and its coast. They're also an excellent way to check out the stunning bioluminescent bays in Vieques and Fajardo. Companies that rent kayaks or offer tours include the following:

San Juan Waterfun
San Juan
Tel: 787-643 4510

Travesías Isleñas Yaureibo
Vieques
Tel: 939-630 1267

Yokahú Kayak Trips
Fajardo
Tel: 787-604 7375

Sailing

Most of Puerto Rico's sailors head to Fajardo or Ponce for weekends on the water. Try one of the charter companies below:

Puerto del Rey Marina
Fajardo
Tel: 787-860 1000

Ponce Yacht and Fishing Club
Tel: 787-842 9003

Ventajero Sailing Charters
Fajardo
Tel: 787-645 9129
Boats of all sizes and descriptions available for rental. Tours.

Scuba-Diving

Puerto Rico is prime scuba territory. Some operators offer sailing, snorkeling, and fishing in addition to scuba-diving. Try: **Caribbean School of Aquatics**, tel: 787-728 6606; 787-383 5700; www.saildiveparty.com.

Located in San Juan, it also serves Fajardo, Culebra, and Vieques. Dive lessons from the following:

San Juan
Caribe Aquatic Adventure
Park Plaza Normandie Hotel,
Puerta de Tierra
Tel: 787-281 8858

Culebra and Rincón
Culebra Divers
Dewey
Tel: 787-742 0803
Taíno Divers
Rincón
Tel: 787-823 6429

Fajardo
Fajardo is probably the island's capital for watersports. Contact:
Catamaran Getaway
Villa Marina Yacht Harbor, Fajardo
Tel: 787-860 7327

Snorkeling

Equipment can be rented or bought at dive shops and department stores. Some companies that offer snorkeling tours are:
Adventures by the Sea
San Juan
Tel: 787-374 1410
Paradise Scuba and Snorkeling
La Parguera
Tel: 787-899 7611

Surfing

Puerto Rico has almost ideal conditions for surfing – warm water, brilliant sunshine, and heavy but even tubular surf. Many of the most popular spots are convenient to San Juan: Aviones, off Route 187 in Piñones, is probably the most renowned, and so named because of the airplanes that fly over from the nearby international airport. La Ocho, in Puerta de Tierra's Escambrón Beach, is also popular and crowded on weekends. In the northwest, Punta Higüero, off Route 413 in Rincón, is famous, while Jobos Beach proves popular among Aguadilla and Isabela residents.

Swimming

Puerto Rico has sandy beaches, some crowded, others secluded and quiet. Many are *balnearios* with public bathing facilities that include lifeguards, refreshment stands, and dressing rooms. Around San Juan most popular are Luquillo and Vega Baja. All beachfront, except the beach at the Caribe Hilton, is public.

Swimmers are advised to be careful of strong surf and undertow at beaches, especially in the northwest. Swimmers should head to Escambrón Beach, a short walk from the Normandie Hotel or the Caribe Hilton in Puerta de Tierra.

Windsurfing and Kiteboarding

Windsurfing and kiteboarding are popular island-wide. Ocean Park in San Juan and La Parguera are ideal places to practice both sports. For rentals and lessons try:

Kiteboarding PR
#2 Santa Ana Street,
1A, Ocean Park
Tel: 787-374 5329
www.kiteboardingpr.com
KitesurfPR
2434 Loíza Street #2,
San Juan
Tel: 787-221 0635
www.kitesurfpr.com
Vela Uno
2430 Calle Loíza,
Punta las Marías
Tel: 787-728 8716
www.velauno.com

Health Clubs and Spas

Bodyderm Spa
Copamarina Beach Resort,
Guánica
Tel: 787-821 0505
Golden Door Spa at Las Casitas Village
El Conquistador Golf Resort and Casino, Fajardo
Tel: 800-468 8365; 787-863 1000 ext. 7300
Mandara Spa
Westin Río Mar Beach, Golf and Resort Spa, Río Grande
Tel: 787-888 6000
N'Spa
Normandie Hotel,
Puerta de Tierra
Tel: 787-729 2929
The Ritz-Carlton Spa
Ritz-Carlton Hotel,
Isla Verde
Tel: 787-253 1700, ext. 4131
Secrets of Eden Spa
331 Recinto Sur Street,
Old San Juan
Tel: 787-721 6400

BELOW: exploring Puerto Rico's extraordinary underwater world.

ABOVE: elegant shopping street.

Zen Spa and Health Studio
1054 Ashford Avenue,
Condado
Tel: 787-722 8433

Spectator Sports

Baseball and Basketball

Puerto Rico's national pastime is baseball. The island has produced some of the great stars of the game.

The Puerto Rico Winter League season runs from November to February, with teams in Santurce, Caguas, Ponce, Manatí, Mayagüez, and Arecibo. The league's official website is www.puertoricobaseballleague.com, although www.hitboricua.com is a good resource sanctioned by the league.

Many aspiring big-leaguers (and not a few has-beens) play in Puerto Rico. Games are almost daily, and tickets generally inexpensive. Those who want to keep abreast of American and National Leagues will find complete box scores in the local papers. Also, cable TV brings a variety of big-league games.

Basketball is another popular team sport. The Superior Basketball League (www.bsnpr.com) has teams in almost all the larger cities.

Horse-Racing

Horse-racing in San Juan is at the Camarero Racetrack in Canóvanas, 10 miles (16km) east of the city. For more information on races, tel: 787-641 6060 or www.hipodromo-camarero.com/mainenglish.html.

Cockfighting

For a truly Puerto Rican sporting experience, cockfighting is hard to match. Although the sport is viewed as inhumane by many, its popularity on the island cannot be denied. In this sport, dozens of the proudest local cocks are matched one-on-one in a tiny ring, or *gallera*. The predominantly male crowds are almost as interesting as the fights themselves. These knowledgeable enthusiasts are familiar with a cock's pedigree through several generations. The shouts are deafening, the drinking is reckless, and the betting is heavy. Betting is done on a gentlemanly system of verbal agreement, and hundreds of dollars can change hands on a single fight.

Galleras are scattered all over, and the fights in even the most rural areas can draw hundreds. Admission can be expensive, but the beer is cheap. For information on cockfighting in the San Juan area:

Club Gallístico de Puerto Rico
Isla Verde Avenue, Isla Verde
Tel: 787-791 1557
Club Gallístico Río Piedras
Route 844, Km 4.2, Trujillo Alto
Tel: 787-760 6815

SHOPPING

Puerto Rico is a great shopping destination. From the streets of Old San Juan to the outlets of Barceloneta and Canovanas, visitors will find everything from jewelry and local crafts to spirits and tobacco.

San Juan alone boasts the largest shopping center in the Caribbean, Plaza Las Américas. This shopping mecca of more than 300 stores features designer clothing, fine jewelry, pottery, a 13-theater multiplex, and more than 40 dining alternatives.

Built in 1968 by Empresas Fonalledas, Inc. on a 48-acre (19-hectare) lot, Plaza's anchor stores include Macy's, Sears, and Borders. It can be easy to spend the day here.

Closer to Old San Juan is the neighborhood of Condado.

Condado is an oceanfront, pedestrian-oriented community. It's also packed with hotels and thrives with its mix of residents and visitors. Famous for high-end shopping, Ashford Avenue features names such as Gucci, Dior, and Ferragamo. Other upscale businesses that have opened in the last year include Cartier, Louis Vuitton, Mont Blanc, and Zen Spa.

For high fashion, visit Hellmuth. Cristóbal Jewelry is also in the area and specializes in couture jewelry. Verovero represents Prada and Miu Miu bags and shoes, and Suola carries none other than famous designer Valentino. Two other notable boutiques across from the landmark La Concha Hotel are Fashion Fitness and Mia.

For a mix of sightseeing, art galleries, small antique shops, and souvenirs, go to Old San Juan. Native handicrafts are good buys, as well as paintings and sculptures by Puerto Rican artists. Among these, the carved wooden religious idols known as *santos* (saints) have been called Puerto Rico's greatest contribution to the plastic arts and are sought by collectors. For the best selection of santos, head for Galería Botello, Olé, or Puerto Rican Arts and Crafts.

There are a lot of T-shirt and souvenir shops, especially along Fortaleza Street and closer to the cruise ship ports, but the major shopping venues are on San Francisco and Cristo streets.

Factory stores for Ralph Lauren, Coach, and Gant are all on Cristo

TRANSPORTATION

ACCOMMODATIONS

EATING OUT

ACTIVITIES

A – Z

LANGUAGE

Street. And for something different, stop by El Galapón for beautiful masks.

Old San Juan is known as a premier destination for quality jewelry at discount prices, and there are many vendors lining Cristo and Fortaleza streets. Some shops worth entering are Joyería Riviera, Club Jibarito and Bared.

Plaza Carolina is a great spot to satisfy mall fever. Operated by Simon Property Group, Inc., Plaza Carolina is the second-largest shopping center in Puerto Rico. Anchored by JC Penney and Sears, it features over 240 stores.

Plaza Carolina is minutes away from San Juan and close to the Luis Muñoz Marín International Airport in Isla Verde. Popular shops include Old Navy, The Children's Place, G by Guess, Aldo Shoes, and bebe.

Puerto Rico has two outlet malls, the Route 66 Outlet Mall in Canóvanas and Prime Outlets in Barceloneta. The Route 66 Outlet Mall is close to Carolina and the metropolitan area, and minutes away from the hotels and beaches of Río Grande and Fajardo.

This outlet opened in 2001 and features more than 80 specialty stores and a food court with over a dozen restaurants. Stores such as Gap Outlet, Calvin Klein, Nike Factory Outlet, Tommy Hilfiger, and Skechers populate the 470,000-sq-ft (43,700-sq-metre) shopping mall.

West of San Juan is the other outlet shopping center – Prime Outlets. Located in Barceloneta and easy to reach via Highway 22, this recently expanded center attracts fashion-conscious locals and tourists alike.

The village-style center stretches out to more than 336,000 sq ft (31,200 sq metres), with its retail mix ranging from discount clothing to electronics games stores. Some of the anchor stores are: Gap Outlet, Polo Ralph Lauren Factory Store.

Mall hours are standard: 9am to 9pm Monday to Saturday and 11am to 5pm on Sundays. Shopping centers with movie theaters have extended food court hours and stand alone restaurants open later as well. Shops in Condado and Old San Juan tend to close earlier, between 6pm and 7pm.

Plaza Carolina
Villa Fontana, Fragoso Avenue, Carolina
Tel: 787-768 0514
Plaza Las Américas
525 F.D. Roosevelt Avenue, San Juan
Tel: 787-767 5202
Prime Outlets
1 Prime Outlets Boulevard (Highway 2, Km 54.8), Barceloneta
Tel: 787-846 5300
Route 66 Outlet Mall
Route 66 and Route 3, Canóvanas
Tel: 787-256-7040

Where to Shop in Old San Juan

Bared (jewelry)
Fortaleza and San Justo streets
Tel: 787-724 3780
Club Jibarito & Hellenis
202 Cristo Street
Tel: 787-724 7797
Joyería Riviera
257 Fortaleza Street
Tel: 787-725 4000
Puerto Rican Arts and Crafts
204 Fortaleza Street
Tel: 787-725 5596
Spicy Caribbee
154 Cristo Street
Tel: 787-725 4690

What to Buy

Cigars are a good purchase, and in spite of laws prohibiting smoking in public, tobacco and cigar shops have sprung up. There are many shops in Old San Juan, such as **The Tobacco Shop** at Plaza Las Américas. It is well stocked, but a bit pricey. **Habana Cuba** is on San Patricio Avenue in San Patricio, and **International House of Cigars** is on Avenida Miranda in Río Piedras. **El San Juan Hotel and Casino** has a "cigar boutique," which sells fine cigars from the Dominican Republic, Honduras, and Jamaica.

Locally made arts and crafts are another good choice. Contact the Puerto Rico Tourism Company's Cultural Affairs Division (tel: 787-723 0682) for advice.

Books

The following have a good selection of books in both English and Spanish:
Bookworm
1129 Ashford Avenue, Condado
Tel: 787-722 3344
Borders
Plaza Las Américas, Hato Rey
Tel: 777 0916
Plaza Escorial, Carolina
Tel: 787-701 6200
Mayagüez Mall
Tel: 787-833 4333
By the Book
304 Ponce de León Avenue, Hato Rey
Tel: 787-777 0485
Castle Books
San Patricio Shopping Center
Tel: 787-774 1790
La Tertulia
204 O'Donnell Street, Old San Juan
Tel: 787-724 8200

BELOW: souvenirs from El Yunque rainforest gift shop.

A – Z

A HANDY SUMMARY OF PRACTICAL INFORMATION, ARRANGED ALPHABETICALLY

A dmission Charges

The average museum admission is $5 for adults. Some nightclubs and pubs have admission fees, between $10 and $15. Public beaches administered by the National Parks Company also charge a small fee for parking ($2 for motorcycles, $3 for cars, $4 for vans), but pedestrians can enter free of charge. Reduced or free admission is widely available for children and seniors (60 and up) at museums, movie theaters and top attractions.

B udgeting for Your Trip

Food is one of the things people spend the most money on while on vacation. A typical meal at a moderately priced restaurant can average $20 per person for an appetizer, entrée, and dessert. Overall, the average cost of an entrée is $20. A glass of wine will set you back between $6 and $9. Domestic and imported beers cost around $5 and desserts $6.

An evening at an all-inclusive resort is around $400 per person, but staying at a country inn or urban villa is between $70 and $120.

A taxi ride from Luis Muñoz Marín International Airport in Isla Verde to a nearby hotel can average $12. Bus admission is $0.75 and Urban Train rides are $1.50. Car rental rates average at $40 for the day.

C hildren

Puerto Rico is a family-friendly destination, and many hotels offer family discounts and children's programs. These may include babysitting services and camp-like activities such as nature hikes, art workshops, and tennis lessons. For older kids, activities can include surfing and scuba-diving lessons, Spanish courses and dance classes.

Most restaurants offer a children's menu, and some have special offers where children can eat for free.

BELOW: Puerto Rico is a family-friendly destination.

CLIMATE CHART

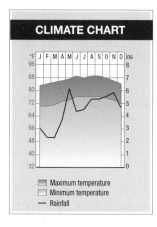

☐ Maximum temperature
☐ Minimum temperature
— Rainfall

Top Five Kid-Friendly Hotels On the Island

1. El Conquistador Resort and Golden Door Spa
2. The Río Mar Beach Resort and Spa: A Wyndham Grand Resort
3. Caribe Hilton
4. The Ritz-Carlton, San Juan Hotel, Spa and Casino
5. Courtyard by Marriott Isla Verde

Climate

Puerto Rico has one of the most pleasant and unvarying climates in the world, with daily highs almost invariably at 70–85°F (9–21°C). The island is at its wettest and hottest in August, with 7 inches (18cm) the average monthly rainfall and 82°F (28°C) the average daily high. During the rainy season, sudden late-afternoon squalls are common.

Regional variations are noticeable: Ponce and the southern coast are

BELOW: keeping Puerto Rico safe.

warmer and drier than San Juan and the north. It is coldest in the higher altitudes of the Cordillera, where the lowest temperature in the island's history was recorded near Barranquitas: 39°F (4°C).

Average daily high temperatures for San Juan range from 75°F (24°C) in January and February to 82°F (28°C) from June through September.

What to Wear/Bring

Puerto Rican dressing is casual yet mostly conservative: jeans, shorts, and long trousers are common. Only in a very small number of clubs are jackets and ties really required, and businessmen often remove their jackets in the course of the workday. However, shed the shorts and tennis shoes when you go out at night, as Puerto Ricans like to dress up. Colorful, medium-length dresses are versatile evening wear for women. Anything more than a light sweater is seldom necessary, even on winter nights in the Cordillera. An umbrella will come in handy, especially in rainy late summer on the island's northern coast.

However, a high-factor sunscreen and a hat are essential for those who plan to spend even a minimal amount of time outdoors.

Crime and Safety

In recent years, the serious crime rate in Puerto Rico has skyrocketed, but following a crackdown by police the annual murder rate has dropped. It is a place with high unemployment and a tourist population that is often gullible and vulnerable. Travelers would be wise to take precautions, such as

staying in well-lit and populated areas when walking at night.

Petty theft and confidence scams are more prevalent than violent crimes. Always lock your room, especially in smaller lodgings. Never leave luggage unattended or out of your sight. Most hotels will store bags at the front desk, as will many restaurants and shops. Never leave any valuables in your room. It is advisable to leave your room key at the front desk when you go out.

Always lock automobiles, regardless of whether you have left any valuables inside, as the radios that come with most rented vehicles are valuable, easily sellable and much coveted by thieves. If you do leave valuables in a vehicle, place them out of sight.

Travelers checks are accepted, so there is no reason to carry more cash than you need.

Puerto Rico has an island-wide emergency number: 911. Most dispatchers understand some English.

Customs Regulations

Customs regulations resemble those of the United States, and are carried out with similar thoroughness. It is illegal to transport perishable foods, plants, drugs, or animals into or out of Puerto Rico except with prior permission. This stipulation applies to those traveling to and from the United States as well. For more information, call the **Transportation Security Administration** (TSA), tel: 787-253 4591, or the **US Department of Agriculture**, tel: 787-253 4651.

Canadians are allowed to bring back duty-free one carton of cigarettes, one can of tobacco, 40 imperial ounces of liquor, and 50 cigars. All valuables should be declared on the Y-38 form before departure from Canada, including serial numbers of valuables already owned, such as expensive foreign cameras. For more information, contact the **Canada Customs and Revenue Agency**, tel: 800-461 9999 in Canada, or 204-983 3500, or visit www.ccra-adrc.gc.ca.

UK citizens have a customs allowance of 200 cigarettes, 50 cigars, or 250 grams of smoking tobacco; 2 liters of still table wine; 1 liter of spirits or strong liqueurs (over 22 percent volume); 2 liters of fortified wine, sparkling wine, or other liqueurs; 60ml perfume; 250ml of toilet water; and $145 worth of all other goods. For more information, contact **HM Customs & Excise**, National Advice Service, Dorset

House, Stamford Street, London SE1 9PY, tel: 020-8929 0152 or visit www.hmce.gov.uk.

Australian citizens can bring in 250 cigarettes or 250 grams of loose tobacco, and 1,125 milliliters of alcohol. If you're returning with valuable goods you already owned, such as foreign-made cameras, you should file form B263. For more information, contact the **Australian Customs Service**, GPO Box 8, Sydney NSW 2000, tel: 02-6275 6666, or see www.customs.gov.au.

The duty-free allowance for New Zealand is 200 cigarettes or 50 cigars or 250 grams of tobacco (or a mixture of all three if their combined weight doesn't exceed 250 grams); plus 4.5 liters of wine and beer or 1.125 liters of liquor. Fill out a certificate of export, listing the valuables you are taking out of the country; that way, you can bring them back without paying duty. For more information, contact the **New Zealand Customs Service**, The Custom House, 17–21 Whitmore Street, Box 2218, Wellington, tel: 04-473 6099, or see www.customs.govt.nz.

Duty-free shops are open for all international flights, and for flights to the United States and US possessions in the Caribbean.

D isabled Travelers

The Americans with Disabilities Act (ADA) applies to all public facilities in Puerto Rico. Most businesses can accommodate travelers with disabilities.

For general information or to file complaints, call the local Handicapped Advocate, tel: 800-981 4125; 787-725 2333. The hearing-impaired can call 787-725 4012 or 787-725 0613. You may also find information at www.oppi.gobierno.pr. The Handicapped Advocate's central office is located on 670 Ponce de León Avenue, Caribbean Office Plaza, 2nd floor, Miramar. Regional offices are also in Aguada, Arecibo, Humacao, and Ponce.

The Handicapped Advocate has a guide of locations and services that can accommodate handicapped travelers, including hotels, *paradores*, vacation centers, restaurants, sights, transportation, and medical services. The guide is available at the central office in Miramar, or it can be mailed if requested.

It is recommended that you call your accommodations ahead of time to verify that they accommodate handicapped travelers.

Electricity

The voltage in Puerto Rico is the same as in the mainland United States (110 volts, 60 cycles a.c.).

Parking for disabled travelers is available in most places, and many towns have ramps that accommodate wheelchairs. However, Old San Juan is known as a difficult place to navigate for travelers in wheelchairs. As of this writing, ferry services were also not accessible to those in wheelchairs.

The public beaches of Luquillo and Boquerón have facilities that allow people in wheelchairs to bathe in the ocean.

For transportation and tours, call Wheelchair Getaway, tel: 800-868 8028; 787-883 0131.

Care Vacations of the Caribbean rents out medical equipment for disabled travelers on cruises or staying at hotels, tel: 877-661 6496; 787-761 8870; www.carevacation.com.

E mbassies and Consulates

Because Puerto Rico isn't an independent nation, it cannot conduct diplomatic relations with anyone. Hence, there are no embassies in San Juan – but plenty of consulates and honorary consulates. These are listed in the yellow pages of the phone book under *Consulados* and in the directory's "Newcomers' Guide," found between the yellow and white pages. You may also call the State Department's Service for the Foreign Citizen, tel: 787-723 2727; www.estado.gobierno.pr.

BELOW: El Capitolio, home of Puerto Rico's legislature.

Consulates include:
Canada, 268 Ponce de León Avenue, Suite 802, San Juan, tel: 787-753 8060.
UK, Chardón Tower, Suite 1236, 350 Chardón Street, tel: 787-758 9828.

Emergency Numbers
San Juan
Emergency, tel: 911.
Police, tel: 787-343 2020.
Fire Department, tel: 787-343 2330.
Medical Center of Puerto Rico, tel: 787-777 3535.
Assist (for medical emergencies), tel: 787-754 2550.
US Coast Guard, tel: 787-729 6770.
Rape Hotline, tel: 787-765 2285; 800-981 5721.
Poison Control Center, tel: 787-726 5660; 800-222 1222.
American Red Cross, tel: 787-759 7979.
Operator/Information, tel: 411.

Etiquette

Puerto Ricans are lively, friendly, and hospitable. Don't be surprised if a group of locals becomes noisy and boisterous while talking, particularly when discussing island politics; it is rarely as argumentative as foreigners assume. Puerto Ricans are also known for gesturing animatedly with their hands while they talk.

Upon meeting one another, Puerto Ricans like to shake hands, then give one kiss on the cheek, and they always greet each other with "*Buenos días*" ("Good morning"), "*Buenas tardes*" ("Good afternoon"), or "*Buenas noches*" ("Good evening), also said upon parting company.

ABOVE: newspaper kiosk on Plaza de Armas, Old San Juan.

G ay and Lesbian Travelers

Attitudes towards gays and lesbians in Puerto Rico are similar to those in the States, though less accepting than in places like New York City, Miami, and San Francisco.

San Juan is the more gay-friendly area of the island, with many bars, restaurants and hotels in Condado, Ocean Park and Old San Juan owned by gays and lesbians. Many have "gay nights." The beach at Ocean Park especially attracts gay travelers.

The first Sunday in June features a gay pride parade in Condado, as well as many activities in the week leading up to it.

Other areas that welcome gays and lesbians are Boquerón (southwest), Fajardo (northeast), and the small island of Culebra.

For listings of gay-friendly bars, accommodations, and places to go, visit www.orgulloboricua.net. When you get to the island, pick up a copy of the free bilingual newspaper *Puerto Rico Breeze*, found at the Atlantic Beach Hotel in Condado and at all Condom World stores. It has current listings of events, restaurants, and stores.

H ealth and Medical Care

Puerto Rico's health care resembles that of the United States in that it has no national health service, and the sick and infirm are cared for on a pay-as-you-go basis.

In practice, however, Puerto Rico's health care is administered on a far more lenient basis than in the United States. In general, fees are much lower and, since many Puerto Ricans have medical insurance, being hospitalized is far less of a financial nightmare than it is in the continental United States. Most hospitals have 24-hour emergency rooms but, if possible, check the yellow pages of the telephone book under *Hospitales*, or search for *sala emergencia* in www.superpagespr.com.

Puerto Rico is full of competent medical professionals. If you could choose where to fall ill, you'd doubtless elect San Juan, as the number of universities and clinics there make it full of doctors and medical personnel. Still, facilities in other areas, though often old and disheartening, are generally run by capable physicians and nurses.

Listed below are some of the larger hospitals with emergency rooms and some of the more popular (not necessarily 24-hour) pharmacies in San Juan. For listings in provincial cities, check the yellow pages in the phone book.

Hospitals

Ashford Presbyterian Community Hospital
Condado
Tel: 787-721 2160
Hospital Auxilio Mutuo, Hato Rey
Tel: 787-758 2000
Hospital San Pablo
Bayamón
Tel: 787-740 4747
Hospital Pavía
Santurce
Tel: 787-727 6060
Río Piedras Medical Center Central Emergency Room
Américo Miranda Avenue, Río Piedras
Tel: 787-777 3535
San Jorge Children's Hospital
Santurce
Tel: 787-727 1000

Pharmacies

San Juan
Puerto Rico Drug
157 San Francisco Street, corner with Cruz Street, Old San Juan
Tel: 787-725 2202
Walgreens
Tel: 787-722 6290
also at 1130 Ashford Avenue, Condado (open 24 hours)
Tel: 787-725 1510
Farmacías El Amal
617 Pavía Street,
Santurce
Tel: 787-728 1760

Mayagüez
Walgreens
Mayagüez Mall (open 24 hours)
Tel: 787-831 9251

Ponce
Farmacias El Amal
Valle Real Shopping Center
(open 24 hours)
Tel: 787-844 5555
Walgreens
Fagot Avenue (open 24 hours)
Tel: 787-841 2135

Special Considerations

Puerto Rico has few dangerous bacteria and diseases, but one deserves a special mention. Almost all of the island's rivers are infected with schistosomes, parasitic flatworms that cause the condition schistosomiasis (bilharzia), which can lead to severe damage to internal organs.

Some people say that river water is safe to drink and swim in on the upper altitudes of mountains, provided it is running swiftly, but this guide does not recommend it. Tap water is safe, however.

Internet

Most of the larger hotels provide guests with internet access either in their rooms or at least in a communal area. Some shopping centers have free WiFi access, such as the food court of San Patricio Shopping Center in Guaynabo. Various restaurants and fast-food chains also offer free WiFi (Denny's, McDonald's and Burger King). More downtown centers are making WiFi available, but the list is still small.

Internet cafés are not very common on the island. But there is a short list below:

CyberNet Café
1128 Ashford Avenue,
Condado
Tel: 787-724 4033, and
5575 Isla Verde Avenue,
Isla Verde
Tel: 787-728 4195

Crew Station Internet Café
111 Paseo Concepción de Gracia, in front of the Old San Juan piers
Tel: 787-289 0345

Lost Property

To contact the Luis Muñoz Marín International Airport police, call 787-791 0098.

For property left in taxis, call the Tourism Transportation booths in the Luis Muñoz Marín International Airport, tel: 787-253 0418, or email: lostandfound@prtourism.com or transportationclaims@prtourism.com.

To report lost or stolen credit cards and travelers checks, call:

American Express, tel: 800-327 1267

MasterCard, tel: 800-307 7309

Visa, tel: 800-847 2911

If you lose your US passport, call the State Department, tel: 787-722 2121; other nationalities should contact the relevant consulate.

For property left on airplanes or in the airline area, call the airline directly.

Media

Print

Puerto Ricans are avid readers of periodical literature, and the national dailies, published in San Juan, cover the spectrum of political opinion.

Of the Spanish papers, *El Nuevo Día* publishes seven days a week and has the highest circulation on the island. Its sister publication, *Primera Hora*, has a more populist slant and mass appeal. It publishes Monday through Saturday. A meaty tabloid with special features and arts

excerpts, *El Vocero* is a trim paper with more local news. *The Puerto Rico Daily Sun*, formed by former employees of the defunct *San Juan Star*, launched in the fall of 2008. It publishes seven days a week and serves as the only English daily on the island.

Puerto Rico produces few magazines, but gets most of the weeklies from the United States and Spain. American newspapers are available here on the day of publication: in Spanish, *Diario Las Américas*, published in Miami; in English, *The New York Times*, *The New York Post*, *The Miami Herald*, and *The Wall Street Journal*.

Television and Radio

Puerto Rico has more than 100 radio stations, including the English-language WOSO (1030 on the AM dial), which is quite versatile, combining fine local coverage with network news. English-language WBMJ is a religious station, and the St Thomas station may be picked up by some radios, particularly in the eastern part of Puerto Rico. Recommended Spanish music stations are Radio Uno and, on FM, Radio Fidelity.

The island has at least half a dozen Spanish-language TV stations of its own, but there are no English-language stations, save for the offerings on cable and satellite TV, which come from the United States and include all the American television networks. The government station, WIPR, broadcasts local programs in Spanish and some Public Broadcasting Service (PBS) programs in English.

Money

All business in Puerto Rico is transacted in US dollars, and visitors are advised to buy travelers checks in that currency if you prefer not to carry cash or withdraw money from cash machines. Travelers checks are accepted all over the island.

Most restaurants, hotels, and stores in well-traveled areas accept the following cards: American Express, MasterCard, Visa, Carte Blanche, Discovery, and Diners Club.

Some American Express Travel Services are offered through the Bithorn Travel agency in Isla Verde Mall, Suite 201, Isla Verde, tel: 787-791 2951. The Banco Popular at the Luis Muñoz Marín International Airport provides currency exchange, tel: 787-791 0326.

Banking

Puerto Rico is the banking center of the Caribbean Basin and as such has branches of almost all of the leading North American banks, as well as many European and Puerto Rican institutions. ATMs (called ATH – *aa-teh-acheh* – in Puerto Rico) are installed in most towns around the island.

Banking hours are Monday to Friday 8.30am–4.30pm. Certain branches of each bank may open for part of the day on Saturday and some evenings.

Tipping

Puerto Rico has a service economy resembling that of the United States, and this means tipping for most services received.

Some hotels and hotel restaurants include a 15 percent to 17 percent service charge to the bill, so always check your bill.

Otherwise, follow the American rules of thumb: 15 percent in restaurants, including *fondas* and *colmados* but not fast-food joints; 10 percent in bars; 10–15 percent for cab drivers, hairdressers, and other services.

Fifty cents per bag is a good rule for hotel porters, and a few bucks should keep the person who cleans your room happy.

Public Holidays

New Year's Day January 1
Three Kings Day January 6
Eugenio María de Hostos Birthday
  Second Monday in January
Martin Luther King, Jr Day
  Third Monday in January
Presidents' Day
  Third Monday in February
Emancipation Day March 22
Good Friday March/April
José de Diego Day
  Third Monday in April
Memorial Day
  Last Monday in May
US Independence Day July 4
Luis Muñoz Rivera Day
  Third Monday in July
José Celso Barbosa Day July 27
Puerto Rico's Constitution Day
  July 25
Labor Day
  First Monday in September
Columbus Day
  Second Monday in October
Veterans' Day November 11
Discovery of Puerto Rico Day
  November 19
Thanksgiving Day
  Fourth Thursday in November
Christmas Day December 25

ABOVE: Puerto Ricans are predominantly Roman Catholics.

O pening Hours

Business hours follow the US rather than the Latin tradition, and the afternoon siesta is generally not practiced. Most stores are open Monday–Saturday 9am–9pm, banks Monday to Friday 8.30am–2.30pm; certain branches of each bank may open on Saturday and evenings. Some selected stores of major supermarket chains are open 24 hours a day, seven days a week.

P ostal Services

Puerto Rican postal services are administered by the US Postal Service. Regulations and tariffs are the same as those on the mainland. Stamps may be purchased at any post office; most are open from Monday to Friday 8am–5pm and on Saturday 8am–noon. They may also be bought from vending machines in hotels, stores, and airports.

The US Postal Service Authorized Abbreviation for Puerto Rico is PR. Visit www.usps.com.

United Parcel Service (UPS) and Federal Express (FedEx) also provide services in Puerto Rico, as do some private mail-service centers.

Phone numbers for the main mail carriers are:
Federal Express: 800-463 3339
General US Postal Office
(information): 787-622 1756
UPS: 800-742 5877

Public Toilets

Restrooms are identified as such in English or in Spanish as *baños*. If identified in Spanish, the ladies' room is marked with *Damas* and the men's room with *Caballeros*.

Some public restrooms are better maintained than others, but a general rule of thumb is not to sit on the toilet seat. Many times you won't find toilet paper in public restrooms, except in good restaurants and larger hotels, so it's always a good idea to carry tissue paper or napkins with you just in case.

All of the public beaches administered by the country's National Parks Company have public restrooms.

R eligious Services

Puerto Rican history is steeped in religion, particularly the Roman Catholic tradition, as the Spanish monarchs at the time of colonization sent *conquistadores* along with priests to convert their new territories.

Roman Catholics still make up the majority of the population, approximately 85 percent, while Protestant churches and other groups such as Muslims and Jews represent about 15 percent of the population.

Most religious denominations on the island offer services in English. For more information, check the listings on the yellow pages under *Iglesias* or in the English-language blue pages under Churches. Some services in English that are close to the San Juan tourist areas follow. Call to verify service times, as they may be subject to change.

Baptist

The Isla Verde Baptist Church
(Sun 11am), tel: 787-726 3055.

Buddhist

Soka Gakkai International USA
Laguna Gardens Community Center, Carolina, tel: 787-791 3118.

Episcopal

St John's Cathedral, Santurce (Sun 8am, 11am), tel: 787-722 3254.

Inter-Denominational

The Union Church of San Juan,
Punta Las Marías (Sun 10.30am), tel: 787-726 0280.

Jewish

The Jewish Reform Congregation of Temple Beth Shalom, Santurce (Fri 8.30pm, Sat 10am), tel: 787-721 6333.
The Jewish Community Center at Shaare Zedeck Synagoge (English/ Spanish/Hebrew on Fri 6.30pm, Sat/ Sun 9am), tel: 787-724 4157.

Lutheran

Grace Lutheran Church, Santurce (Sun 10.30am), tel: 787-722 5372.

Methodist

The Holy Trinity Methodist Church,
Old San Juan (Spanish with English translation on Sun 11am), tel: 787-722 5372.

Presbyterian

O'Neill Memorial Presbyterian Church, Old San Juan (Sun 9am), tel: 787-977 2405.

Roman Catholic

Nuestra Señora del Perpetuo Socorro, Miramar (Sun 10.30am), tel: 787-721 1015.
Stella Maris, Condado (Sun 9.30am, 12.30pm), tel: 787-723 2240.

S moking

Smoking is banned in virtually all public areas since 2007. The law doesn't allow businesses to designate areas for smokers, as was previously the case on the island. According to the regulation, smoking is prohibited in restaurants, bars, casinos, clubs, pubs, and liquor stores. It is also not permitted in businesses dedicated to the sale of food, public buildings and transportation vehicles, convention centers, shopping malls, and outdoor cafés if an employee takes an order there, among other places.

People may smoke in areas that are in the open air, out of work areas, in private homes, in vehicles when a child under the age of 13 is not present, and in freestanding tobacco shops. Fines for violating the law start at $25 for individuals.

Smoking is also prohibited in hotel common areas. Check with your hotel for individual smoking policy in rooms.

T ax

For the first time in its history, Puerto Rico implemented a 5.5 percent commonwealth sales tax in 2006. Municipalities also charge an additional sales tax of up to 1.5 percent. The sales tax is applicable to jewelry, electronics, rental vehicles, and most goods and services. Medical services, prescription medicine, products derived from petroleum, and non-processed foods are exempt from the tax. Other groceries are subject to the sales tax. There are additional taxes on alcohol and cigarettes, though these are included in marked prices and do not appear as surcharges. An excise tax applies to incoming automobiles.

There is also a room tax in Puerto Rico, which varies according to type of accommodation and facilities.

BELOW: most stores stay open until 9pm.

Telephones

International area codes for Puerto Rico are **787** and **939**. All numbers listed in this guide require a 787 area code unless otherwise indicated.

Coin-operated telephones are common and cost 50¢ for local calls, depending on the particular pay phone. When you hear the dial tone, you may dial the area code followed by the seven-digit number. If the call is outside the area you are calling from, you will need to dial 1-787 followed by the seven-digit number. If the call is long-distance within Puerto Rico, extra charges will apply. For calls to the US Virgin Islands, dial 1-340 and the number; to the Dominican Republic, dial 1-809 and the number. Every Caribbean island now has its own area code; check your directory for the complete list. For calls to the US and Canada, dial 1, then the area code, then the number. An operator will tell you how much money to deposit.

If you wish to place a call through an operator, dial "0." Directions are usually printed on the phone, and are always printed in the first pages of the phone directory.

The phone directories in Puerto Rico are in Spanish, with a special wine-and-blue-colored section in English providing commercial and government telephone numbers and giving translations of the Spanish headings under which information can be found.

Telegraph facilities are available through Western Union or Telex. Western Union telegraphs (tel: 800-325 4045) and cash transfers arrive at food stores of the Pueblo chain.

Time Zone

Atlantic Time Zone, four hours behind GMT and one hour ahead of Eastern Standard Time.

Tourist Information

Tourist Offices Abroad

On the US mainland, call the Puerto Rico Tourism Company toll-free at 800-223 6530 (toll-free). Offices are located in Miami, tel: 800-815 7391, and Los Angeles, tel: 800-874 1230.

Outside the United States:
Canada
(postal address)
6-295 Queen Street East, Suite 465, Brampton, Ontario, L6W4S6
Tel: 416-580 6287
UK
c/o Activate Sales and Marketing, 2nd Floor, 67a High Street, Walton-on-Thames, KT12 1DJ
Tel: 01932-253 302
Email: puertoricouk@aol.com

Local Tourist Offices

The Puerto Rico Tourism Company has its main office at:
La Puntilla Building, 2 Paseo de La Princesa, Old San Juan
Tel: 787-721 2400
Tourists may also get information at La Casita, Dársenas Plaza, next to Pier 1, Old San Juan
Tel: 787-722 1709
There is a Tourism Company Information Center at the airport, on the first level of concourse C (tel: 787-791 1014).

Websites

Arecibo Observatory:
www.naic.edu
Casa Bacardi Visitor Center:
www.bacardi.com
Culebra Island: www.culebra-island.com, www.culebra.org
Puerto Rico Coliseum:
www.coliseodepuertorico.com
Puerto Rico Convention Bureau:
www.meetpuertorico.com
Puerto Rico Convention Center:
www.prconvention.com
Puerto Rico Golf Association:
www.prga.org
Puerto Rico Hotel and Tourism Association: www.prhta.org
Puerto Rico Information:
www.enjoypuertorico.com
www.puertorico.com
Puerto Rico Tourism Company:
www.gotopuertorico.com
San Juan Tourism: www.sanjuan.org
Vieques Island: www.enchanted-isle.com

Tour Operators and Travel Agents

Tour Operators

Aquatica Dive and Surf
Tel: 787-890 6071
www.aquaticadive-surf.com
Scuba, surf, and bike package.
Three days of activities: 1 scuba dive
(Discover Program); 1 surf lesson;
1 bike tour in Porta del Sol region.

Ecoquest Adventures and Tours
Tel: 787-616 7543
www.ecoquestpr.com
Rappelling and ziplining adventure.
Ecoquest Adventures and Tours
specializes in organizing adventures
and tours that include ziplining,
rappelling, hiking, and kayaking.
This exciting action tour includes
a pristine river hike, rappelling,
and ziplining across breathtaking
canyons with scenic views of rivers
and waterfalls.

Kayaking Puerto Rico
Tel: 787-564 5629
www.kayakingpuertorico.com
Reef and rainforest full-day tour.
Kayak along Puerto Rico's
northeastern coastline, snorkel
through the underwater gardens,
and hike the El Yunque rainforest,
all in one day.

Pure Adventure Puerto Rico
Tel: 787-202 6551
http://pureadventurepr.com
Scuba-diving, kayak, snorkeling,
diving, and birdwatching. Experience
adventures like no other tour in
Mother Nature.
 This company offers a crash
course in scuba-diving, kayak
adventures, bird watching
expeditions, and more.

For certified divers, discover the
excellent diving waters off Puerto
Rico's eastern coast.

Travesías Isleñas Yaureibo, Inc.
Tel: 939-630 1267; 787-447 4104
This company is owned and operated
by bilingual Vieques natives, who
guide visitors to explore the best
Vieques has to offer: includes
historical attractions, bio bay
kayaking, and snorkeling.

Travel Agents

For a list of travel agencies in Puerto
Rico endorsed by the Tourism
Company, visit www.gotopuertorico.com/
pdf/travel-agents-list.pdf. The following
is a partial list:

Condado Travel
MCS Plaza, 255 Ponce de León
Avenue, Suite 721, Hato Rey
Tel: 787-754 7000
www.condadotravel.com

Continental Travel
268 Ponce de León Avenue, Suite
705, San Juan
Tel: 787-753 5480
www.continentaltravelpr.com

Darlington Travel Agency
Darlington Building, Río Piedras
Tel: 787-765 1760

Modern Travel
5555 Ashford Avenue, Condado
Tel: 787-721 3984
www.moderntravel.com

Miranda Travel and Tours, Inc.
809 Fernández Juncos Avenue,
Santurce
Tel: 787-725 5577
www.mirandatravel.com

Viajes Coquí
418 Agüeybaná Street, San Juan
Tel: 787-754 7757
www.viajescoqui.com

Weights and Measures

Throughout the island of Puerto
Rico distances are measured in
kilometers, but speed limits are
indicated in miles.
 Weight is measured in
pounds and gas is sold in liters;
most other things use the British
Imperial system.

Visas and Passports

No visa or passport is required for US
citizens entering Puerto Rico from
the United States.
 Visitors and cruise passengers
planning to go to other Caribbean
islands, excluding the US Virgin
Islands, must have a valid passport
to return to US territory.
 Those with permanent residence,
however, are advised to bring their
green cards.
 Foreign nationals are required to
present the same documentation
and papers required for entry into
the continental US.
 Countries whose citizens are
exempted from tourist visa
requirements, for stays of up to
90 days, include Australia, Ireland,
New Zealand, and the UK.
 To qualify for visa-free travel,
you need an unexpired passport,
must hold a return or onward ticket,
a completed form I-94W and enter
aboard an air or sea carrier
participating in the Visa Waiver Pilot
Program if entering by air or sea
(lists of participating air or sea
carriers are available from most
travel agents).

BELOW: flights link the Islands with Fajardo and San Juan; travel agents will help with the bookings.

L ANGUAGE

UNDERSTANDING THE LANGUAGE

General

The language of Puerto Rico is Spanish. While it is by no means true that "everyone there speaks English," a majority of Puerto Ricans certainly do, especially in San Juan. Almost everyone in a public-service occupation will be able to help in either language.

The Puerto Rican dialect of Spanish resembles that of other Antillean islands, and differs from the Iberian dialect in its rapidity, phoneme quality, and elisions. For a more detailed look at this rich tongue, *see The Language of Puerto Rico on page 82*.

There are many excellent Spanish-English dictionaries for sale, but Barron's, edited at the University of Chicago, is particularly recommended for its sensitivity to the vocabulary and syntax of the Latin American idiom. Cristine Gallo's *The Language of the Puerto Rican Street* is an exhaustive lexicon of the kind of Puerto Rican slang that most dictionaries would blanch at printing.

Basic Rules

English is widely spoken in most tourist areas, but even if you speak no Spanish at all, it is worth trying to master a few simple words and phrases.

Generally, the accent falls on the second-to-last syllable, unless it is otherwise marked with an accent (´).

Vowels

a as in father
e as in bed
i as in police
o as in hole
u as in rude

Consonants

Consonants are almost like those in English, the main exceptions being:
c is hard before a, o, or u (as in English), and is soft before e or i, when it sounds like s. Thus, *censo* (census) sounds like senso.
g is hard before a, o, or u (as in English), but where English g sounds like j – before e or i – Spanish g sounds like a guttural h; g before ua is often soft or silent, so that *agua* sounds more like awa, and Guadalajara like Wadalajara.
h is silent.
j sounds like the English h.
ll sounds like y.
ñ sounds like ny, as in the familiar Spanish word *señor*.
q is followed by u as in English, but the combination sounds like k instead of like kw.
r is often rolled.
x between vowels sounds like a guttural h, as in México or Oaxaca.
y alone, as the word meaning "and", is pronounced ee.

Note that **ch** and **ll** are separate letters of the Spanish alphabet; if looking in a phone book or dictionary for a word beginning with ch, you will find it after the final c entry. A name or word beginning with ll will be listed after the l entry.

When addressing someone you are not familiar with, use the more formal *usted*. The informal *tú* is reserved for relatives and friends.

Words and Phrases

Hello Hola
How are you? ¿Cómo está usted?
How much is it? ¿Cuánto es?
What is your name? ¿Cómo se llama usted?
My name is... Yo me llamo...
Do you speak English? ¿Habla inglés?
I am British/American Yo soy británico/norteamericano
I don't understand No entiendo
Please speak more slowly Hable más despacio, por favor
Can you help me? ¿Me puede ayudar?
I am looking for... Estoy buscando...
Where is...? ¿Dónde está...?
I'm sorry Lo siento/Perdón
I don't know No sé
No problem No hay problema
Have a good day Que tenga un buen día
That's it Eso es
Here it is Aquí está
There it is Allí está
Let's go Vámonos
See you tomorrow Hasta mañana
See you soon Hasta pronto
See you later Hasta luego
Show me the word in the book Muéstreme la palabra en el libro

BELOW: Puerto Ricans speak Spanish.

TRANSPORTATION • ACCOMMODATIONS • EATING OUT • ACTIVITIES • A – Z • LANGUAGE

At what time? ¿A qué hora?
When? ¿Cuando?
yes sí
no no
please por favor
thank you (very much) (muchas) gracias
you're welcome de nada
excuse me con su permiso
OK bien
goodbye adiós
good evening/night buenas tardes/ noches
here aquí
there allí
today hoy
yesterday ayer
tomorrow mañana (note: mañana also means "morning")
now ahora
later después
right away ahora mismo
this morning esta mañana
this afternoon esta tarde
this evening esta tarde
tonight esta noche

On Arrival

I want to get off at... Quiero bajarme en...
Is there a bus to the museum? ¿Hay un autobus al museo?
What street is this? ¿Qué calle es esta?
How far is...? ¿Cuán lejos queda...?
airport aeropuerto
customs aduana
baggage claim reclamo de equipaje
suitcase maleta
train station estación de tren
bus station estación de autobuses/ guaguas
metro station estación de tren urbano
bus autobus/guagua
bus stop parada de guaguas
ticket boleto/taquilla
round-trip ticket boleto de ida y vuelta
hitchhiking auto-stop/pon
toilets servicios/baños
This is the hotel address Esta es la dirección del hotel
I'd like a (single/double) room Quiero una habitación (sencilla/ doble)
... with shower con ducha
... with bath con baño
... with a view con vista
Does that include breakfast? ¿Incluye desayuno?
May I see the room? ¿Puedo ver la habitación?
washbasin lavabo
bed cama
key llave
elevator/lift ascensor/elevador

wheelchair silla de ruedas
stairs escaleras
wheelchair ramp rampa de impedidos
air conditioning aire acondicionado
internet connection conección a la red cibernética
trip viaje
business negocio
pleasure placer
vacation vacación

Emergencies

Help! ¡Socorro!/¡Auxilio!
Stop! ¡Alto!/¡Pare!
Call a doctor Llame a un médico
Call an ambulance Llame a una ambulancia
Call the police Llame a la policía
Call the fire brigade Llame a los bomberos
Where is the nearest telephone? ¿Dónde está el teléfono más cercano?
Where is the nearest hospital? ¿Dónde está el hospital más cercano?
I am sick Estoy enfermo/a (male/ female)
I have lost my passport/purse (bag) He perdido mi pasaporte/ cartera

On the Road

Where is the spare wheel? ¿Dónde está la rueda de repuesta?
Where is the nearest garage? ¿Dónde está el taller más cercano?
Our car has broken down Nuestro carro se ha dañado
I want to have my car repaired Quiero que reparen mi carro
It's not your right of way Usted no tiene prioridad/derecho de paso
I think I must have put diesel in my car by mistake Me parece haber echado combustible de motor diesel por error
the road to... la carretera a...
left izquierda
right derecha
straight on derecho
far lejos
near cerca
opposite frente a
beside al lado de
parking lot estacionamiento
over there poralli
at the end al final
town map mapa de la ciudad
road map mapa de carreteras
street calle
square plaza
give way ceda el paso
exit salida

dead end calle sin salida
wrong way va contra el tránsito
no parking prohibido estacionar/no estacione
expressway autopista
toll highway autopista/expreso
tire goma/llanta
speed limit límite de velocidad
gasoline station gasolinera
gasoline gasolina
unleaded sin plomo
diesel diesel
water/oil agua/aceite
air aire
puncture pinchazo
bulb bombilla
lights luces
breaks freno

On the Telephone

How do I make an outside call? ¿Cómo hago una llamada al exterior?
What is the area code? ¿Cuál es el código de área?
I want to make an international (local) call Quiero hacer una llamada internacional (local)
I'd like a wake-up call for 8 tomorrow morning Quiero que me despierten a las ocho de la mañana
Hello? ¿Díga?/¡Aló!
Who's calling? ¿Quién llama?
Hold on, please Un momento, por favor
I can't hear you No le oigo
Can you hear me? ¿Me oye?
He/she is not here Él/ella no está aquí
The line is busy La línea está ocupada
I must have dialed the wrong number Debo haber marcado un número equivocado

Shopping

Where is the nearest bank? ¿Dónde está el banco más cercano?
I'd like to buy Quiero comprar
How much is it? ¿Cuánto es?
Do you accept credit cards? ¿Aceptan tarjetas de crédito?
Can I pay with a check/cheque? ¿Puedo pagar con cheque?
I'm just looking Sólo estoy mirando
Have you got...? ¿Tiene...?
I'll take it Me lo llevo
I'll take this one/that one Me llevo este/ese
What size is it? ¿Que talla es?
size (clothes) talla
small pequeño
large grande
cheap barato
expensive caro

enough suficiente
too much demasiado
a piece una pieza
each cada uno/la pieza/la unidad
bill la factura (shop), la cuenta (restaurant)
bank banco
bookshop librería
pharmacy farmacia
hairdressers peluquería
post office correo
department store tienda por departamentos
closed cerrado
open abierto
on holiday feriado
business hours horas de oficina

Market Shopping

Supermarkets (supermercados) are self-service, but often the best and freshest produce is to be had at the town market (mercado) or the street market (mercadillo).
    Prices are usually by the pound (por libra) or by the unit (por unidad).

fresh fresco
frozen congelado
organic orgánico
basket cesta/canasta
bag bolsa
bakery panadería
butcher's carnicería
cake shop repostería/pastelería
fishmonger's pescadería
grocer's verdurería
tobacconist tabaquero/estanquero
thriftshop tienda de segunda mano

Sightseeing

mountain montaña
hill colina
valley valle
river río
lake lago
lookout mirador
old town casco antiguo
monastery monasterio
convent convento
cathedral catedral
church iglesia
palace palacio
hospital hospital
town hall alcaldía
nave nave
statue estatua
fountain fuente
tower torre
castle castillo
Iberian ibérico
Phoenician fenicio
Roman romano
Moorish moro
Romanesque románico
Gothic gótico
museum museo

art gallery galería de arte
exhibition exposición
tourist information office oficina de turismo
free gratis
admission/admission fee entrada/precio de entrada
every day diario/todos los días
all day todo el día
swimming pool piscina
to book reservar

Dining Out

breakfast desayuno
lunch comida/almuerzo
dinner cena
meal comida
snack merienda
appetizer aperitivo
first course primer plato
main course plato principal
dessert postre
drink included bebida incluída
wine list carta de vinos
the bill la cuenta
fork tenedor
knife cuchillo
spoon cuchara
plate plato
glass vaso
wine glass copa
napkin servilleta
ashtray cenicero
straw sorbeto
Waiter, please! ¡Camarero, por favor!
coffee café
...black negro
...with milk con leche
...decaffeinated descafeinado
sugar azúcar
tea té
herbal tea infusión
milk leche
mineral water agua mineral
...fizzy con gas
...non-fizzy sin gas
juice (fresh) jugo (natural)
beer cerveza
soft drink refresco
with ice con hielo
wine vino
red wine vino tinto
white blanco
rosé rosado
dry seco
sweet dulce
house wine vino de la casa
sparkling wine vino espumoso
Where is this wine from? ¿De dónde es este vino?
Cheers! ¡Salud!

Table Talk

I am a vegetarian Soy vegetariano
I am on a diet Estoy a dieta

What do you recommend? ¿Qué recomienda?
Do you have local specialties? ¿Hay especialidades locales?
I'd like to order Quiero pedir
That is not what I ordered Ésto no es lo que pedí
May I have more wine? ¿Me da más vino?
Enjoy your meal Buen provecho
That was delicious Eso estuvo delicioso/sabroso/rico

Menu Decoder

Breakfast and Snacks

azúcar **sugar**
bocadillo **sandwich in a bread roll**
bollo **bun/roll**
jalea/mermelada/confitura **jam**
huevos **eggs**
...cocidos **boiled, cooked**
...fritos **fried**
...revueltos **scrambled**
tocineta **bacon**
mantequilla **butter**
pan **bread**
integral **whole wheat/wholemeal**
avena **oatmeal**
pimienta **black pepper**
sal **salt**
sandwich **sandwich in square slices of bread**
tostada **toast**
yogúr **yoghurt**

Main Courses

Carne/Meat
cabrito **kid**
carne picada **ground meat**
cerdo **pork**
chorizo **paprika-seasoned sausage**
chuleta **chop**
conejo **rabbit**
cordero **lamb**
costilla **rib**
cuerito **roast suckling pig's skin**
entrecot **beef rib steak**
filete **steak**
jamón **ham**
jamón cocido **cooked ham**
jamón serrano **cured ham**
lechón asado **roast suckling pig**
lengua **tongue**
lomo **loin**
morcilla **black pudding**
rez **beef**
riñones **kidneys**
salchichón **sausage**
sesos **brains**
solomillo **fillet steak**
ternera **veal or young beef**
a la brasa/parilla **charcoal-grilled**
a la plancha **grilled**
al horno/asado **roast**
bien cocido **well done**
en salsa **in sauce**
frito **fried**

guisado **stew**
parrillada **mixed grill**
pincho **skewer**
poco cocido **rare**
relleno **stuffed**
término medio **medium**

Pollo/Poultry
codorniz **quail**
faisán **pheasant**
pato **duck**
pavo **turkey**
perdiz **partridge**
pintada **guinea fowl**
pollo **chicken**

Pescado/Fish
almeja **clam**
anchoas **anchovies**
anguila **eel**
atún **tuna**
bacalao **cod**
besugo **sea bream**
boquerones **fresh anchovies**
caballa **mackerel**
calamar **squid**
camarones **shrimp**
cangrejo **crab**
caracol **sea snail**
carrucho **queen conch**
cazón **dogfish**
centollo **spider crab**
cigala **Dublin Bay prawn/scampi**
dorado **dolphin fish, mahi mahi**
fritura **mixed fry**
gamba **prawn**
jibia/chopito **cuttlefish**
jueyes **land crab**
langosta **spiny lobster**
langostino **large prawn**
lenguado **sole**
lubina **sea bass**
mariscada **mixed shellfish**
mariscos **shellfish**
mejillón **mussel**
merluza **hake**
mero **grouper**
ostión **large oyster**
ostra **oyster**
pescadilla/pijota **small hake**
pez espada **swordfish**
pulpo **octopus**
rape **monkfish**
rodaballo **turbot**
salmón **salmon**
salmonete **red mullet**
sardina **sardine**
trucha **trout**
tiburón **shark**
viera **scallop**

Vegetables/Cereals
ajo **garlic**
alcachofa **artichoke**
apio **celery**
arroz **rice**
berenjena **eggplant/aubergine**
cebolla **onion**

cereal **cereal**
champiñón/seta **mushroom**
coliflor **cauliflower**
crudo **raw**
ensalada **salad**
espárrago **asparagus**
espinaca **spinach**
garbanzo **chick pea**
guisante **pea**
haba **broad bean**
habichuela **bean**
habichuela colorada/roja **red bean**
judía **green bean**
lechuga **lettuce**
lenteja **lentil**
maíz **corn/maize**
papa **potato**
pepino **cucumber**
pimiento **pepper/capsicum**
puerro **leek**
rábano **radish**
repollo **cabbage**
tomate **tomato**
verduras **vegetables**
zanahoria **carrot**

Fruit and Desserts

aguacate **avocado**
albaricoque **apricot**
cereza **cherry**
china **orange**
ciruela **plum**
frambuesa **raspberry**
fresa **strawberry**
fruta **fruit**
granada **pomegranate**
guineo **banana**
higo **fig**
limón **lemon**
limón verde **lime**
mandarina **tangerine**
manzana **apple**
melocotón **peach**
melón **melon**
pasa **raisin**
pera **pear**
piña **pineapple**
plátano **plantain**
sandía **watermelon**
toronja **grapefruit**
uva **grape**
flan **caramel custard**
helado/mantecado **ice cream**
natilla **custard**
pastel **pie**
postre **dessert**
queso **cheese**
tarta/torta/bizcocho **cake**

Numbers, Days, and Dates

0	cero
1	uno
2	dos
3	tres
4	cuatro
5	cinco
6	seis
7	siete
8	ocho
9	nueve
10	diez
11	once
12	doce
13	trece
14	catorce
15	quince
16	dieciséis
17	diecisiete
18	dieciocho
19	diecinueve
20	veinte
21	veintiuno
30	treinta
40	cuarenta
50	cincuenta
60	sesenta
70	setenta
80	ochenta
90	noventa
100	cien
200	doscientos
500	quinientos
1,000	mil
10,000	diez mil
1,000,000	un millón

week semana
weekday día de semana
weekend fin de semana
Monday lunes
Tuesday martes
Wednesday miércoles
Thursday jueves
Friday viernes
Saturday sábado
Sunday domingo

January enero
February febrero
March marzo
April abril
May mayo
June junio
July julio
August agosto
September septiembre
October octubre
November noviembre
December diciembre

Weather

sunny soleado
cloudy nublado
rain/rainy lluvia/lluvioso
humid húmedo
umbrella paraguas/sombrilla
storm tormenta
hurricane huracán
wind viento
waves olas

FURTHER READING

General

Emotional Bridges to Puerto Rico: Migration, Return Migration, and the Struggles of Incorporation (Perspectives on a Multiracial America) (paperback), by Elizabeth M. Aranda, Rowman & Littlefield Publishers (2006). *Emotional Bridges to Puerto Rico* is about Puerto Ricans' struggles of incorporation into US society, and the conditions under which members of the Puerto Rican middle class move back and forth between the mainland and island. The book illustrates how structures of inequalities based on race, class, and gender affect Puerto Ricans' subjective assessments of incorporation: Puerto Ricans do not feel like they fully belong in mainland society.

None of the Above: Puerto Ricans in the Global Era (New Directions in Latin American Culture), edited by Frances Negrón Muntaner, Palgrave Macmillan (2007). *None of the Above* is about current debates regarding Puerto Rico and Puerto Ricans, both in the US and on the island. The title simultaneously refers to the results of a non-binding 1998 plebiscite held to determine the island's political status, the ambiguities that have historically characterized Puerto Rican political agency, and the complexities of Puerto Rican ethnic, national, and cultural identifications.

The Puerto Ricans: A Documentary History, by Kal Wagenheim and Olga Jiménez de Wagenheim, Markus Wiener Publishers, revised edition (2008). "An essential sourcebook for a better understanding of the Puerto Ricans." *The New York Times*.

Puerto Rico, by José Javier López, Charles F. Gritzner (Editor), Chelsea House Publishers (2006). "Part of the series "Modern World Nations," this title focuses on the geography, history, and politics of Puerto Rico. The organization, significant information, straightforward terminology, and colorful pictures with helpful captions contribute to a useful geography or history book.

Puerto Rico in the American Century: A History since 1898, by César J. Ayala and Rafael Bernabé, University of North Carolina Press (2007). Offering a comprehensive overview of Puerto Rico's history and evolution since the installation of US rule, Ayala and Bernabe connect the island's economic, political, cultural, and social past of residents of the island as well as the many Puerto Ricans in the diaspora. The authors discuss a wide range of topics, including literary and cultural debates and social and labor struggles that previous histories have neglected.

Puerto Rico: Island in the Sun, by Roger A. LaBrucherie, Imágenes Press (2008). A hardcover pictorial book in the coffee-table book format with color photos and English-language text. The photos and accompanying captions present the scenery, beaches, architecture, geography, culture, and history of Puerto Rico, with a special emphasis on aerial photographs and Old San Juan.

Puerto Rico Mio, Four Decades of Change, photographs by Jack Delano (1990). A collector's item for lovers of Puerto Rico. Black-and-white photographs tell the story of Puerto Rico from the 1940s to the 1980s by one who loved the island and its people dearly.

Taíno Revival: Critical Perspectives on Puerto Rican Identity and Cultural Politics, by Gabriel Haslip-Viera, Markus Wiener Publishers (2001). This stimulating and timely collection examines the Taíno revival movement, a grassroots conglomeration of Puerto Ricans and other Latinos who promote or have adopted the culture and pedigree of the pre-Columbian Taíno Indian population of Puerto Rico and the western Caribbean.

The Taínos: Rise and Decline of the People Who Greeted Columbus, by Irving Rouse, Yale University Press (1993). A noted archeologist and anthropologist tells the story of the Taínos of the northern Caribbean islands, from their ancestry on the South American continent to their rapid decline after contact with the Spanish explorers.

Witchcraft and Welfare: Spiritual Capital and the Business of Magic in Modern Puerto Rico, by Raquel Romberg, University of Texas Press (2003). Persecuted as evil during colonial times, considered charlatans during the nation-building era, Puerto Rican *brujos* (witch-healers) today have become spiritual entrepreneurs. Drawing on fieldwork among practicing *brujos*, this book presents a masterful history and ethnography of Puerto Rican *brujería* (witch-healing).

Fiction

Eccentric Neighborhoods, by Rosario Ferré, Plume (1999). Elvira loves her daddy, the man who bravely remade Puerto Rico, but she's got to come to terms with her long-dead mother. From the author of *The House on the Lagoon*, a National Book Award nominee.

Macho Camacho's Beat, by Luis Rafael Sánchez. Dalkey Archive Press (2001). Originally published in 1976, it was first translated to English in 1980. Sánchez's comic novel is told in snippets as it follows the lives of several inhabitants of San Juan, Puerto Rico: a crooked senator, his mistress, and his idiot child; the senator's wife; and a son in love with his car. The text is presented as verbal wordplay replete with ad slogans, puns, and pop culture references, which the author uses to show the influence a large country (the USA) can have on a small one (Puerto Rico) and how a fad in one can alter the culture of the other.

The Meaning of Consuelo, by Judith Ortiz Cofer, Beacon (2005). *La niña seria*, the serious child. That's how Consuelo's mother has cast her pensive, book-loving daughter, while Consuelo's younger sister, Mili, is seen as vivacious – a ray of tropical sunshine. Two daughters: one dark, one light; one to offer comfort and consolation, the other to charm and delight. But something is not quite right in this Puerto Rican family. Coming of age when American influence threatens to dilute the island's traditional Spanish customs as well as to harm, perhaps irreparably, its fragile ecology, Consuelo watches her family and culture being torn asunder – much like the island itself.

TRANSPORTATION   ACCOMMODATIONS   EATING OUT   ACTIVITIES   A – Z   LANGUAGE

Cuisine

Puerto Rican Cookery, by Carmen Aboy Valldejuli, Pelican Publishing (1993). Now in its 15th printing, *Puerto Rican Cookery* has become the standard reference on traditional native cookery *(cocina criolla)*. Accurate and easy-to-follow recipes assure the success of every dish. "Considered today to be the definitive book on island cooking." *The New York Times*.

Puerto Rican Cuisine in America, by Oswald Rivera, Four Walls Eight Windows (1993).

Puerto Rican Dishes, by Berta Cabanillas and Carmen Ginorio, Editorial de la Universidad de Puerto Rico (1993).

Puerto Rico True Flavors, by Wilo Benet, Tropical Dining Press (2007). Chef Benet presents traditional recipes of Puerto Rican cuisine, updated for the modern home cook, while remaining grounded in indigenous ingredients. A must for anyone interested in Latino cooking.

Rice and Beans and Tasty Things: A Puerto Rican Cookbook, by Dora Pomano, Ramallo Brothers (1986).

The Spirit of Puerto Rican Rum: Recipes and Recollections, by Blanche Gelabert, Discovery Press (1992).

Arts, Customs, and Social

Antonin Nechodoma, Architect 1877–1928, by Thomas S. Marvel, University of Florida Press (1994).

Contemporary Puerto Rican Installation Art: The Guagua Aerea, the Trojan Horse, and the Termite, by Laura Roulet, Editorial de la Universidad de Puerto Rico (2001). "Addressing volatile issues of sexism, racism, Puerto Rico's relationship with the United States and the dual nature of Puerto Rican existence, [installation artists] transcend the formally conservative, nationalistic character of Puerto Rican art as defined by earlier generations," writes Laura Roulet, a curator and freelance writer from Washington DC. Here she traces the movement from its radical inception in the 1960s through to the mode's present incarnations, where artists like Antonio Morales explode "otherness" with industrial detritus and other found objects.

Divided Borders: Essays on Puerto Rican Identity, by Juan Flores, Arte Público Press (1993). A collection of the essays on history, literature, and culture by the most celebrated

commentator on Puerto Rican and Caribbean culture in the United States, the winner of the Casa de las Américas award for his monograph on Puerto Rican identity.

Puerto Rican Culture: An Introduction, by Raoul Gordon, Gordon Books (1982).

Puerto Rican Woman, by Edna Acosta-Belén and Eli H. Christensen, Praeger (1979).

Puerto Rico 1900: Turn-of-the-Century Architecture in the Hispanic Caribbean, by Jorge Rigau, Rizzoli (1992).

Taíno: Pre-Columbian Art and Culture from the Caribbean, by Ricardo Alegría and José Arrom, Monacelli (1998). Organized by El Museo del Barrio in New York to coincide with a major exhibition, this is the first comprehensive English-language publication on the fascinating legacy of Taíno art and culture. This volume showcases over 100 rare and beautiful artworks of this ancient culture, including quality colour prints.

Trapped: Puerto Rico Families and Schizophrenia, by Lloyd H. Rogler and August B. Hollingshead, Waterfront Press (1985).

When I Was Puerto Rican, by Esmeralda Santiago, Addison-Wesley Publishing (1993).

Send Us Your Thoughts

We do our best to ensure the information in our books is as accurate and up-to-date as possible. The books are updated on a regular basis using local contacts, who painstakingly add, amend, and correct as required. However, some details (such as telephone numbers and opening times) are liable to change, and we are ultimately reliant on our readers to put us in the picture.

We welcome your feedback, especially your experience of using the book "on the road." Maybe we recommended a hotel that you liked (or another that you didn't), or you came across a great bar or new attraction we missed.

We will acknowledge all contributions, and we'll offer an Insight Guide to the best letters received.

Please write to us at:
**Insight Guides
PO Box 7910
London SE1 1WE**
Or email us at:
insight@apaguide.co.uk

Other Insight Guides

Apa Publications offer the discerning traveler more than 400 titles in its three series of travel guidebooks. **Insight Guides** provide a full cultural background and top-quality photography; **Insight Compact Guides** combine portability with encyclopedic attention to detail and are ideal for on-the-spot reference; and **Insight Pocket Guides** highlight recommendations by a local host and include a full-size pull-out map.

Insight Guide: Caribbean
The vivid text and spectacular photography in *Insight Guide: Caribbean* brings to life the serenity, the allure, and the diversity of this part of the world – from the beauty of a Caribbean sunset to the charm of the Caribees.

Insight Guide: Belize
Discover the beauty of Belize with the aid of breathtaking photography and articles written by local experts.

Insight Guide: Jamaica
This is a fascinating book full of creative pictures and information about Jamaica, its people and customs.

Insight Pocket Guide: Barbados
A perfect companion, this book offers tailor-made itineraries to help get the most out of a short stay in Barbados.

Insight Compact Guide: St Lucia
It's the ultimate quick-reference guide to the island, from its spectacular rainforest to its fine beaches.

ART AND PHOTO CREDITS

INDEX

Punta
del Morro

Port of
San Juan
Lighthouse

El Morro

City Walls
(Murallas de San Juan)

Bastión de
San Antonio

SAN JUAN
CEMETERY

Batería
San Fernando

Bastión de
Santa Rosa

CEMENTERIO
DE SANTA MARIA
MAGDALENA DE PAZZIE

LA PERLA

Calle Lucila Silva

Bastión de
Santo Domingo

Bastión de
Santa Elena

Old City Walls
(Murallas de
San Juan)

Escuela de
Artes Plásticas

Calle Norzagaray

Plaza
del Quinto
Centenario

Dominican Convent,
Institute of Puerto
Rican Culture

Bastión de
las Animas

Museo de Arte e
Historia de San Juan

C. Virtud

Cuartel de
Ballajá

Plaza
de Ballaia

Totem
Telúrico

San José

San José

Museo
Pablo Casals

Museo de
las Américas

C. de Beneficencia

Plaza
San
José

Antiguo Asilo
de Beneficencia

C. San Sebastián

Iglesia
Metodista

Calle Sol

Dios de
Pentecostal

Bastión de
San Augustín

Casa
Rosa

Casa
Blanca

Calle Sol

Museo del Niño
(Children's Museum)

Calle Luna

Caleta de las Monjas

Hotel
El Convento

La Rogativa

C. de San Juan

Plaza
de las
Monjas

San Juan
Cathedral

City Hall
(Casa Alcaldía)

Plaza de
Armas

San Juan Gate

Museo Felisa
Rincón de Gautier

Calle R. Cordero

Calle Fortaleza

Recinto del Oeste

Palacio
Rojo

Centro Nacional de Artes
Populares y Artesanías

La Fortaleza

Casa del
Libro

Cristo Chapel
(Capilla del Cristo)

Calle Tetuán

Old
City Walls

Siervas
de Marín

PARQUE DE
LAS PALOMAS

La
Princesa

Bastión de
las Palmas

Paseo de la Princesa

Bahía de
San Juan

Calle Presidio

Frente

Portuario

US Coa

N

Old San Juan

0   200 yds

0   200 m